# alternative
# natural

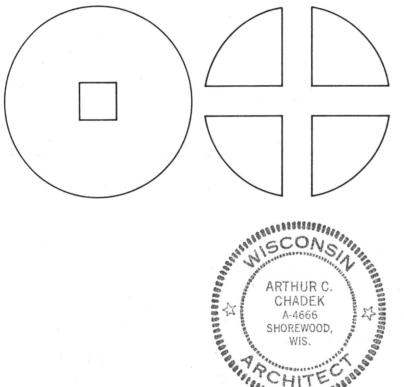

# energy

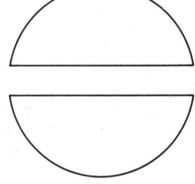

# sources

## in building design

## davis + schubert

VAN NOSTRAND REINHOLD COMPANY

NEW YORK  CINCINNATI  TORONTO  LONDON  MELBOURNE

Davis/Schubert:  Alternative
Natural Energy Sources

Copyright (c) 1974 by Albert
 J. Davis & Robert P. Schubert

First printing October 1974
Second printing February 1976

Library of Congress Catalog
 Card Number   76-54002

ISBN  0-442-22008-1

Printed in the United States
of America

Published in 1977 by Van
Nostrand Reinhold Company.
A division of Litton Educa-
tional Publishing, Inc. 450
West 33rd Street, New York,
NY  10001,  U.S.A.

Van Nostrand Reinhold Limited
1410 Birchmount Road
Scarborough, Ontario  M1P
2E7,  Canada

Van Nostrand Reinhold
Australia  Pty. Ltd.
14 Queen Street
Mitcham, Victoria  3132,
Australia

Van Nostrand Reinhold
Company Limited
Molly Millars Lane
Wokingham, Berkshire,
England

12 11 10 9 8 7 6 5 4 3 2

*The validity of information
is not so much measured
by weight, time or space
extension, but by the
threads it offers for
connections within the
condition of man.*

*Paolo Soleri*

**Library of Congress Cataloging in Publication Data**

Davis, Albert J
    Alternative natural energy sources in building design.

    Includes index.
    1.  Architecture and energy conservation.  I.  Schubert,
Robert P., joint author.  II.  Title.
NA2542.3.D38  1977      721      76-54002
ISBN 0-442-22008-1

# Contents

# Thanks.

Brinley Schubert     typing

Diane Jaeger     editing

Kae Greenwalt     editing

Mark Driscoll     graphics

D. Davis

Zane Hurst

Linda Davis

Virginia Polytechnic Institute
and State University

Charles Burchard, Dean, College of Architecture
Olivio C. Ferrari, Assistant Dean,
         College of Architecture

# Preface

Since the first printing of *Alternative Natural Energy Sources in Building Design* in October 1974, many volumes have been published on the utilization of solar energy (in all of its manifestations) for the heating and cooling of buildings. Some of these are quite complete and many others are inadequate. On the occasion of this third printing, the authors have attempted to update to a certain degree the primary concerns when energy conservation and alternative natural energy sources are integral and decisive components of building design.

There has been no attempt to relate in depth the specifics of chemical and mechanical principles but rather to outline the parameters of concern. A selected reference listing has been included to extend to the reader information which deals more specifically with the outlined criteria and relevant areas of research beyond the scope of this book.

It is now three years since the so-called "energy crisis" when public concern over future energy sources was at its peak. The changes are still continuing even though the immediacy of the problem is seemingly reduced. The future changes are dependent as much on mental awareness and balance as hardware and technological practicality. Without the former no amount of technological wizardry is going to solve the issues of energy demand. This text focuses on the design and hardware issues while leaving open the simultaneous development of an approach and philosophy as to their usage.

*Alternative Natural Energy Sources in Building Design* is organized so that a portion focuses on energy conservation, because without those basic principles inherent in the design, any attempt to utilize alternative energy sources would be futile.

There are cases where one energy source may satisfy the demands of the building but in many applications several natural energy sources may be needed to supply the diverse requirements inherent in the function of the building. For this purpose the last chapter has been included to give the criteria necessary when the integration of natural energy sources are to be used.

It is of the utmost concern to us that this information be communicated. We further suggest that this text be used as a workbook in which you make additions and subtractions as your concerns and information change.

Blacksburg, Virginia
October, 1976

*The ancient Christian symbols, represent in the order they are shown; water, sun, earth and air.*

The world environmental "energy crisis" goes far deeper than simply the depletion of fossil fuels. The crisis is one that is generated at the core of a culture bent on wastefulness. The past technological development has attempted to improve the standard of living which is a necessary and vital part of evolution. However, when in the process it generates unnatural contingencies that tend to destroy the very environment which sustains life, then this form of development must be questioned. The utilization of alternative natural energy sources and basic energy conservation principles will inevitably alter the present energy use patterns that have led us to the current dilemma. Furthermore, their application offers the opportunity to show concern for the earth, its people and the environment as a holistic, nonseparable entity.

This chapter attempts to discuss energy and its relationship to the built environment, contemporary technological solutions

to the energy situation and practical alternatives to the present technological (technocratic) base.

## 1.1 *Energy and Its Relationship to the Built Environment*

The term energy is derived from the Greek term *energos*, which means active. It is defined by Webster as the capacity to perform work. Power is the term generally applied to the rate at which energy is used or the rate work is done. Energy can be observed in many forms. Some of these forms are: *kinetic* energy, the energy of mechanical motion; *thermal* energy, which is the temperature difference between two substances, and; *potential*, or stored energy.

Lately our capacity to perform work has been given varying time limits. Depending upon who authorizes the research, and what sources of energy are being investigated, estimates of available potential run between near-depletion, at one extreme, and indefinite or unlimited supply at the

other. It is very difficult to locate unbiased data; however, in some contexts, it is not the time element that is critical. There are other considerations, such as the moral vacuum created by technology, the high capital and social cost, the exponential growth rate of pollution and overall wastefulness.

Many of the industrialized nations have established themselves as parasites on the remaining parts of the world. To the developing countries, the attitude is one of welcoming, in the hope that any future development is better than the misery and suffering of the present. This is a highly controversial subject, and clearly beyond the scope of this book. It can be debated as to whether the industrialized countries are helping or hurting and whether the energy use patterns established by the built environment can afford to continue their current trend. The position assumed here is that they cannot.

To be more specific, we can analyze the energy

pattern of the United States. The U.S. alone consumes 35% of the world's energy, yet comprises only 6% of the population of the world.[1] This amounts to over 9 tons of coal per person, just about 6 times the world's average.[2] Table 1.2 gives the breakdown of energy usage in the United States as of 1968.

Overcoming this awesome consumption rate is not easy. During the "energy purge" of the 60's, half of the world's production of petroleum took place.[3] Fossil fuels currently supply 95% of the energy in the U.S. This is broken down as to coal, 20%; oil, almost 40%; natural gas, around 30%; and natural gas liquids and hydroelectric power about 4%. By mid-1973, it was estimated that 17.6% of the total energy consumption was lost in electricity generation due to transmission and electrical inefficiencies. The building industry alone created energy use patterns that will last for decades. The built environment has a staggering affect on the environment. Table 1.1 indicates energy use affect-

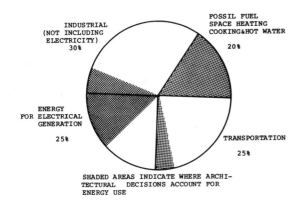

INDUSTRIAL (NOT INCLUDING ELECTRICITY) 30%

FOSSIL FUEL SPACE HEATING COOKING&HOT WATER 20%

ENERGY FOR ELECTRICAL GENERATION 25%

TRANSPORTATION 25%

SHADED AREAS INDICATE WHERE ARCHITECTURAL DECISIONS ACCOUNT FOR ENERGY USE

TABLE 1.1   ENERGY USE AFFECTED BY ARCHITECTURAL DECISIONS. *Source: Richard Stein in Architectural Forum, July-August 1973.*

ed by the architect's decision-making.  Because of the nature of technology, the building industry has been involved in perpetuating the depletion of fossil fuels, pollution and other unnatural processes.  The term unnatural, as applied here, relates to those practices that are in opposition to the cycles of the biosphere.  This reference also includes the large-scale combustion of fossil fuels, though they are naturally derived, when combusted, fuels cause a disequilibrium in the en-

| Sector | Percent of National Total |
|---|---|
| Residential: | |
| Space heating | 11.0 |
| Water heating | 2.9 |
| Cooking | 1.1 |
| Clothes drying | .3 |
| Refrigeration | 1.1 |
| Air conditioning | .7 |
| Other | 2.1 |
| TOTAL | 19.2 |
| Commercial: | |
| Space heating | 6.9 |
| Water heating | 1.1 |
| Cooking | .2 |
| Refrigeration | 1.1 |
| Air conditioning | 1.8 |
| Feedstock | 1.6 |
| Other | 1.7 |
| TOTAL | 14.4 |
| Industrial: | |
| Process steam | 16.7 |
| Electric drive | 7.9 |
| Electrolytic processes | 1.2 |
| Direct heat | 11.5 |
| Feedstock | 3.6 |
| Other | .3 |
| TOTAL | 41.2 |
| Transportation: | |
| Fuel | 24.9 |
| Raw materials | .3 |
| TOTAL | 25.2 |
| NATIONAL TOTAL | 100.0 |

*TABLE 1.2   U.S. Energy Consumption by End Use, 1968.*
Source:  Stanford Research Institute, **"Patterns of Energy Consumption in the U.S. '72."**

vironment, upsetting
natural cycles and damaging
living systems.

The energy cycle as shown
in figure 1.1 shows the
process by which fossil
fuels are produced and
consumed by industry.
There are alternative
natural sources of energy
that utilize the sun
directly, eliminating
many steps through which
potential energy is lost.
These sources essentially
are taking off the top of
the energy cycle. By
utilizing the different
manifestations of the
sun's energy directly
(i.e., solar heat or
photovoltaic, wind energy
and processing organic
matter once sustained by
photosynthesis), the
massive thermal, solid
particle and gaseous
pollution of the environ-
ment, not to mention the
depletion of fossil fuels
can be eliminated. All
the alternative energy
sources discussed here are
not bound by time limita-
tions, such as those de-
pending on fossil fuels.
What retards the develop-
ment of alternative technology is our present system
of economical priorities

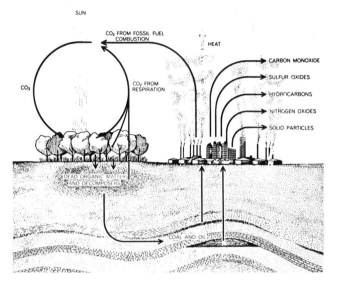

FIGURE 1.1  From "Human Energy Production as a Process
in the Biosphere" by S. Fred Singer.  Copyright © 1970
by Scientific American, Inc.  All rights reserved.

and restraints imposed by
policy-makers.  This is
discussed further in the
next section.

The controversial book,
*Limits to Growth*,[4] has
placed time limits on some
of the fossil fuels; these
are as follows.  With the
continuing of our present
growth rate, natural gas
will be used up in 38 years.
If we are to discover five
times the known resources,
it will only last 49 years.
The figures for petroleum
are 31 years with the
known reserves and 50 years

with the discovery of
five times the known amount.
Coal could be expected to
last 2300 years.  However,
if the other fuels exhaust
themselves, increasing the
demand and then with the
present growth rate, it
could only be expected to
satisfy the needs for 111
years.  This exploitation
would inevitably continue
to increase the degradation
of the environment through
strip mining and pollution.
Whether these figures are
exactly correct have little
bearing on the issue.  The
fact remains that fossil

fuel-derived energy is intrinsically polluting, bound by specific time limit parameters and increasing in capital cost due to scarcity, researching for new finds, and the fluctuating price of capital.

"Big business" and clients of architects and other designers of our built environment are reluctant to accept the present slight increase in initial cost of either a building designed with energy conservation principles in mind or utilizing alternative energy sources. What is not taken into account is the life-cycle cost. This would obviously indicate the savings in fuel costs which will inevitably continue to rise considerably. What this saves the environment can only be conceptually projected and generally is not transferred to monetary equivalents. In life cycle cost figuring, initial cost and material replacement are some of the factors considered.

When industry begins to shift its concerns to the production of elements

OIL

| Year of Estimate | Lifetime (years) | Depletion Date |
|---|---|---|
| 1920 | 81 | 2001 |
| 1920 | 57 | 1977 |
| 1933 | 19 | 1952 |
| 1935 | 12 | 1947 |
| 1935 | 18 | 1953 |
| 1937 | 26 | 1953 |
| 1948 | 22-160 | 1970-2108 |
| 1950 | 30 | 1980 |
| 1951 | 25 | 1976 |
| 1952 | 100 | 2052 |
| 1952 | 123 | 2075 |
| 1952 | 136 | 2088 |
| 1952 | 159 | 2111 |
| 1953 | 23 | 1976 |
| 1955 | 25 | 1980 |
| 1957 | 118 | 2075 |
| 1959 | 38 | 1997 |
| 1960 | 38 | 1998 |
| 1960 | 40 | 2000 |
| 1961 | 33 | 1994 |
| 1962 | 36 | 1998 |
| 1963 | 32 | 1995 |
| 1963 | 35 | 1998 |
| 1964 | 31 | 1995 |
| 1965 | 30 | 1995 |
| 1966 | 35 | 2001 |
| 1968 | 35 | 2003 |
| 1969 | 35 | 2004 |
| 1971 | 30 | 2001 |

NATURAL GAS

| Year of Estimate | Lifetime (years) | Depletion Date |
|---|---|---|
| 1952 | 84 | 2036 |
| 1962 | 48 | 2010 |
| 1969 | 48 | 2017 |
| 1970 | 38 | 2008 |
| 1971 | 20 | 1991 |

COAL

| Year of Estimate | Lifetime (years) | Depletion Date |
|---|---|---|
| 1913 | 5940 | 7853 |
| 1913 | 5820 | 7733 |
| 1937 | 3730 | 5667 |
| 1937 | 217 | 2154 |
| 1948 | 2200 | 4148 |
| 1948 | 3420 | 5368 |
| 1948 | 3600 | 5548 |
| 1949 | 4948 | 6728 |
| 1949 | 3780 | 5728 |
| 1952 | 500 | 2452 |
| 1952 | 258 | 2210 |
| 1953 | 3850 | 5803 |
| 1955 | 3846 | 5801 |
| 1957 | 700-843 | 2657-2800 |
| 1961 | 1270 | 3231 |
| 1968 | 3300 | 5268 |
| 1969 | 3700 | 5669 |

TABLE 1.2  A SURVEY OF FORECASTS OF THE DEPLETION OF FOSSIL FUELS.  *Source: The Futurist.*

utilized in alternative energy systems (or passive energy systems) then these initial price restraints will dissolve. In most cases life cycle costs already place them in a competitive position on the market.

When investigating our built environment within the context of energy use, it becomes readily apparent that the energy is used wastefully with the existing knowledge of heat recovery processes, insulation techniques, simple orientation concerns and basic form response principles available, there is no excuse for designers to continue to neglect the impact of the built environment on the ecosphere.

Architectural lighting and space heating are two of the largest and most visable consumers of energy that the designer should concern himself with. Since the advent of completely sealed buildings, the amount of energy utilized has grown considerably. Schools are often the largest consumers of lighting energy. Much of this is due to the use of only a few, often inoper-

able, windows. Two of the most prodigious wastes of energy through lighting are in high level lobby and facade lighting. An extraordinary example of the massive waste of energy can be seen in the newly completed World Trade Center towers. These two towers alone demand the energy input of a city of 100,000.[5] Continual air conditioning is required due to metabolic heat build-up, lighting and penetration of solar radiation. The building is a completely sealed volume,

relying upon a massive mechanical system dependent upon fossil fuels.

The materials used and the way they are used by the building industry constitutes a major dilemma for energy conservation. The recent dependence on plastics and other synthetics that are produced at a much higher energy cost than that of the materials they are replacing, has accounted for a lot of energy usage that should be questioned. This questioning should also apply to situations where

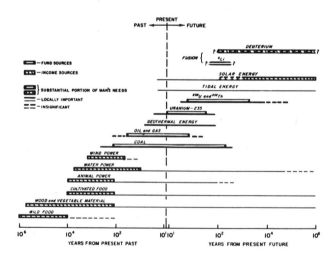

FIGURE 1.2 MAN'S USE OF ENERGY THROUGH THE MILLENIA.
*Reprinted with permission from The Futurist, published by the World Future Society, P.O. Box 30369 (Bethesda), Washington, D.C. 20014.*

aluminum is used. Aluminum has been predicted to last, at best, 100 years and at an exponential rate of growth, 31 years, according to a Bureau of Mines study. Copper is predicted to last 36 years and only 21 at an exponential growth rate. Both of these minerals are used in alternative natural energy mechanical systems. Hopefully, through further research, their usage can be eliminated.

During the design and construction phase, the designer(s) and those who carry forth the design, should pay careful attention to a building's

    orientation
    bioclimatic concerns
    climatic data
    physiogomy of the site
    building form response
    choice of materials
    construction practices
    potential use of passive
      energy sources

The end result will be as much as a 50% savings of the energy that would be consumed under current normal standards. The proper manipulation of these elements is a direct function of the bioclimatic needs which are the basis for criteria used in heating, cooling and lighting design and all are synergetic with the synthesizing of our built environment and Nature.

It may be possible to justify this grandoise waste of energy with the fallacy that our standard of living has increased, but has it? All that is necessary to disprove that hoax is to look at non-subsidized housing in the lower middle income market; for instance, the mobile home industry and much of the cheap tract housing presently being constructed. Both of these use cheap building materials, creating high energy usage per square foot, rapid rate of deterioration, and a high regeneration rate. All of this is contained within a culturally deficient, dormitory-like, suburban sprawl.

Under conditions such as those, and many more, the question can be justifiably raised as to whether it is necessary to build a new structure when it may be cheaper and less energy consuming to utilize an al- ready existing structure. The question of the necessity for a new building is a difficult and ambiguous one that should be carefully analyzed by both client and designer.

In the initial phases of design, large offices quite frequently separate aspects of the design work into distinct packages which are to be carried out by independent teams of designers. If there is very little communication between designers, mechanical and structural engineers and other consultants, then the building is likely to lack the cohesion required for an energy-conservative design. This design concept grew from the attitude that a building is a compilation of parts. For a building to function in coordination with the environment, there can exist no illusion of independence between the interior and exterior environment, the sun, the building form, fenestration, materials, mechanical and electrical systems and the bioclimatic needs of the users.

## 1.2 Contemporary Solutions (technology)

The industrial nations have been addicted to and subjugated by technology. In its overwhelming obsession with material comforts, society has overlooked such paramount concerns as the psychological, social and political aspects of human existence. It is not a question of whether or not technology should exist, but rather the manner in which it is administered, by the policy-making power base, which should be revised. Technological issues cannot be dealt with as specific, isolated subjects removed from the holistic framework of necessary change.

As problems associated with contemporary technology have previously been discussed, a summary will assist us in a discussion of the current and alternative solutions. Basically, fossil fuel-derived energy has an intrinsically high pollution rate, a wasteful exploitation of its fuels, and high capital cost where only "big business" can afford the price economically but humanity pays the price

socially. There is a continual feedback loop between the powerful, detached policy-makers and the technical specialists' elite, determining the direction technology assumes. This feedback loop has little connection with the "average" citizen. This stimulates his dislike for large scale, centralized production of energy that puts a limitation on the individual's control of his own energy. However, there are substantial arguments against individual energy production. Large scale production of energy has its advantages. Unlike the current trend in technology, large scale production can build interdependence between countries, unifying their efforts. This interdependence is grossly misused today, but the potential for such a relationship exists.

The most obvious, current solution to the energy dilemma is the "fix-it" response.[6] This is a response derived from within the feedback loop mentioned earlier that stimulates more technology rather than a reorientation of existing technology or less technology. There are

two very clear examples of this reaction. The most simplistic example is the automobile anti-pollution device. This device minimizes the direct air pollution from the auto itself, but creates a need for increased gasoline requirements. This places demands on industry to increase gasoline production which in turn increases air pollution and the depletion of a fossil fuel. This device obviously did not solve the air pollution problem; it merely placed it out of sight. One might say that essentially system B is built to rectify the effects of system A. This kind of progression may never have an ending.

Another example is nuclear energy (fission). When it was first realized that our continuation of the present lifestyle would create a need for a new energy source, nuclear energy seemed to be the best possible solution to keep from altering the present trend. The lifestyle itself was never questioned nor were alternatives analyzed that would discontinue the pollution, time parameters and depletion of non-renewable

resources. The amount of thermal pollution and radioactive waste created from nuclear fission reaction is staggering. If 70% of our energy needs are satisfied by nuclear energy in year 2000, 30 million pounds of radioactive waste per year will have to be "disposed of."[7] This material has a half life of 2500 years and to date no completely safe material casing has been designed that can withstand the effects of radioactivity. All the "System B's" that will be necessary to counteract the dangerous effects of nuclear energy in the future will prove to be ridiculous. One such reaction to the nuclear waste problem is the breeder reactor. It should be realized that no matter how successful the breeder is, it cannot create fissionable material beyond the physical volume of the non-renewable metal.

Current solutions to the energy situation do not justifiably attach the underlying sources creating the problems. Should they continue in their overt blindness, the crisis will eventually reappear and with it more difficult and potentially dangerous dilemmas.

## 1.3 Alternative Solutions

The current situation clearly dictates the need for a directional pattern of technology that is essentially nonpolluting, not exploitative of natural resources, simplistic in principles, socially and culturally rejuvenating (due to the potential intensive involvement by the community or individuals in the preservation of the environment), generates no danger to the annihilation of humanity through misuse, and denotes a significant step on the ever-continuing evolutionary path.

The alternative technologies have quite often been associated with primitive aspects aligned with increasing physical hardship and danger to life. By no means do passive energy sources do away with technology or 200 years of scientific knowledge. However, they are not afraid to admit that much can be gained from vernacular architecture, which consists of shelters consciously designed in harmonious response to the environment. Vernacular architecture can be associated with cultures who treated and respected the earth as the sustainer of life. To these people, antagonistic reactions to her are the same as to one's mother. Utilizing alternatives to the contemporary solutions can only be classified as civilizing.

Begining with Chapter five, four alternative solutions and their characteristics are thoroughly discussed. Water is more limited in it's availability due to it's predominately rural locations.

The characteristic attributes of solar energy are almost obvious. There is no thermal pollution because no heat energy is being added. The only heat energy is that which is coming in from the sun. There are no by-products or physical waste from its utilization. Solar energy can easily be integrated at community and village

scales, thereby encouraging community involvement in the environment. By virtue of the nature of solar energy, its potential for misuse is reduced.

Unequal distributions of solar energy over the world create varying wind patterns. These general wind patterns flow over the earth and can vary according to microclimate. Although wind energy is less evenly distributed and more difficult to store than some other forms of power, in many areas of the world its potential has already been proven. Wind energy is also nonpolluting, because it uses the energy that is always available. There are no time parameters on solar and wind energy as long as the sun is shining.

The processing of organic matter through anaerobic decomposition produces a natural gas called methane. Its BTU factor is lower than conventional forms of natural gas, but it still remains a renewable resource. The use of methane determines its potential for pollution. This is inherently very low. When stored, then processed in a fuel cell set-up, the waste by-product is fresh water.

The data gathering, analyzing and developments of these three alternatives have been, in the past, performed at relatively small scales. The data however, is invaluable for any scale. Its past applications, though associated with small scale and rural utilization, do not indicate that with some alterations the urban scale cannot be explored using the same basic principles. There have been several proposals for supplying, through solar energy, the demands of a nation or continent. These proposals should be carefully considered in terms of the ecosystem of the area involved and the climatic alterations that could occur when covering so much land with solar collectors. Other proposals suggest a spacecraft which would use photovoltaic conversion principles to produce electricity which is relayed back to earth. These proposals also lend themselves to potential misuse which should be carefully dealt with. Many of the major developments and reforms will be generated at the urban scale. These passive energy systems will ultimately change the direction in architecture from the ludicrous games of "who can build the tallest," to a regional, non-homo-generic (by the nature of the energy source and regional climatic requirements) and socially responsive morphology.

Many of these alternative solutions easily adapt to aspects of what Soleri calls miniaturization. This is the process of reducing the complexities affecting man and his environment to a more human dimension by increasing the reaching power of man. It is an evolution of matter to mind, from the haphazard to the coordinated. This can be seen when a higher organism, such as man, takes with him a form of reality and a high degree of complexity to a multilevel, human ecology.[8]

In the Fall of 1973 a new approach for dealing with the value of energy in our society emerged. It is most frequently referred to as the concept of *net energy*. Dr. Howard Odum, Graduate Research Professor at the University of Florida, first brought

forth the term in a paper presented to the Royal Swedish Academy of Sciences. The concept of net energy may be simply stated as "it takes energy to get energy."

For example, a heating or cooling system design is completely analyzed in energy equivalents as to the man-made and natural materials and processes necessary for its production, and weighed against the services it would provide, it would then be evident over time whether the system would yield an excess of net energy. This universal concept may be applied to eliminate many incorrect design decisions. This concept presents a "whole-system view" of the environment with all its interactions. Dr. Odum's energy system analysis brings out the realities of design decisions in energy terms.

The operation of taking a concentrated source of energy such as nuclear fuel and diluting it to usefulness, requires a tremendous amount of energy in the form of natural materials mining and processing as well as the energy in the form of natural forces in the environment.

The reverse, going from a dilute energy form to a concentrated form, is just as wasteful. This may be seen when solar energy, a dilute energy source, is concentrated to perform functions well beyond its natural boundaries.

By following the principles of the net energy approach there are many instances where the use of solar energy actually consumes more energy in the production of equipment and installation than will ever be recovered by the system. Consequently, many alternative energy system designs yield no net energy and actually waste energy. The designer is urged to make an investigation into net energy calculations prior to making a decision on a system design. It is necessary that each system and energy source be optimally matched for its function.

It was stated in the beginning and is now repeated, that reforms in our contemporary technological framework will only occur at the policy-making level. Alternative technologies have the potential to be catalytic agents in accelerating the rate of development within the feedback loop. Other catalytic determinants within the sociological and psychological frameworks further accelerate this broad-based reform. The danger of intensive specialization has the potential to contradict and disintegrate the concept of the inter-relationship of the whole. These changes cannot be assumed to be partial or arbitrary but basic to survival of a major ecosystem.

FOOTNOTES:

1. Anderson, Bruce. *Solar Energy and Shelter Design*, M.I.T. Thesis, January 1973, p. 6.

2. Schurr, S.H. and B.C. Netschert. *Energy in the American Economy 1850-1975*, Johns Hopkins Press, Baltimore, Md., 1960, p. 1.

3. *Op.cit.* Anderson, p. 6.

4. Meadows, Dennis, et.al. *Limits to Growth*, Cambridge, Mass., M.I.T. Press, 1972.

5. Stein, Richard. "Architecture and Energy," *Architectural Forum*, July-August 1973, p. 46.

6. Clark, Robin. "The Pressing Need for Alternative Technology," *Impact of Science on Technology*, vol. 23, no. 4, 1973.

7. *Op.cit.* Anderson, p. 6.

8. Soleri, Paolo. *Matter Becoming Spirit*, Anchor Press, Garden City, New York, 1973.

REFERENCES:

"The Biosphere," *Scientific American*, vol. 223, no. 3, September 1970.

Bender, Tom. *Environmental Design Primer*, Schocker Books, New York, 1973.

Citizen's Advisory Committee on Environmental Quality, *Citizen Action Guide to Energy Conservation*, Washington, D.C., September 1973.

Cook, Earl. "Energy Sources for the Future," *The Futurist*, August 1972, pp. 142-152.

Dubin, Fred. "Energy for Architects," *Architecture Plus*, July 1973, pp. 39-49, 74-75.

Harper, Peter. "In Search of Allies for the Soft Technologies," *Impact of Science on Technology*, vol. 23, no. 4, 1973, pp. 287-301.

Landsberg, H.H. and Schurr, S.H. *Energy in the United States*, Random House, New York, 1968.

Odum, Howard T. *Environment, Power and Society*, John Wiley & Sons, Inc., New York, 1971.

Odum, H.T. *Energy Basis for Man and Nature*, McGraw-Hill Co., New York, 1976

Schumacher, E.F. *Small Is Beautiful*, Harper & Row, New York, 1973.

Southwest Florida Planning Team, Department of Architecture, University of Florida.

# 2. Regional and Site Adaption

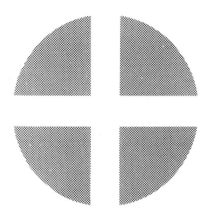

There are certain climatic elements at work at any given instant which directly influence both the external and internal spaces of a building. This chapter attempts to outline the basic nature of these factors, their integration of certain microclimatic levels and their influence on human comfort. For more information it is sug-gested that further readings be made into standard cli-matological books. The primary sources of informa-tion used here are B. Givoni's *Man, Climate and Architecture*; "Solar Energy in Housing" in *Architectural Design*, October 1973, pp. 634-661 and *Design with Climate* by Victor Olgyay. Other references have been made accordingly. These are excellent sources for more complete information on the relationship of climatic elements to the human body within the context of building design.

## 2.1 Man's Biological Relationship to His Surroundings

The basis of human comfort in the design of an internal

space is the combination of two primary elements: the external climatic conditions and, secondly, the demands placed upon the internal climate by the activity that will be occurring in the space. The interaction of the internal and external climates occurs at the barriers between them, these being the outer walls, the floor and the roof. Since the two-way flow of energy occurs at those points, it is obvious that this is where the regulation of energy must be controlled. The barrier can be so designed to fluctuate due to variations in the environmental conditions, either internal or external, or be of a stable design when conditions are known not to vary. Since these surfaces regulate heat gain and loss, they also offer the potential for utilizing the external environment at times and completely inhibiting its intrusion at other times. One of the more frequent contributors to wasteful energy consumption occurs when a stable condition is assumed in a building design (such

as a sealed volume type as discussed in Chapter 1) in an area where a manipulation of the external environment for either ventilation, heating, cooling or all three could allow for less energy expenditure. Conventional design techniques fail to acknowledge the biological potentials that the surroundings have to offer Man.

D.H.K. Lee[1] has summarized the human body's heat gains and heat losses into seven categories. These categories basically involve four processes of heat exchange: radiation, conduction, convection and evaporation. Of these processes, it is estimated that radiation accounts for about 2/5 of the heat loss from the body, convection for 2/5, and evaporation for 1/5; however, these proportions change with variations in the thermal conditions. Table 2.1 gives the seven categories and exemplifies the types of exchanges made in day-to-day living. The definite data as to internal climate temperatures vary with the climatic conditions of the area and the activity occurring within

the building. There are many publications of data available with regard to internal environmental conditions which should be investigated prior to completing any aspect of a final design. It is up to the designer to produce an environment that is comfortable to the users and will not place undue stress on the body's heat compensating mechanism.

## 2.2  Forms of Heat

*Latent heat* is the thermal energy released when a substance changes state as in fusion or vaporization. This is to a large degree involved in evaporation and in many mechanical systems where a gas changes into a fluid or the reverse. *Sensible heat* is the energetic property of matter whereby the degree of molecular excitation of a given mass is its temperature. When materials are given an identical energy input at the same initial temperature, then the measurement of their different thermal capacities

TABLE 2.1 HEAT EXCHANGE
BETWEEN MAN AND SURROUNDINGS;
reprinted with permission
from *Design with Climate* by
Victor Olgyay.

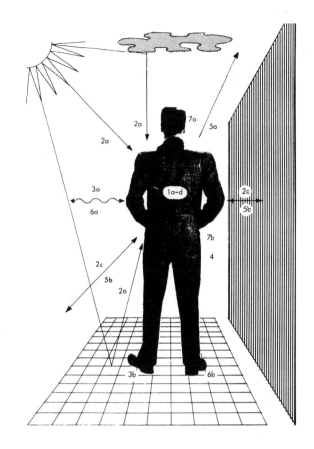

GAINS

1.  Heat generated by:

    a) Basal processes
    b) Activity
    c) Digestive, etc.
       processes
    d) Muscle tensing and
       shivering

2.  Absorption of radiant
    energy:

    a) From the sun directly
       and reflected
    b) From glowing radia-
       tors
    c) Other hot objects

3.  Heat conduction toward
    the body:

    a) From air above skin
       temperature
    b) By contact with
       hotter objects

4.  Condensation of atmos-
    pheric moisture (occa-
    tional)

LOSSES

5.  a) Outward radiation
       to the sky
    b) To colder surround-
       ings

6.  Heat conduction away
    from the body:

    a) To air below skin
       temperature

    b) By contact with
       colder surfaces

7.  Evaporation

    a) From the respiratory
       tract
    b) From the skin

is their *specific heat.*
*Thermal capacity* is the
volumetric expression of
a material's specific
heat.

*Conduction* occurs when molecular excitation spreads
from one mass to another
(or through it) going from
one of higher temperature
to one of a lower temperature. *Convection* occurs
in gases and fluids when
they loose their density
due to thermal energy
gain, and rise to form
currents. This is an im-
portant principle of
natural ventilation,
natural cooling and in
the use of wind energy.
*Radiant heat* is energy in
motion. All radiation
travels in straight lines
at the speed of light
(186,000 miles per second).
It is important to remember
that the shorter the wave
length, the more energy
content. This basic prin-
ciple is evident in the
process of trapping solar
energy for heating pur-
poses. A black body is the
most efficient absorber/
emitter of radiation. The
wave length of radiation
emitted from a body is in-
versely proportional to its

temperature measured in °K.
Radiation is either transmitted, where it continues
on its way through a material, reflected, where the
radiation is deflected, or
absorbed, where the radiation comes to an end. A
unique quality of glass and
some plastics is that they
have potential to do all
three simultaneously or
under certain conditions,
independently.

## 2.3  Solar Radiation

Solar radiation is measured
in langleys per minute,
which is equivalent to one
calorie of radiated energy
per square centimeter per
minute or 221 BTU per
square foot per hour. De-
pending upon geographical
location, time of day and
year, and atmospheric conditions, the intensity of
solar radiation reaching
the surface of the earth
will vary from 0-1.5 langleys per minute.

Solar radiation is electromagnetic radiation emitted
from the sun.[2] In general,
the solar spectrum of light
is divided into three categories of varying wave

length. These regions are
the ultra violet, the
visible range, and the
infrared. The maximum
intensity of solar radiation
occurs in the visible range,
but over half of the energy
is in the infrared. Absorption, scattering and reflection by the atmosphere,
decreases the spectral
distribution (figure 2.1).
Much of the shorter wave
lengths' energy is scattered
by water droplets in the air
in the blue and violet
spectrum, giving a blue sky.
At times long wave radiation
is scattered in the yellow
and red range, and when
mixed with that scattered in
the blue range, the sky
assumes a white appearance.
This often occurs when there
is a large percentage of
dust particles in the air,
such as over dense city
areas.

The mean value of solar
radiation falling on the
earth's atmosphere perpendicular to the sun's rays is
generally accepted as 420
$BTU/ft^2/hr$. The amount
falling on the earth is
less, subject to the atmospheric conditions.[3] The
intensity of radiation gain
on the earth's surface is

subject to the height above sea level, where less is lost to the atmosphere.

According to Victor Olgyay in *Design with Climate*, radiant heat transfer is divided into five main areas. These are, in order of importance:[4]

1. direct short wave radiation from the sun,
2. diffuse short wave radiation from the sky vault,
3. short wave radiation reflected from the surrounding terrain,
4. short wave radiation from the heated ground and nearby objects, and
5. outgoing long wave radiation-- exchange from building to sky.

Roughly twice as much solar energy falls on a horizontal surface during overheated times as on a vertical surface.[5] A lot of this heat is in turn reflected into buildings. Table 2.2 gives the estimated percentage of incident solar radiation diffusely reflected from various surfaces. The importance of this is for

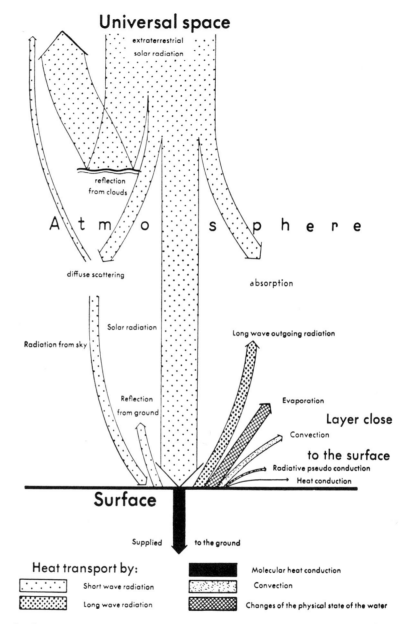

**Heat transport by:**

| | | |
|---|---|---|
| Short wave radiation | Molecular heat conduction | |
| Long wave radiation | Convection | |
| | Changes of the physical state of the water | |

FIGURE 2.1   HEAT EXCHANGE AT NOON FOR A SUMMER DAY
*Reprinted with permission from Climate and Architecture*

**23**

% OF INCIDENT SOLAR RADIATION
DIFFUSELY REFLECTED.

| Type of Surface | Est. % |
|---|---|
| Bare ground, dry | 10-25 |
| Bare ground, wet | 8-9 |
| Sand, dry | 18-30 |
| Sand, wet | 9-18 |
| Mold, black, dry | 14 |
| Dry grass | 32 |
| Green fields | 3-15 |
| Green leaves | 25-32 |
| Dark forest | 5 |
| Desert | 34-28 |
| Salt flats | 42 |
| Brick, depending upon color | 23-48 |
| Asphalt | 15 |
| City area | 10 |

TABLE 2.2    PERCENTAGE OF
INCIDENT SOLAR RADIATION
DIFFUSELY REFLECTED from
*Design with Climate*, V.
Olgyay.

the designer to be totally aware of the surroundings and the possible advantages and disadvantages that could occur with so much potential energy radiating onto (or into) a building.

Long wave radiant heat is emitted by the surface of the earth to the atmosphere and outer space. The amount emitted varies as the temperature differs between the earth's surface and the atmosphere. Cloud cover is an important consideration in determining the transmission of the long wave energy. The long wave radiation emitted in overcast conditions, is returned by the clouds, which in turn raises the ambient air temperature. Water vapor is highest in long wave radiation absorption and emission. When the sky is clear the surface of the earth is cooler because the long wave radiation can travel to outer space.

*Humidity* is the measurement of the water vapor content of the air. It is critical to control humidity through the designs of the heating and cooling system and wall structure. Failure to

regard this can result in a "wet wall" due to condensation. This obviously accelerates the deterioration rate and human discomfort. Humidity levels may vary due to the activities occurring within the space and the varying climatic concerns of the region.

When the earth's surface cools more than the surrounding air, a "surface inversion" can occur where the air closer to the earth's surface is cooler than the air higher above it. When this lower air containing a certain amount of water vapor is cooled, its moisture-holding capacity is reduced, increasing its relative humidity until it becomes saturated. This saturation temperature is called the *dew point*. Any further cooling below this dew point causes the moisture in the air to condense on the colder surface. When this colder surface is the ground, then the more familiar form of condensation known as dew is present. When it mixes with cooler air, fog is the result. When expansion due to rising currents causes

the cooling of the air, large scale precipitation is the result.

Colder air tends to collect in a lower valley or other low topographical situations such as ditches or low areas next to a building. This raises the potential for fog to form. Long wave radiative heat loss which will cool the surface of the earth also stimulates fog, dew and frost conditions.

Solar radiation has an indirect effect on air temperature. Air is essentially transparent to direct solar radiation.[6] The primary factor involving air temperature is the heating and cooling of the earth's surface upon which solar radiation has direct influence.

Air layers close to the surface of the earth are warmed and rise by convection creating breezes and more powerful winds. During the winter and at night when the sky is clear, long wave radiative heat loss to the atmosphere cools the surface of the earth, consequently cooling

the air in contact with it. When vapor condenses into liquid droplets, the latent heat involved tends to warm the air and reduce cooling. This and other factors stimulate mountain and sea breezes and forms of precipitation that are discussed under microclimate (2.5).

Insolation is the rate at which solar energy is received on a horizontal surface per unit of measurement. The determination of insolation effects is an important tool to the designer in determining shading effects, insulation, fenestration location, orientation, building configuration and mechanical systems.

Charts showing the average solar energy received on a horizontal plane at the earth's surface are excellent for gross purposes. However, when dealing with designs requiring specific data on the amount of solar radiation to be received, as for collector design, these charts do not include the variations that can occur in microclimatic conditions.

## 2.4  Sun Path Diagrams and Sundials

Sun path diagrams allow one to project the location of the paths of the sun for each date and time required along with altitude and bearing data. The diagrams project the imaginary sky vault on a plane parallel to the horizon. The observer is assumed to be at the center, facing south for northern latitudes and north for southern latitudes. Many sun path diagrams for the north latitudes are located in *Graphics Standards*. The sun's position at any date and hour can be calculated. The altitude angles are in 10° intervals by equidistant concentric circles. The bearing angles are also at 10° intervals by equally spaced radii. They range from 0° south meridian to 180° north meridian. Figure 2.2 shows a view aiding in the understanding of a sun path diagram.

The earth's axis is inclined 23°27' and rotates 15° hourly in its orbit around the sun.[7] The declination of the sun occurs in the extremes between the summer solstice and winter solstice.

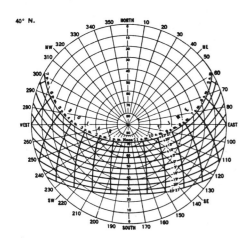

40° N.

Figure 55.—Solar altitude and azimuth for selected days of the year at 40 degrees north latitude.

Sun Path Diagram for 40°
North Latitude

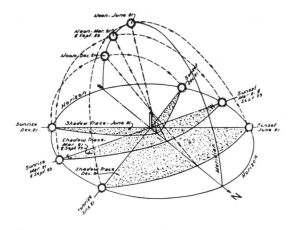

FIGURE 2.2  A GRAPHIC
PROJECTION OF A SUN PATH
DIAGRAM. *Reprinted with
permission from Climate
and Architecture.*

The sundial can be an invaluable tool to the designer when attempting to calculate altitudes and bearing angles where data is unavailable.  The sundial can also be utilized in cooperation with a model in determining shadow angles.  Appendix B covers the process of making a sundial, its calculations and application.

*2.5  Microclimate*

Have you ever noticed how spring seems to come earlier on one slope of a hill than the others, or when climbing a mountain in the early morning, that breezes flow up the side of the mountain as the sun rises?  These effects are the result of microclimatic conditions which may vary considerably in very short distances due to factors such as topography, elevation, soil, precipitation and many others. When extracting exact climatic data to choose a favorable location on a site, it is critical to investigate the microclimate.  Much of the weather

data available is compiled for the aviation industry. When this is the case, the data is compiled away from the earth's surface, sometimes in congested areas, on large buildings or at airports, so it applies little to ground area of normal capacity.[8]  The thin membrane we generally occupy is subject to fluctuations in wind, temperature, humidity and precipitation due to topography, water bodies, forests, paved areas, park areas and other buildings. Proper management in designing around existing microclimatic conditions can offer economics in heating, cooling, lighting, and cleaning of buildings.

To understand the impact climate has on the relationship between the built environment and nature, it is essential that a simultaneous processing of climatic data occur at both the micro and macro scales within generalized principles that can transcend any scale.

Elevation is one of the more influential factors in determining free air temperature.  Meteorologists in

certain parts of the world customarily give weather data according to feet above sea level because of the influence of elevation on vegetation. At certain times of the year "frost holes" will occur where cold air during the night drained into the lowest point in the terrain causing changes in temperature often as much as 11° and 20% differential in humidity. At all times of the year, colder air will exist often accompanied by a thin sheet of fog.

The crest of a hill is more exposed to wind conditions than the surrounding terrain. This may be favorable in some areas, but in many it would call for greater insulation of buildings, careful placement of openings and a building form which minimized the heat loss surface area in the direction of the prevailing winds during the underheated periods. Further discussion of designs requiring wind for natural ventilation and natural cooling will be given in Chapter 4. Just below a crest on the leeward side of a hill, protected from the prevailing winds, a completely different envi-

ronment may exist in contrast to that on the windward slope below the crest. The crest will receive higher velocities of wind in both the horizontal and vertical directions. High velocity areas also exist below and at the sides of the crest, with the lowest speeds near the bottom on the leeward side.

In the areas of the world where the underheated period determines the design, the most favorable location is in a south or southeasterly slope between bottom and top.[9] It might be remembered that a sloped site receiving 40% more winter radiation may be three and a half weeks ahead of other slopes when spring arrives. In many areas of steep terrain, breezes can occur on particular slopes, usually of a south or southeastern orientation. Solar radiation is absorbed by the earth, and the air close to the surface is heated and rises, thus creating breezes. These breezes are shallow winds flowing up the mountain during the day, varying as to slope orientation, and down at

night due to cold air drainage (figure 2.3). Breezes also occur between land and sea. During the day the air is heated over land more so than over large water surfaces of the same latitude. The warmer air rises, creating a suction effect, drawing in cooler air close to the surface of the water (figure 2.4). The process is reversed at night but since the temperature differential is greater in the daytime, the onshore breezes are stronger. Any major global pressure or wind system may alter the regularity and force of these breezes.

Precipitation has a direct relationship with wind flow, air temperature and relative humidity. Each variable fluctuates from month to month, season to season, as does precipitation. The length of precipitation time, its intensity and the frequency of its many manifestations dictate various building and site responses.

Precipitation is caused by rising air masses cooling by expansion as they rise, reaching their dew point.

This induces large scale condensation. These form clouds containing tiny water droplets and sometimes ice crystals. As heavier droplets form, they begin to fall. Should they survive the evaporative loss during the descent, precipitation occurs.[10]

One of the first principles of climate and precipitation interrelationships is illustrated by rising air mass phenomena. When air masses are made to rise for different reasons, three main types of precipitation are produced: convectional, convergent and orographic.[11]

Convectional precipitation is caused by ascending humid air masses that were heated by contact with warmer surfaces. As condensation occurs, latent heat is given off, reducing the rate of cooling and aiding the ascent. Convectional rain usually descends in heavy, short duration showers. In many mountainous areas known for their high humidity, convectional storms can be created almost daily under ideal conditions.

Convergent precipitation occurs with the rising of air in areas where air masses converge at low pressure zones or fronts. The rising air then follows the process of cooling and condensing to form clouds and finally precipitation.

Orographic precipitation emanates from air masses rising over mountain slopes due to pressure gradients. When those air masses strike static air in front of the mountains, orographic rains may begin. However, they may begin changing with elevation.

The rainfall is greatest on the windward side, sometimes never going beyond the ridge of large mountains. This often creates sharp differences in the landscape. On the microclimate level, precipitation can also vary due to the topography. Precipitation can be carried by the wind over a hill or small mountain from the windward side and deposited on the leeward side.

The soil also influences the air temperature. According to Helmut Lands-

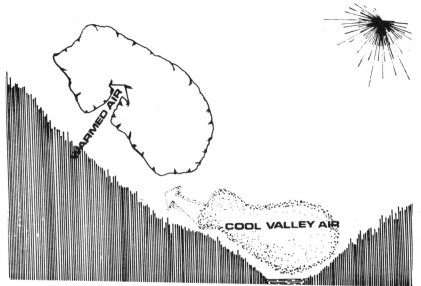

FIGURE 2.3  MOUNTAIN BREEZES.

berg,[12] it is frequently found that in summer at about one foot above the soil surface on a sunny day, there may exist as much temperature variation as 8° to 10° F, with the soil surface being lower. Exposed soil, depending upon its color, and grass covered ground may differ as much as 10° to 14°, with the grassy area being cooler. The shaded surface obviously shows variant temperatures, frequently differing as much as 5° F at six feet off the ground.

Sizable bodies of water can exert subtle influences on the microclimate. Water has a higher specific heat than that of land and will tend to be warmer in winter than the surface of the land, and cooler in the summer than land. This further applies to night when water is generally warmer and in the day, cooler. This will have an effect on the air temperatures in the zone of most human activity. Locating near water can have its advantages but if wind is not taken into account, these advantages can be lost. Areas on the leeward side of a water body will tend to have less extreme weather than that on the windward side. Water will also raise the humidity in the immediate vicinity. The larger the water body, the less subtle the influences become. This has been shown earlier by the relationship between ocean and shore. In the region of the Great Lakes, the average January temperature rates approximately 5° F higher and the average July temperatures decreased by about 3° F.[13]

The usage of highly sophisticated measuring equipment to determine microclimate variations is not necessarily needed. Nature herself, can be a very sensitive indicator of inherent stresses placed on the natural systems by the climate. Nature offers the unique opportunity to view simultaneously, the variations in climate within a regional environment.

According to Lynch,[14] the location of common trees like red maple, alder, topelo, hemlock and willow, indicate wet ground that is poorly drained. Oak and hickory, when growing next

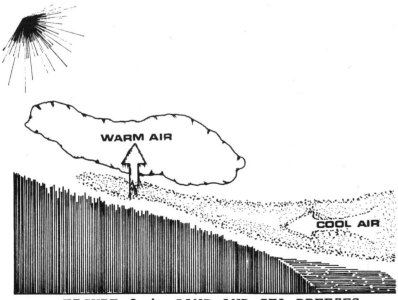

FIGURE 2.4   LAND AND SEA BREEZES.

to each other, indicate warm, dry land. Spruce and fir, growing near each other, are indicative of a cold and moist area. Pitch pine and scrub oak are evidence of very dry land with perfect drainage. Red cedars designate poor soil. Plant suitability depends upon drainage, acidity, humus, temperature, sunlight, moisture and wind flow.

When specific natural flora is to be saved, then an intensive analysis should be made as to where machinery is to be on the site and where roads will be located. The microclimate will be severely altered once heavy machinery starts compacting the earth, restricting the role of roots and the porosity of the soil. The water table will begin to fall and forms of pollution will gradually appear. Appendix F gives a synopsis of Malcom Wells' concepts of minimum impact construction practices. These are worthy of including, for if the designer is not sensitive, knowledgeable and aware, the damage he allows may render the

site unsuitable for the many forms of vegetation and ground cover which may have been desirable

The microclimate of the built environment is of a completely different nature. Natural ground cover has a tendency to balance and stabilize temperatures and decrease extremes, but the man made environment almost invariably exaggerates them. Plants will tend to reradiate much less heat than inorganic materials and are much cooler due to evaporation occurring on their surfaces. Landsberg sites an example where the air temperature in a meteorological shelter read 98° F and asphalt pavement nearby had a reading of 124° F. This, of course, influenced the zone of human activity (approximately four feet above the surface) which had a temperature of 108° F. A concrete surface was 14° cooler than the asphalt. Similar effects were noted when radiant temperatures were measured rather than air temperatures.

In terms of light reflectivity, concrete reflected between 25 to 35% of the

incident light, while grass surfaces reflected only 10 to 15%. A fully leaved tree may inhibit 25 to 30% the light that would fall on a horizontal surface in an unshaded area.

City areas demonstrate a remarkable difference in microclimate from surrounding areas. Few cities have been designed where climate played a significant role in its morphology. Slow and subtle changes have occurred in many city microclimates due to rapid, haphazard growth. If designed without regard for wind, buildings and streets can accidentally produce by a funneling effect, powerful winds from mild breezes. Skyscrapers have a profound effect when designed in ignorance of climatic factors. Meteorologists say that not only is the wind pattern altered, but also the rainfall and the entire microclimate.

The number of excessively tall buildings is increasing. Fighting climatic factors rather than designing in cooperation with them can produce disastrous results. A recent victim of such a

conflict is the $100 million, all glass, John Hancock Tower in Boston. After the building was exposed to a hard wind, well-known to occur in the Boston area, 5000 thermoglass panels, each 4-1/2 x 12 feet and totaling 16 acres of glass, cracked and fell out.[15] They were replaced with the amount of plywood that it might take to build 30 houses, until the $6 million worth of new glass was installed. What caused this rather ludicrous event can be easily guessed, although the reports have not yet been made public. Presumably, the wind, striking on the high pressure side, created a very powerful vacuum, pulling the glass out of the frames. This is a high price to pay, economically and ecologically, for attempting a standoff with Nature.

It should be noted that the effect of large air currents rising by conduction due to a heated surface, such as that caused by a sunlit valley wall, can also happen to large building surfaces that are exposed to the sun. These air currents can be beneficial where natural ventilation is concerned, but they will alter potential cooling breezes on the street. Dense city areas generally have higher temperatures year round, sometimes by as much as 12° over the surrounding suburban areas. This is due to heat-absorptive masonry surfaces and heat generated by traffic, people, machinery, wasted space-heating and lighting.

Smog can have a substantial affect on the microclimate and has a direct detrimental influence on the human mechanism. It can raise the temperatures in cities by preventing heat escape. It also reduces the amount of visible solar radiation by as much as 30% and biologically important ultraviolet light by 50%.[16] When this excessive heat is combined with high humidity, human comfort is greatly reduced.

Precipitation as an element of city microclimate is of less significance than other elements but indeed should be regarded. The asphalt, concrete and masonry surfaces absorb little water, accenting the water run-off. Those surfaces do not benefit from evaporative cooling, except following a shower, so they generally add heat during already overheated periods. One advantage of city heat during the winter affects precipitation. When radiant heat passes into the atmosphere, it can raise the temperature of storm clouds enough to change snow to freezing rain, should the storm front be moving slowly enough.

In the northern hemisphere winter sunshine is almost always desired. Cityscapes invariably inhibit the penetration of sunlight. The ratio of street width to building height is a primary determinant in the amount of light striking the street. Obviously, this is regulated by the solar angles, but the composite percentages give an indication of progressive decreases in available solar illumination. On a surface behind a top floor window, no more than 50% of the potential illumination can be expected. At a height

below the roof line of a southern adjacent building, at about half the width of the street, the value of solar illumination is reduced to 35%, at one street width below the roof line only 25%, two street widths only 15% and four street widths, 8%.[17] This affects the required amount of artificial illumination.

Since glass can act as a radiation trap, the location of skylights and fenestration is critical in places where an excess amount of solar radiation could build up due to either direct or reflected solar radiation. (This will be discussed more specifically in Chapter 7.) The way to avoid excessive heat build-up is to have either a sun screen or a retractable shading device *outside* the glass surface. This is important to remember in cases where no build-up is desired. It is possible to allow some penetration for the purpose of raising internal air temperature by having variable shades or curtains on the inside. Careful decision-making should be made in the initial phases of development, to specify the particular needs of each space exposed to direct sunlight.

## 2.5 *Orientation*

Orientation is one of the most important principles in energy conservation design. Its effects on indoor climate should have a significant role in determining the type of activity to occur within the internal space in coordination with the functional and thermal considerations of the activity.

Initial investigations into orientation, precluding a final design, can by the nature of the subsystems involved, anticipate a synergetic approach to design. The information about microclimate should be combined with the concepts outlined in this section to give a more complete understanding of the principles affecting orientation.

There are two distinct climatic considerations whose manipulation influences or regulates indoor climate. The first of these is solar radiation and its heating effect on walls and rooms, the second being ventilation, which is directly associated with the relationship of building orientation and form to the prevailing winds. Both of these considerations will fluctuate according to microclimate effects, whether natural or induced. The final decision on orientation should be made after an evaluation of the quantitative physiological advantages of each element has been done. This will vary with the functional requirements of the building.

If the orientation is to be determined by factors other than climate, a thorough understanding of the climatic impact is necessary to make structural and morphological responses to modify the effects of temperature and wind.

The wall, roof and floor are the critical interfaces between the external and internal environment. The regulation of their external surface temperature has a direct influence on the materials, structure, durability and weathering

potential of each interface. The quantitative effect of radiation on a surface is dependent on two principles: color of the external surface and the air velocity closest to the external surface.[18] Only when calculations require accuracy, should the air velocity closest to the external surface be considered. For general information all that would be necessary is the general surface temperature which will depend on ambient air temperature and solar radiation incidence. The color of an external surface will directly influence the internal temperatures. When the external surface is light, absorption by the surface is low and ambient air temperature determines the thermal effect rather than incident radiation. However, if the surface is dark, the influence of irradiation dominates.[19] The heat flow through a wall, roof or floor is determined by the materials used. In all parts of the world solar radiation is distributed on a building unevenly. Once it is calculated where and when solar radiation will strike a building surface, decisions can be made as to color and building materials. Table 2.2 gives the percent of the reflectivity and emissivity of surfaces. This data can be of considerable importance in choosing materials and their colors according to the climatic determinants of the region. For example, a southern exposure at 40° north latitude receives nearly three times the solar energy from winter sunlight as the eastern or western exposures.[20] At lower latitudes, the difference may be greater.

Approximate external surface temperature can be determined empirically by the formulae

$$ts = ta + \frac{aI}{12} - 5$$

for a horizontal surface and

$$ts = ta + \frac{aI}{12} - 2$$

for a vertical surface.

ts = exterior temperature of the surface
ta = outdoor air temperature
a = absorptivity of the surface (dependent on color)
I = intensity of solar radiation.

These formulae were reprinted from Givoni's *Man, Climate and Architecture*.

The magnitude of temperature elevation above that of the ambient air temperature is related to wind velocity. In areas where a westerly wind prevails, the temperature elevation of the east wall will be higher than that of the west wall, even though almost the same amount of radiation falls on the surfaces at the same respective periods of time.

The external surface is less responsive to orientation concerns when the resistance of the wall material is higher, thus inhibiting the flow of heat into the internal space. There are two methods to decrease high surface temperature build-up: whitewashing the surface and increasing the thermal resistance of the small structure. Each have distinct, qualitative differences. Whitewashing reduces the absorptivity of the wall surface, minimizing the effect of solar radia-

tion on internal climate and tends to stabilize the internal temperature. A white or other light surface roof can reflect 70% of the sun's heat. Aluminum foil, when applied just under the roof, can reflect 95% of the heat away from the internal space.[21]

Increasing the thermal resistance of the wall moderates the heat transfer to the internal space, lowers the maximum temperature gradient and raises the minimum by inhibiting internal heat transfer to the external.

Orientation and location of fenestration is critical to internal temperatures. The location is variable depending upon those requirements of the internal space specified by the type of activity occurring within it. Quite often a conflict arises when designing for ventilation requirements and either attempting to retard or promote the flow of solar radiation into the space. Careful considerations of sunscreens and shading devices are important in such a conflict. Exterior shades, baffels and blinds reduce the internal heat gain and increase the effectiveness by as much as 35%.[22]

Solar energy is magnified as it penetrates a glazed surface. This heat could be dissipated by long wave radiation or convection to the exterior, but glass is opaque to both. In overheated periods, glass areas should be carefully shaded. As mentioned before, this is optimally done by exterior applications of sunshades, overhangs, vertical projections, awnings, vegetation, trees or any other potential external shading device. Information given in sun path diagrams or a sundial can be important in plotting the angles of the sun at particular times of the year.

The sol-air temperature[23] gives the combined thermal effect on the building exterior surface due to solar radiation and the ambient air conditions. The sol-air temperature includes three component temperatures: the ambient outdoor air, the fraction of the solar radiation absorbed by the surface

Differences Between Indoor and Outdoor Maxima (deg C)

| Shading variant | Ventilation variant | East | West | North | South | Average east-west | Average north-south |
|---|---|---|---|---|---|---|---|
| None | Window and opening closed | 5.9 | 11.3 | 3.5 | 3.5 | 8.6 | 3.5 |
| | Window open, opening with slot | 0.0 | 0.9 | -0.4 | 0.4 | 0.45 | 0.45 |
| | Window closed, opening open | 4.0 | 7.7 | 2.2 | 5.7 | 5.85 | 3.95 |
| External Dark | Window and opening closed | 0.0 | 0.5 | -0.3 | 0.0 | -0.15 | 0.25 |
| | Window open, opening with slot | 0.3 | 0.45 | 0.25 | 0.65 | 0.45 | 0.38 |
| External Light | Window and opening closed | -0.3 | 0.3 | -0.3 | -0.1 | 0.0 | -0.05 |
| | Window open, opening with slot | 0.1 | 0.3 | -0.2 | 0.0 | 0.2 | -0.1 |
| Internal Dark | Window and opening closed | 2.6 | 8.0 | 1.6 | 3.0 | 5.3 | 2.3 |
| Internal Light | Window and opening closed | 1.7 | 6.5 | 0.6 | 1.5 | 4.1 | 1.05 |

TABLE 2.3 TEMPERATURE VARIATIONS IN AN INTERNAL SPACE.
*Source: Man, Climate and Architecture.*

and the net long wave radiant heat exchange between the exterior surface and the environment. This is a theoretical external air temperature which aids in heat transfer calculations. The sol-air temperature can be found by the following simplified formula:[24]

$$t_{sa} = t_O + a(I) r_O + Qr$$

where:

$t_{sa}$ = the sol-air temperature

$a$ = the absorptivity of the external surface

$I$ = the intensity of total incident solar radiation on the surface

$r_O$ = overall external surface coefficient (resistance)

$t_O$ = outdoor air temperature °F

$Qr$ = 7 BTU/ft$^2$/hr for horizontal surfaces
= 0 for vertical surfaces (approximate values

The quantitative effect of solar radiation entering an internal space is related to the thermal properties of the structural materials. Window shading and ventilation must be considered in an overall assessment. Table 2.3 gives temperature variations in an internal space depending upon shading and ventilation. The degrees Centigrade (°C) can be changed to degrees Fahrenheit (°F) by the following formula:

$$C° (1.8) + 32 = F°.$$

The primary factors determining window design for ventilation are discussed more comprehensively in Chapter 4, but for the purposes of orientation some factors should be mentioned here. When depending upon the prevailing wind direction to induce natural ventilation, an opening should be located on the windward or high pressure side and on the leeward (low pressure) side. The design and placement of internal walls is critical in determining air flow.

Regional considerations in choosing a proper orientation are covered in Table 2.4. According to Olgyay, the thermal impact of solar radiation is measured over at least a one-year period. In the New York, New Jersey area, the total maximum insolation would come from an orientation due south. However, in the colder, underheated months, the maximum gain is from the east of south. During the summer or overheated period the biggest gain is from the southwest. His evaluation combining those findings and compromising harsh summer conditions and best winter conditions, is an orientation of 17.5° east of south. In this area a favorable site would then be a southeasterly slope with possible evergreen trees to the north and northwest and deciduous trees to the southwest, placed so as not to inhibit summer breezes but shade out harsh summer sun.

For the Phoenix, Arizona area, the same series of investigations were performed, stimulating a different orientation. In this analysis the compromise of the optimum sol-air orientation was 25° east of south. Table 2.4 indicates the orientations arrived at for the cool

**35**

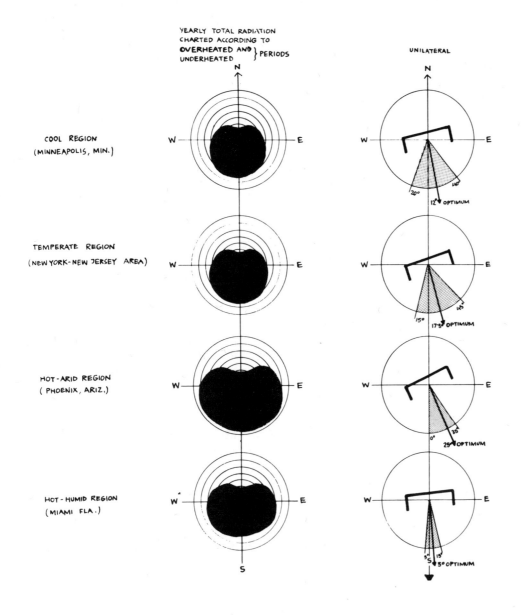

YEARLY TOTAL RADIATION
CHARTED ACCORDING TO
OVERHEATED AND } PERIODS
UNDERHEATED

UNILATERAL

COOL REGION
(MINNEAPOLIS, MIN.)

TEMPERATE REGION
(NEW YORK-NEW JERSEY AREA)

HOT-ARID REGION
(PHOENIX, ARIZ.)

HOT-HUMID REGION
(MIAMI FLA.)

region and the hot, humid region. In areas where the underheated period is dominant, materials of low reflectivity of solar radiation is advantageous. Table 2.2 gives data for determining the amount of reflectivity of materials.

It should now be clear that when a site is chosen, many interacting variables determine its potential. Some of these variables are elevation, topography, soil, amount of solar radiation, wind patterns, precipitation, water and vegetation. These factors then interact with other factors such as roads, power distribution, drainage, building code restrictions and any symbiotic parameters affecting the site. The climate of the internal space is then a function of the synthesis of all the factors mentioned, including the types of material used in the structural make-up of the walls, roof and floor, as well as exterior color and overall orientation.

TABLE 2.4   REGIONAL ORIENTATION CHART.   *Reprinted with permission from Design with Climate.*

In the U.S., modern buildings tend to look very much the same whether they are in northern or southern climates and regardless of their orientation on a particular site. This is because buildings have been designed largely to keep natural phenomena outside, to separate conditions inside from the outdoors as much as possible, relying on mechanical systems to do much of the work. Not only is this wasteful in terms of energy consumption, but it also seems quite boring in terms of regional esthetics.

*Richard Stein*

FOOTNOTES:

1. Lee, D.H.K. *Physiological Objectives in Hot Weather Housing*, U.S. Housing and Home Finance Agency, Washington, D.C., 1953, p. 2.

2. Givoni, B. *Man, Climate and Architecture*, Elsevier Publishing Co., New York and London, p. 1.

3. Olgyay, Victor. *Design with Climate*, Princeton University Press, Princeton, New Jersey, 1963, p. 32.

4. *Ibid*, p. 33.

5. *Ibid*, p. 33.

6. *Op.cit.* Givoni, B., p. 6.

7. American Institute of Architects. *Graphics Standards*, John Wiley & Sons, New York, p. 71.

8. Landsberg, Helmut. "Microclimate Research in Relation to Building Construction," *Architectural Forum*, March 1947, pp. 114-119.

9. *Op.cit.* Olgyay, p. 155.

10. *Op.cit.* Givoni, p. 17.

11. *Ibid*.

12. *Op.cit.* Landsberg, p. 116.

13. *Op.cit.* Olgyay, p. 51.

14. Lynch, Kevin. *Site Planning*, M.I.T. Press, Cambridge, Mass., 1965, p. 81.

15. "Scraping the Sky," *Washington Post*, May 7, 1974.

16. *Op.cit.* Landsberg, p. 118.

17. *Ibid.*, p. 119.

18. *Op.cit.* Givoni, p. 192.

19. *Ibid.*, p. 193.

20. *Op.cit.* Olgyay, p. 53.

21. Pratt Institute, *Investigation of the Small House*, School of Architecture, Brooklyn, 1957.

22. *Op.cit.* Olgyay, p. 70.

23. Mackey, C.O. "Summer Weather Data and Sol-Air Temperature," *ASHVE Transactions* (50) 1945, p. 75.

24. Hoskins, Edward. *Solar Energy and the Natural House* (Preliminary Draft), Cogswell/Hausler Assoc., Chapel Hill, North Carolina.

REFERENCES:

Angus, T.C. *The Control of the Indoor Climate,* Pergamon Press, England, 1968.

Aronin, J.E. *Climate and Architecture,* Reinhold, New York, 1953.

Geiger, Rudolph. *The Climate Near the Ground,* Harvard University Press, Cambridge, 1950.

Leckie, J., et.al. *Other Homes and Garbage,* Sierra Club Books, San Francisco, 1975.

"The Climate," *Architectural Forum,* March 1951, pp. 180-193.

# 3. Energy Conservation

It is time for a new ethic based upon the concept of survival in a finite world. We must control the one factor for which we are responsible, the demand for energy.

## 3.1  Introduction

As architects, we are responsible for over one third of all energy used in the United States, more than 50% of which is being inefficiently expended.
It is time for us to develop a new energy ethic directed toward the goal of achieving minimum use of energy in building design.

The architectural process must be viewed as a consumer of energy and materials. We have to realize that energy consumption of a building originates with the initial design decisions and continues throughout the life of the building. Energy conservation practices not only manifest themselves through a decrease in energy demand but also a reduction in environmental pollution and the rate of use of our non-renewable resources.

Our attitude in the past has been toward dividing the design process into distinct packages, each independent of the others, i.e., the mechanical system considered as separate from the building design-- thus, leading to an overuse of energy. Depending upon the attitude we develop, the building industry can effect positive changes in the energy usage patterns of modern society.

The recycling of a building is one approach to conserving energy. The re-use and modification of an existing structure is quite often less in terms of energy expenditure than the construction of a new building. If the recycling of a building is considered, detailed economic and energy evaluations need to be done.

### 3.1a Life Cycle Costs

Principles of high energy consumption are largely incorporated into buildings to reduce initial costs. Clients are interested in systems that show an early return on initial investment and are inexpensive to install. Energy conservation systems and practices generally have high initial cost. However, if a comparative cost analysis were to be done over a period of time, the overall cost and energy expenditure would be lower.

### 3.1b Conservation through Use of Materials

General concensus holds that most structures contain more material than is needed for either stability or safety requirements. Codes and other related design standards provide generalized information to suit a wide degree of situations. As a result, they can suggest escalated use of material for a given situation. "More rigorous structural analysis eventually revised theory and codes, plus components responding in their cross section to varying structural demands will immediately allow substantial energy savings."[1] An overuse of material comes from economic pressure to reduce labor time at the cost of more material.

The factor of disposability in building supplies is another factor leading to excessive energy usage. There is a tremendous output in energy and labor for materials and procedures incorporating the principles of "planned obsolescence." Rather than this, energy should be invested in the production of more durable goods, ultimately a savings in time and upkeep.

The use of building materials which require less energy for their production should be encouraged. For example, it requires six times as much electric energy to produce a ton of aluminum than a ton of steel. Every material should be accompanied by an energy expenditure rating to aid in the selection of low energy usage materials.

The recycling of materials requires less energy than the refinement of new materials. For example, it takes only 5% as much energy to produce recycled aluminum as virgin aluminum.

Building materials should be chosen for their multifunctional uses; for example, the

use of panels which integrate thermal acoustical, electrical and structural facilities.

## 3.1c Exclusion or Inclusion of the Natural Environment

There are two opposing viewpoints regarding energy consumption and the natural environment. One focus considers the building as an enclosed envelope to be isolated from natural phenomena. The objective is to create a space with the minimum amount of thermal transfer. This attitude rides on the assumption that air is a consumer of energy and that in order to be used, it has to be cleaned and either cooled or heated. The solution to operating under a minimum amount of air infiltration requires odor absorbing devices and effective air filtration. The space is habitable as a result of extensive mechanical intervention. Should there be a mechanical or electrical failure, the space would become unusable.

The second viewpoint perceives the outside environment as an advantage because it contains beneficial phenomena (solar heat, natural ventilation, natural light, etc.). These external processes can be utilized in a manner that provides services which would ordinarily be done by mechanical equipment. The main concern should be to bring the building as close to a natural balance as its program, technology and skill will allow and to rectify those few incident imbalances with mechanical intervention.

## 3.2 Fenestration

Windows are one of the largest single factors affecting building energy consumption, and they have much potential for energy conservation. Large expanses of glass can be responsible for as much as 20 to 30% of the energy used for heating and cooling in residences. The architect can design an effective usage and placement of windows and external and internal shading devices, to allow an overall reduction of glazing material and the use of insulating glass.

## 3.2a Natural Illumination

As the reduction of window area takes place it will necessitate that the placement of windows optimize the benefits of natural illumination. The more effective natural illumination is, the greater the reduction of heat loss. The utilization of natural illumination in place of electrical lighting wherever possible, results in a conservation of energy through the reduction of heating and cooling loads.

In order to effectively deal with natural light, the basic principles of lighting and the dynamics of the sun must be analyzed. The path of the sun and its relationship to the value of light must be understood in order to intelligently determine the placement of windows. The sun's angle to the horizon, the latitude of the site, the seasonal variations, and the diurnal motion will all be factors

in calculating the suit-
able quantities and
qualities of light which
is expected to enter the
space.

One device which illus-
trates the variables of
the sun path is the sun-
dial. A description on
how it can be constructed
will be found in Appendix
B. By attaching a sundial
to a three-dimensional
model of the building and
site, the site can be
manipulated in front of
a light source so that the
shadow cast by the sundial
corresponds to the hour
and season. This can be
used as an indicator as to
what type of light will be
entering an interior space
during a certain period of
time.

There are three basic types
of light. First, there is
*direct* sunlight, which
originates from the southeast to southwest (high
angle), and east to west
(low angle). *Ground* light,
a secondary source, is
reflected from the earth's
surface and varies in
intensity in relationship
to ground surface, angle
toward the sun, and the

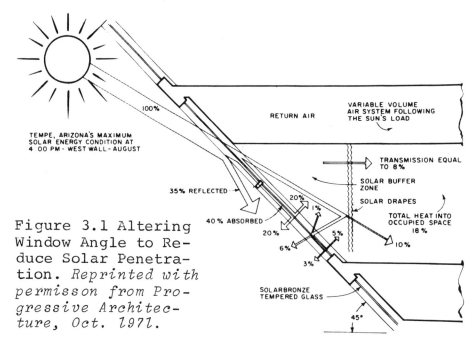

Figure 3.1 Altering
Window Angle to Re-
duce Solar Penetra-
tion. *Reprinted with
permisson from Pro-
gressive Architec-
ture, Oct. 1971.*

slope of the ground. *Diffused* light or skylight is
direct light diffused by the
particles in the atmosphere.
Each of the aforementioned
have certain qualities and
characteristics. Activities,
focal points, and moods are
determined by its penetration
into the internal space.
The type of light that is
admitted is dependent on
what type of fenestration is
used. Skylights will admit
a diffused light, as will
clerestories. Typical windows like those discussed in
Chapter 4 will admit a combination of the three different components of sunlight.

The type of light that will
penetrate the space will be
determined by the window's
orientation. Lower windows
will admit the reflected
ground light, while narrow
vertical windows will admit
very localized light.

In the cold climates of the
northern hemisphere, windows
should be excluded from the
north wall and concentrated
on southern walls for sunlight and the minimum amount
of heat loss. If a certain
quality of northern light is
desired, solar controls on
the southern facade can provide the same quality light

without the heat loss of north facing windows.

It is important to remember that (by the manipulation of type, placement, surface deformation and shading devices) any interior natural lighting quality can be provided.

### 3.2b Solar Control through External Shading

External shading is one of the most effective means for controlling thermal build-up on a surface. If solar radiation can be reduced before it reaches interior space, it can be beneficial in reducing energy consumption.

Vegetation can provide an effective means for shading. Several factors should be considered when selecting decidious and evergreen trees for their shading effects. The shape and characteristics of the tree are important, and the configuration of the shadow produced should be considered. In planting new trees one must consider that there will be a minimum of five years before shading effects will be noted. Shading by vines can be greatly improved by properly controlling their growth patterns on a trellis arrangement which can be utilized as an overhang.

The use of vegetation is two-fold; not only does it provide shading by reducing heat loads on exposed surfaces by blocking direct solar radiation but it also improves the microclimate by filtering and cooling air, reducing sound, and modifying air-flow patterns.

Another method of shading is the sunscreen. By using different configurations, it is possible to control the heat-producing sunshine and still keep the benefits of natural lighting. There are many different varieties of sunscreens. They can be categorized in three basic types: the first is the overhang or horizontal. These units control heat build-up by excluding the summer sun. They may be solid, as a louvered type, or canvas-covered. The overhang is more effective in southern orientations; another type is the vertical sunscreen which excludes thermal build-up in windows with an east-west orientation; the third is a combination of both the vertical and horizontal sunscreens such as an egg crate design. This incorporates the better features of the other two.

Sunscreens do not have to be stationary to make them more effective. They should be allowed to be adjusted to exclude a greater amount of thermal build-up under a variety of situations. For further discussion on the variations in existing sunscreens, consult Victor Olgyay's book, Design with Climate.

### 3.2c Glazing Types for Energy Reduction

Heat-absorbing glass or tinted glass can absorb 4.5% of the solar heat striking them. The heat that is absorbed will be re-radiated. Some means for handling this re-radiated heat will have to be provided. It can either be carried off by the installation of a mechanical

**43**

FIGURE 3.2 NATURAL VENTI-
LATION USED TO CARRY AWAY
RERADIATED HEAT FROM HEAT
-ABSORBING GLASS. *Reprint-
ed with permisson from
Progressive Architecture,
October 1971.*

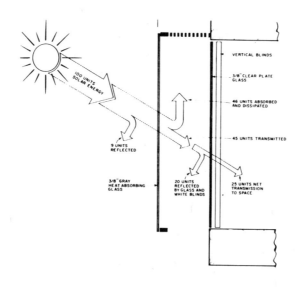

system (which consumes)
energy) or it can be placed
so that natural ventilation
will carry the heat away.

An effective use of wind
for carrying away re-radiated heat was devised for the
Norfolk, Virginia Civic
Center.  (See Figure 3.2.)
Heat that is absorbed by
the heat-absorbing glass is
re-radiated into the air
space between the screen
and building.  The air
circulates through aluminum
louvers which carry the
re-radiated heat away.  The
reflection from window
glazing and blinds further

reduces the amount reaching
the building to only 25% of
the available solar heat.

There has been a recent
development by Ernest Wild
of a device called Protecta-
Sol which is similar in
operation to that used in
the Norfolk Civic Center.
It is dependent upon the
high-pressure, climatized
air that is normally ex-
hausted to the exterior.
This is instead exhausted
to the interior space at
ceiling level, where it
then flows down a double-
walled window and out at the
bottom.  This creates an air

curtain that covers the
walls of the building,
carrying away heat during
hot months before it is
re-radiated into the space.
The operation is basically
the same for winter-time
utilization, during which
the climatized air pro-
vides a warmed-air curtain
that heats its surround-
ings.[2]

Glass applied with reflective metallic coating can
be an effective means to
block solar radiation.
The thickness to which the
metallic coating is applied
controls the amount of
transmission and reflection.
The glass can be manufac-
tured with variable transmittance ratings varying
from 8 to 26%.  Libbey
Owens-Ford did a detailed
computer study comparing
chromium-coated dual wall
insulating glass against
conventional 1/4" plate
glass.  The results show
that a building having
metallic insulating glass
would have a 64.7% reduc-
tion in capacity of the
refrigeration system, 67.7%
reduction in the distribution system and a 53.2%
reduction in heating equipment.

### 3.2d *Variable Thermal Barriers in Fenestrations*

A variable thermal barrier is one whose thermal characteristics would be dictated by the outside environment. The thermal barrier would present a physical change in state when outside conditions vary; for example, a curtain can be opened or closed to admit or exclude sunlight when desired. The curtain also presents a thermal barrier that prevents heat loss from an interior space at night. A thermal barrier that could be operated automatically would considerably cut down on mechanical loads.

Zomeworks, Incorporated, a New Mexico-based firm, has been recently dealing with the development of glazed areas that vary in thermal characteristics with a given situation. One is the beadwall, in which styrofoam beads are blown between two panes of glass to prevent heat loss at night or heat gain in summer. The filling and removal of the anti-static beads is accomplished with an ordinary vacuum cleaner. The beadwall is an effective means of cutting heat loss by a factor of ten. Three inches of styrofoam beads give the window section a U value of approximately .1. (Fig. 3.3)

The Skylid, another product of Zomeworks, consists of a set of insulated rotating louvers that can be used with a skylight or large windows. The louvers automatically close or open when they sense a thermal imbalance. The louvers will close during the night or periods of heavy overcast to prevent a thermal discharge from the interior to exterior space. This is accomplished by the use of freon in two identical cylinders mounted to a set of louvers. One cylinder monitors the inside temperature while the other monitors the exterior. When a thermal imbalance exists, say at nighttime when heated interior air is trying to escape from the interior space, it will flow past the interior cannister causing the gas to evaporate. The evaporated gas will move to the cooler exterior cannister where it will condense. The imbalance in the weights

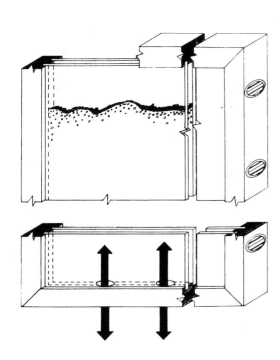

FIGURE 3.3  THE BEADWALL.
*Patented by Zomeworks, Inc.*
*P.O. Box 712, Albuquerque,*
*New Mexico, 87103.*

of the cylinders will tip the louvers closed.  In the daytime the whole process will be reversed with the exterior cannister being heated first, causing the louvers to open and allowing thermal heat to enter. There is a manual override for exceptional conditions. (See Figure 3.4.)

## 3.3 Collection, Distribution and Utilization of Waste Heat

Large quantities of energy are allowed to "leak" out of the natural energy system at the point of consumption.  These "leaks" are the result of inefficiencies at the points of production and consumption. These inefficiencies are represented as reject waste heat.  There are energy conservation devices and practices that transfer this wasted heat to useful purposes.  At the point of power production and distribution you will find total energy and underground heat distribution systems. At the point of consumption for the purpose of waste heat reclamation you have heat pipes, rotary heat ex-changers, and coil type or run-around exchangers.

### 3.3a Total Energy Systems

A total energy system is one in which a building or small complex of buildings contains its own electric generating system.  The rejected heat from the electrical production process is captured and diverted back to the hot water or steam for comfort-conditioning.  The promise of reducing the total fuel requirements of building complexes by 25 to 50% has been shown to be possible in principle. [3]  Generally, there are three criteria which must be met to justify a total energy plant: (1) high and fairly constant electrical demands during most of the day and over most of the year, (2) building function should be such that heating and cooling demands will occur simultaneously with, and in relative proportion to, lighting and electrical power demands, and (3) gas or liquid fuel rates in the area should compete with prevailing electric rates. [4] Total energy plants are, of

FIGURE 3.4 " SKYLID"
*Reprinted with permisson from Zomeworks.*

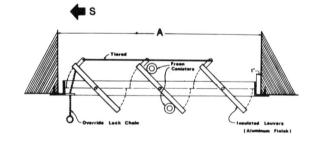

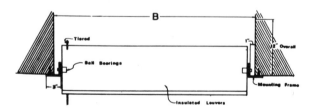

**46**

necessity, small installations and, as a rule, the effective temperature of combustion of a small plant is less than that in a large central power station. By using efficient central station power generators and employing heat pumps to reclaim waste and provide comfort-conditioning, it is possible, in principle, to gain greater effectiveness of fuel consumption than by using small scale total energy plants which operate under limited thermal efficiencies.[5]

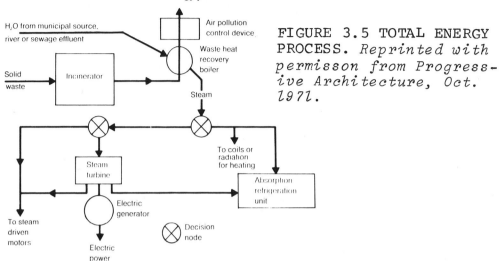

**Waste heat — total energy process**

FIGURE 3.5 TOTAL ENERGY PROCESS. *Reprinted with permisson from Progressive Architecture, Oct. 1971.*

### 3.3b Underground Heat Distribution Systems

While these systems are widely in use at college campuses, military bases, and small communities, not until recently have they been considered applicable at the urban scale. The basic idea involved is that effective utilization can be made of waste heat from central electric power-generating plants and the heat generated from waste incinerators by collecting and distributing waste heat into underground distribution systems.

### 3.3c Heat Reclamation at Point of Consumption

An incandescent lamp converts 90% of the input electrical energy into heat and only 10% into useful illumination. The conversion efficiency of fluorescent light is higher than incandescent but still leaves a large percentage of energy as waste heat. While heat generated by lighting may decrease the heating load during the colder part of the year, it also represents a burden during the cooling season. Waste heat can be a useful

commodity if it can be reclaimed. Instead of depositing waste heat into the living space it can be exhausted into a ceiling plenum. At this point the heat can be used as a reheat source to condition air or it can be drawn away and exhausted to reduce cooling loads. There is another system in which water is used to cool the light fixtures. The water transfers the heat to a refrigeration unit through a heat exchanger. Water, in turn, reheats supply air and also warms window louvers. (See Figs. 3.6, 3.7,

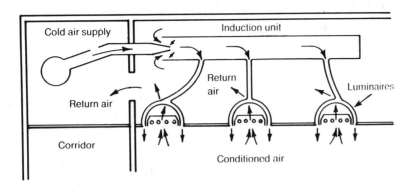

FIGURE 3.6   HEAT OF LIGHT RECLAMATION (AIR). *Reprinted with permission from Progressive Architecture, October 1971.*

and 3.8)   There is a second benefit from using heat of light, in that lamp and ballast life is greatly increased in cooled fixtures. Light efficiency is also improved. An ordinary 40 watt fluorescent lamp operating at 100° F produces 12% less light output than when operated at 77° F.

FIGURE 3.7   ROTARY HEAT EX-CHANGER.

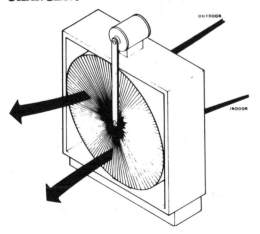

### 3.3d   Heat Pipes

Heat pipes are another means to recapture and transfer wasted heat from one point to another. The heat pipe works as an air to air recovery system. When installed in a system, the airstream or recovery duct runs counterflow to the waste heat or exhaust duct while heat is transferred by the heat pipe from air-stream to airstream.

The heat pipe consists of a sealed tube containing a fluid (ammonia, acetone, or water). One end of the tube is heated by the waste heat duct, thus causing the fluid inside the sealed tube to evaporate. The opposite end, which is in the incoming duct, is cooler, allowing the evaporated liquid to condense. The vapor carries the latent heat from one end of the pipe to the other, requiring that the supply and exhaust duct be in close proximity to each other. One system that alleviates this situation and allows heat transfer from supply to exhaust systems in widely separated locations is the coil exchanger. Coils need only be installed in each of the ducts and connected by piping and a pump to move the liquid heat transfer

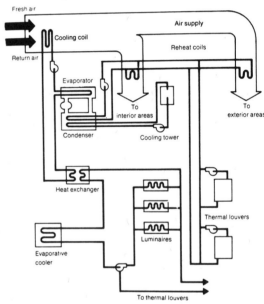

FIGURE 3.8   HEAT OF LIGHT RECLAMATION (WATER). *Reprinted with permission from Progressive Architecture.*

medium from coil to coil. This piping is relatively easy to run within any structure and, in fact, can connect any number of separate exhaust and fresh air systems (or reheat terminal units) into one loop. Coil-type heat exchangers are normally more economical for small or heating-only installations, or as modifications in existing buildings. Figure 3.10

In most buildings you will find reheat air conditioning systems. They operate in such a way that air is cooled constantly to a temperature of about 55° F and then reheated to the temperature required by the various zones. There is an energy expenditure for both heating and cooling with this type of system. The zone requiring the least amount of cooling could use the most energy. With the installation of a heat recovery device, energy consumption could be markedly reduced. Heat exchangers can take care of all fresh air intake preheat requirements in the winter and can reduce air conditioning tonnage in the summer.

Heat exchangers installed to recover heat from escaping flue gas can cut the overall energy requirements of a furnace. For example, most flue gas leaves the furnace from

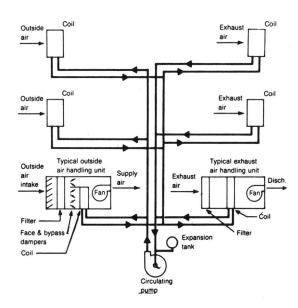

FIGURE 3.10 HEAT RECOVERY SYSTEM. *Source: Progressive Architecture.*

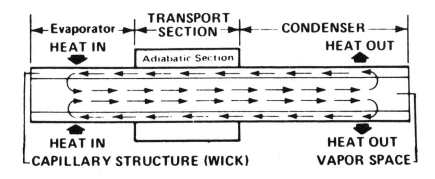

FIGURE 3.9 HEAT PIPE SCHEMATIC. *Source: Popular Science.*

450° F to 560° F. Reducing the temperature to 140° F results in a fuel saving of 13%.

Isothermics, Incorporated markets a heat pipe device called the Air-O-Space which recovers waste heat escaping from flues. Finned heat pipes are installed on the furnace flue so they protrude into the flue gas path. A small fan blows air over the heat pipes to remove

the heat and to circulate it into the duct-work of the air-handling system.

Hot water heating accounts for approximately 4% of all energy consumption. This represents a significant amount of energy that is lost due to expended hot water going down the drain. The hot water discharge should be recovered from kitchens, laundries, and lavatories and passed through heat exchangers. The recovered heat could be used as a preheat for incoming water for hot water service.

### 3.4  *Illumination in Buildings*

Illumination of residences and commercial buildings accounts for 1.5% of the national energy consumption. In office buildings in the United States the illumination provided often exceeds, by as much as a factor of 2, the amount of illumination used in similar European buildings.[6]

Many recent experiments confirm that lighting levels between 10 and 40 foot candles are sufficient for visual activity and physiological needs where levels of 60 to 150 foot candles are now being provided.[7] An intense and comprehensive research program should be initiated as to the consideration of lowering the overall illumination average.

Unnecessary illumination imposes double energy costs. The first and most obvious is that an increase in illumination causes an increase in electrical consumption. Secondly, the heat generated by illumination increases air conditioning loads; for every two excessive watts of lighting, one excessive watt of cooling is needed. "A 50 percent reduction in electrical usage for lighting would be a three percent reduction in nationwide energy use. This is equivalent to the output of over thirty 1,000-megawatt generating plants.[8]

The modification of existing illumination systems for the reduction of energy consumption is much more easily accomplished than the modification of other existing building components such as heating, cooling and ventilation systems.

Richard Stein in his article, *Architecture and Energy*, suggests that the characteristics of a flexible lighting system with minimum energy expenditure have the following characteristics: "A more efficient light source; a lighting component capable of being easily plugged in and removed as requirements change; one capable of delivering a number of levels of light; one easily controlled locally; one fitted with a light sensitive device that will turn if off if the ambient light level is adequate; and one that will accept screening devices when necessary." He goes on further to suggest a universal ceiling grid in which fixtures could be plugged in or removed to change the light delivery system for different activity requirements.[9]

The above criteria suggest a flexible lighting system that could easily adapt to a variety of illumination situations. This counters our present attitude of evenly illuminating a space with large quantities of

light. Our hallways and storage areas are as well lit as our work spaces. Selective lighting or task lighting is one approach in which the space is lighted for the activity to take place. The illumination level occurring in lesser-occupied areas would be considerably lower than the task area.

### 3.4a Lighting Energy Recommendations[10]

The Illuminating Engineering Society prepared twelve recommendations for saving energy in illumination systems without sacrificing visual performance and visual requirements established through research. The recommendations are as follows:

1. Design lighting for expected activity. It is necessary to determine what types of activities are expected, their duration and where they occur. Lighting should be provided for the seeing tasks with less light on surrounding non-working areas such as corridors, storage and circulation area. There should be capability to relocate or alter lighting equipment where changes in the use of the space are anticipated.

2. Design with more effective luminaires and fenestration. Select lighting equipment and windows capable of providing proper visibility for performing tasks. This includes selecting lighting equipment designed to avoid ceiling reflections and glare, and windows with controls for sun and sky light.

3. Use efficient light sources. The various lamps available today have different properties including light output per watt input. This ranges from less than 10 lumens per watt to over 100. The choice should be the most efficient source that appropriate to the application (light source color, life, physical size are characteristics also to be considered).

4. Use more efficient luminaires. More efficient luminaires produce a greater amount of light for the wattage consumed; however, consideration should also be given to ceiling reflections and glare and the ease of cleaning and relamping.

5. Use thermally controlled luminaires. Recognize lighting heat. Design the heating and cooling system to use lighting heat to reduce heating energy and to control lighting heat for minimal effect on cooling.

6. Use care in choosing finish on ceilings, walls, floors and furnishings. Dark finishes absorb light, while very light finishes can cause glare. Follow IES reflectance recommendations.

7. Use efficient incandescent lamps. Higher wattage incandescent lamps are more efficient. Thus, using fewer higher wattage lamps can save power. The less efficient long-life lamps consume more energy than general service lamps for the

same light output.

8. Provide flexibility in the control of lighting. Use separate and convenient switching or dimming devices for areas that have different activity patterns. Photo-electric control of the electric lighting should be considered where adequate daylighting is possible. Turn off lights when not needed. Institute a program that will remind occupants to turn off lights as they leave an empty room or when daylighting is adequate.

9. Design fenestration to control heat-producing radiation entering a space. This will reduce the cooling load while still making use of available daylight.

10. Design fenestration to use daylighting as practicable to produce the required illumination either alone or with an electric lighting system.

11. Select luminaires with good cleaning capability and lamps with good lumen maintenance. Select lighting servicing plan to minimize light loss during operation and thus reduce the number of luminaires required. Keep lighting equipment clean and in good working order through a well-planned program of regular cleaning, relamping and servicing.

12. Post instructions covering operation and maintenance. These initially should be based on the design criteria but may be modified later as more efficient, newer replacement equipment is installed. As activity locations change, modify the lighting system and instructions accordingly.

3.5  *Thermal Performance and Insulation of Buildings*

The major consumers of energy in buildings are space heating, air conditioning and hot water heating. Space heating of residences accounts for 11% of the total natural energy consumption while space heating of commercial installations represents an additional 6.9% of that total. Air conditioning in commercial and residential buildings represents 2.5% of the total natural energy consumption.[11] The inefficiencies that influence the above mentioned consumption rates deal with heat loss and heat gain of a structure. The major sources responsible for excessive heat loss and heat gain are inadequate insulation, excessive ventilation, high rates of air infiltration from outside and excessive fenestration. "Because few buildings are designed to exceed the standard requirements for thermal insulation, one may assume that most of the residential buildings in use today may consume approximately 40% more energy for heating and air conditioning than they would had they been insulated and sealed in accordance with present day minimum property standards."[12]

The fundamental purpose of insulation is to retard heat flow inwardly and outwardly. How effectively it accomplishes this is dependent upon the insulating materials' thermal properties, its thickness,

**52**

the type and quality of construction in which the insulation is located, the wall area exposed and the difference between inside and outside temperatures.

Air spaces and reflective surfaces can be employed as insulators. To be effective air spaces must be at least 3/4 inch wide, but effectiveness is not increased by additional air space up to 4 inches. The air gap can be further improved by a factor of 3-1/2 by applying metal reflective foil on one of the adjacent surfaces. The foil substantially reduces heat radiation across the air gap by reflecting heat waves back toward the warm inner areas, and slowing down the heat loss from the warm areas. The foil also provides the function of a vapor barrier. A vapor barrier is designed to prevent moisture-laden air from condensing on the inner surface of the outer wall. Reflective type insulation consists of aluminum foil attached to the back of wall board or bonded to insulation batts.

An accordian type of reflective insulation is manufactured for placement between wood studs and wood joists.

Insulation is available in a variety of forms; they consist of rigid boards, blanket or batt, blown or poured, and foamed-in place.

It is considered technologically and economically feasible to reduce heat losses from buildings to 700 BTU per thousand cubic feet-degree day through the use of insulation. If these estimates prove to be correct, it would be feasible to reduce total energy requirements of buildings by more than 50% through well-designed insulation and careful control of ventilation.

The infiltration of outside air accounts for approximately 25 to 50% of the heating and cooling requirements of individual buildings. Air infiltration is a serious contributor to heat loss, yet some is necessary to provide ventilation and "fresh air" for furnace and fireplaces. One does not want to achieve an

airtight space, yet the sensible use of weather-stripping thermopane glass and insulation can trim infiltration to acceptable limits. Total fuel requirements for space heating and air conditioning can be reduced by providing control of ventilation in critical areas (i.e., toilet facilities, kitchens) so that high rates are supplied only when required.

Wind plays a large role in the volume of air that infiltrates a space. Victor Olgyay, in *Design with Climate*, states that a 20 mph wind doubles the heat load of a house that is normally exposed to 5 mph winds. Trees as a wind break can represent an effective means of controlling heat transfer loss. Exposed surfaces can be built below grade or earth berms can be employed to reduce transmission losses.

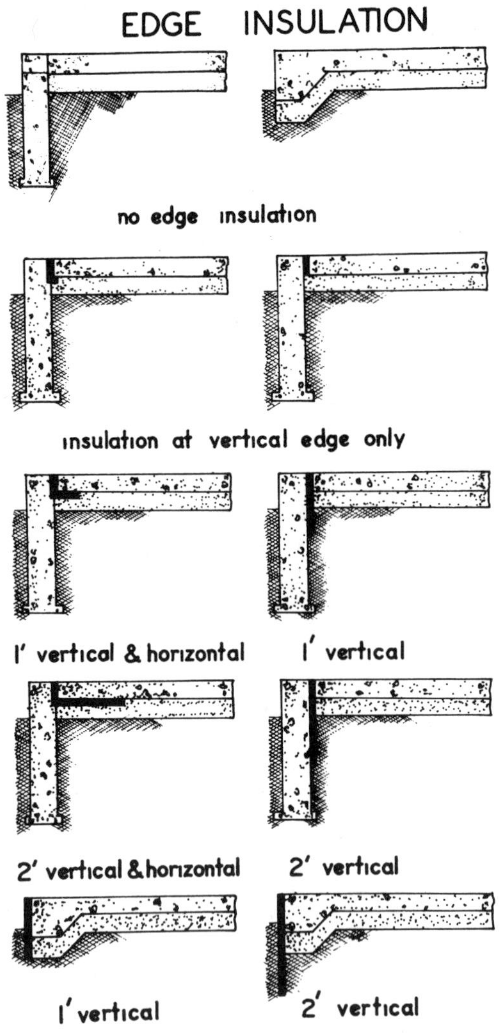

## EDGE INSULATION

no edge insulation

insulation at vertical edge only

1' vertical & horizontal          1' vertical

2' vertical & horizontal          2' vertical

1' vertical          2' vertical

FIGURE 3.11 VARIATIONS IN EDGE INSULATION. *Source: ASHRAE.*

## 3.6 Heat Transmission Coefficients

In dealing with heat transmission the only concern of the designer is human comfort. The physiological factors of importance are outlined by Seville and Fellows.[13]

-production and regulation of heat in the human body
-heat and moisture losses from the human body
-the effects of cold and hot surfaces in the space
-the stratification of air
-effective temperature: the combination of the effects of air temperature, moisture content and air movement

All of these are affected by the materials that make up the physical interface between the internal and external environment. It is this barrier that modifies the thermal effects of climatic conditions.

The building envelope may be separated into two categories: the opaque surfaces (wall structure, roof and floor) and the transparent surfaces (glazing). The opaque surfaces are subject

| Material | Thickness Inches | Time lag, Hours |
|---|---|---|
| Stone | 8 | 5.5 |
| | 12 | 8.0 |
| | 16 | 10.5 |
| | 24 | 15.5 |
| Solid Concrete | 2 | 1.1 |
| | 4 | 2.5 |
| | 6 | 3.8 |
| | 8 | 5.1 |
| | 12 | 7.8 |
| | 16 | 10.2 |
| Common Brick | 4 | 2.3 |
| | 8 | 5.5 |
| | 12 | 8.5 |
| | 16 | 12.0 |
| Face Brick | 4 | 2.4 |
| Wood | 1/2 | 0.17 |
| | 1 | 0.45 |
| | 2 | 1.3 |
| Insulating Board | 1/2 | 0.08 |
| | 1 | 0.23 |
| | 2 | 0.77 |
| | 4 | 2.7 |
| | 6 | 5.0 |

TABLE 3.1 TIME LAGS OF SPECIFIC MATERIALS. *Source: Design with Climate.*

to successive heating and cooling of their various layers. Each layer receives less heat and experiences less temperature rise than the layer externally adjacent to it. As a result, the internal surface experiences a much less pronounced oscillation (or wavelike amplitude) than the external surface. This also creates a lag in the transmission of externally absorbed heat and that which reaches the internal surface. Besides structural and thermal characteristics of each layer, color plays a significant role in the absorptive ability of the external surface. Depending upon the particular concerns of the designer the surface color can aid in nighttime heating. This can be done by absorbing solar radiation on a black exterior surface during the day and releasing it to the internal space within a specified time lag at night. Those materials which reflect rather than absorb and which more easily emit longwave thermal radiation will cause lower temperatures within the internal spaces.

Table 3.2 gives the absorptivities of various surfaces.

Just as the heat of the day can be absorbed and released in the cool of the night, so can the nighttime coolness be released in the daytime. This is referred to as thermal balance. A complex south facing wall (That is, one with several penetrations or an undulating surface) will greatly increase the difficulty in calculating the time lag. Time lag is directly affected by orientation. In a hot, dry region the horizon-

tal surfaces may be designed for a 12-hour lag time to inhibit the high thermal build-up from affecting the internal space until the early morning. The east face may have a minimal lag time to allow for the small amount of thermal energy to be felt immediately. The west wall which receives its load late in the afternoon may have a short lag time of between 5-10 hours and the south face, which in the summer receives the least amount of heat due to the angle of the sun at the hottest time of the day, may have a lag time of about

| Material or color | Shortwave absorptivity | Longwave absorptivity |
|---|---|---|
| Aluminum foil, bright | 0.05 | 0.05 |
| Aluminum foil, oxidized | 0.15 | 0.12 |
| Galvanized steel, bright | 0.25 | 0.25 |
| Aluminum paint | 0.50 | 0.50 |
| Whitewash, new | 0.12 | 0.90 |
| White oil paint | 0.20 | 0.90 |
| Grey color, light | 0.40 | 0.90 |
| Grey color, dark | 0.70 | 0.90 |
| Green color, light | 0.40 | 0.90 |
| Green color, dark | 0.70 | 0.90 |
| Ordinary black color | 0.85 | 0.90 |

TABLE 3.2 ABSORPTIVITIES (EMISSIVITIES) OF VARIOUS SURFACES. *Source: Man, Climate and Architecture.*

7-10 hours.[14] All of these figures may vary according to the general and micro-climatic conditions with which the designer is working. To understand more fully the transmission characteristics, the following definitions are given. They are derived primarily from the ASHRAE *Handbook of Fundamentals*.

*BTU*-(British Thermal Unit) This unit represents the actual heat loss through a structure or a material. One BTU is required to raise the temperature of one pound of water one degree fahrenheit.

*U*-The overall coefficient of heat transmission usually applied to combinations of materials or to single materials, such as glass, is an expression of the time rate of heat flow. It is expressed in the units of BTU per hour (square foot) (°F temperature difference between air on the inside and air on the outside of a wall, floor, roof or ceiling).

*K*-Thermal conductivity. The measure of a material to "permit" the flow of heat through a homogeneous material under steady-state conditions per unit area and temperature. It also is expressed in BTU/hr (sq.ft.) (°F per inch of thickness).

*C*-Thermal Conductance. Similar to $K$ but measures the heat flow through a given thickness of material. If a material's $K$ is known and to identify $C$, just divide by the thickness. The lower the $K$ or $C$, the higher the insulating value.

*f*-film or surface conductance given by the time rate of heat exchange with its surroundings. The surroundings must have air or other medium for radiation and convection to take place.

*R*-Thermal resistance, the measure of ability of a material to resist the flow of heat. It is

the mathematical reciprocal of both $C$ and $U$. $R = 1/C = 1/U$, which depends on whether the thermal resistance of a piece of insulation or an entire wall section is the issue.

For calculating overall coefficients with the resistance method, the following equations are used. For homogeneous materials: (1) $R_T = R_1 + R_2 + \ldots + R_n$, where $R_T$ is the total resistance made up of component individual resistances. A wall of a single homogeneous material could be expressed as: (2) $R_T = \dfrac{1}{f_i} + \dfrac{x}{k} + \dfrac{1}{f_o}$ where k is the conductivity of the material for a thickness x. $f_i$ and $f_o$ refer to indoor and outdoor surface conductances, in BTU/sq.ft. (hr) (F). When an air space of conductance C exists in the wall cavity, the formula is: (3) $R_T = \dfrac{1}{f_i} + \dfrac{x_1}{k_i} + \dfrac{1}{C} + \dfrac{x_2}{k_2} + \ldots + \dfrac{x_n}{k_n} + \dfrac{1}{f_o}$ (4) The overall coefficient is then $U = 1/R_T$.

For building materials having

non-uniform sections such as clay tile or concrete blocks, the conductance C given by the manufacturer should be used instead of conductivity K.

In most cases the wall components are arranged so that parallel heat flow paths of different conductances would result. The overall Heat Transfer per hour is:

(5) $H_{Th}=U(t_i-t_o)$ where $H_{Th}=$ overall heat transfer, BTU/sq.ft.(hr); $t_i=$ inside temperature (°F) often assumed as 65°F; $t_o=$ outside temperature (F)

(6) The combined ceiling/ roof transmission equation is: $U=\dfrac{U_R U_C}{U_R+(U_C/N)}$

where $U_R=U$ factor for roof in BTU/hr/sq.ft./°F; $U_C=U$ factor for ceiling in BTU/sq.ft./hr/°F.

The general procedure for calculating heat transmission coefficients could be summarized as follows:[15]

A. Determine the materials and their combination for the given wall, roof, ceiling or floor.
B. Identify the heat flow path and direction.
C. Select the resistance for air from Table 3.3
D. Select the conductance or resistance for each material from appendix C.
E. Calculate the total thermal resistance by using equation 3.
F. Calculate the U factor by using equation 4.

The best ways to inhibit heat loss through the building envelope is to use large amounts of insulation, never use just single glass, cover win-dows at night (Zomeworks: bead wall) and use the earth for insulation where possible.

To retard excess heat gain, interior shading devices should be designed to give maximum reflectance so that much of the incident radiant energy is not converted to sensible heat and then released to the interior space. As a summary, the rate of heat flow through opaque construction materials is a product of the:

-intensity of solar energy

Surface Conductances and Resistances

| Position of Surface | Direction of heat flow | Surface Emissivity | | | | | |
|---|---|---|---|---|---|---|---|
| | | Non-reflective = 0.90 | | Reflective = 0.20 | | Reflective = 0.05 | |
| | | $f_i$ | R | $f_i$ | R | $f_i$ | R |
| STILL AIR | | | | | | | |
| Horizontal | Upward | 1.63 | .61 | .91 | 1.10 | .76 | 1.32 |
| Sloping-45° | Upward | 1.60 | .62 | .88 | 1.14 | .73 | 1.37 |
| Vertical | Horizontal | 1.46 | .68 | .74 | 1.35 | .59 | 1.70 |
| Sloping-45° | Downward | 1.32 | .76 | .60 | 1.67 | .45 | 2.22 |
| Horizontal | Downward | 1.08 | .92 | .37 | 2.70 | .22 | 4.55 |
| MOVING AIR (any position) | | $f_o$ | R | $f_o$ | R | $f_o$ | R |
| 15 mph wind (for winter) | Any | 6.00 | .17 | | | | |
| 15 mph wind (for summer) | Any | 4.00 | .25 | | | | |

TABLE 3.3 SURFACE CONDUCTANCES AND RESISTANCES FOR AIR. *Source: ASHRAE.*

VERTICAL PANELS (EXTERIOR WINDOWS, SLIDING PATIO DOORS, AND PARTITIONS)-- FLAT GLASS, GLASS BLOCK, AND PLASTIC SHEET

| Description | Exterior | | Interior |
|---|---|---|---|
| | Winter | Summer | |
| Flat Glass | | | |
| single glass | 1.13 | 1.06 | 0.73 |
| insulating glass-double[a] | | | |
| 3/16" air space | 0.69 | 0.64 | 0.51 |
| 1/4" air space | 0.65 | 0.61 | 0.49 |
| 1/2" air space | 0.58 | 0.56 | 0.46 |
| 1/2" air space, low emissivity coating[b] | | | |
| emissivity = 0.20 | 0.38 | 0.36 | 0.32 |
| emissivity - 0.40 | 0.45 | 0.44 | 0.38 |
| emissivity - 0.60 | 0.52 | 0.50 | 0.42 |
| insulating glass-triple[a] | | | |
| 1/4" air spaces | 0.47 | 0.45 | 0.38 |
| 1/2" air spaces | 0.36 | 0.35 | 0.30 |
| storm windows | | | |
| 1" - 4" air space | 0.56 | 0.54 | 0.44 |
| Glass Block[c] | | | |
| 6 X 6 X 4" thick | 0.60 | 0.57 | 0.46 |
| 8 X 8 X 4" thick | 0.56 | 0.54 | 0.44 |
| --with cavity divider | 0.48 | 0.46 | 0.38 |
| 12 X 12 X 4" thick | 0.52 | 0.50 | 0.41 |
| --with cavity divider | 0.44 | 0.42 | 0.36 |
| 12 X 12 X 2" thick | 0.60 | 0.57 | 0.46 |
| Single Plastic Sheet | 1.09 | 1.00 | 0.70 |

[a]Double and triple refer to the number of lights of glass.

[b]Coating on either glass surface facing air space; all other glass surfaces uncoated.

[c]Dimensions are nominal.

[d]For heat flow up.

[e]For heat flow down.

[f]Based on area of opening, not total surface area.

[g]Refers to windows with negligible opaque area.

TABLE 3.4   COEFFICIENTS OF TRANSMISSION (U) OF WINDOWS. *Source: ASHRAE.*

on the buildings' surfaces
-temperature of the surrounding air
-temperature of the exposed surface
-heat storage capacity of the material
-indoor design temperature[16]

### 3.7   Calculating Heating and Cooling Loads

The following procedure for calculating heat loads and cooling loads is not as complete as an analysis by a mechanical engineer might be, but it allows the designer the opportunity to respond to the issues which will directly influence the design. Following a preliminary design, a detailed comprehensive procedure should be outlined. For more complete information, consult the ASHRAE *Handbook of Fundamentals, 1972.*

There are two means by which heat loss occurs: by transmission through the walls, glass, floor, ceilings and roof and by infiltration losses through cracks and crevices around doors and windows, and through open doors and windows. The usual responses to the latter group are

storm windows and a double set of doors. The following procedure is based on maintaining a desired indoor air temperature during those periods of recommended design outdoor weather conditions.

1. Select the outdoor design air temperature, wind direction and speed for both summer and winter heating and cooling both standard and irregular conditions, including microclimatic variables must be considered. Remember that weather data is not always ac-

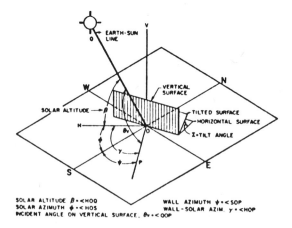

FIGURE 3.12 SOLAR ANGLES FOR VERTICAL AND HORIZONTAL SURFACES. *Source: ASHRAE.*

**58**

curate to the specific site.

2. Depending upon the activity to occur within the space and the human comfort conditions, choose a desired indoor temperature for both summer and winter.
3. Estimate the temperatures in the surrounding spaces such as basement, attic, ground temperature and any unheated adjacent spaces.
4. Calculate infiltration, both the *sensible heat loss* which is the heat required to warm the outdoor air entering in,

and *latent heat loss* which is the heat equivalent of any moisture that needs to be added. The sensible heat loss can be computed by:

$$H_s = 0.018 \ Q \ (t_i - t_o)$$

$H_s$ = amount of required heat to raise $t_o$ to $t_i$ in BTU/hr

$Q$ = volume of outdoor air entering the space in cubic ft/hr

$t_i$ = indoor design temperature

$t_o$ = outdoor design temperature

The latent heat loss can be computed by:

$$H_l = 79.5 \ Q \ (W_i - W_o)$$

$H_l$ = amount of heat required to increase the moisture content from $W_i$ to $W_o$ in BTU/hr

$W_i$ = humidity ratio of outdoor air, pounds per pounds of dry air

$W_o$ = humidity ratio of outdoor air, pounds per pounds of dry air

$Q$ may be found by estimating the number of air changes rather than by the crack method. Table 3.6 gives the information for residences.

For other spaces or buildings, it is recommended to use the coded ventilation requirements. In many cases six air changes per hour are recommended for most public and industrial buildings where 50 or more occupancies occur and mechanical ventilation is required.[17]

5. Calculate the heat transmission coefficients (3.6) for walls, partitions, roof, ceilings, floors, and glass.
6. Computer the net area of outside wall, glass and roof adjacent to heated spaces, other walls, floors or ceilings next to unheated spaces. This

Estimated Heat Lost from Building by Infiltration

*The tabulated factors when multiplied by room or building volume (cu.ft.) will result in estimated heat loss (BTU/hr) due to infiltration and does not include the heat needed to warm ventilating air.*

| Room or Building Type | No. of walls with windows | Temp. difference, F deg | | | |
|---|---|---|---|---|---|
| | | 25 | 50 | 75 | 100 |
| A | None | 0.23 | 0.45 | 0.68 | 0.90 |
| | 1 | 0.34 | 0.68 | 1.02 | 1.36 |
| | 2 | 0.68 | 1.35 | 2.02 | 2.70 |
| | 3 or 4 | 0.90 | 1.80 | 2.70 | 3.60 |
| B | Any | 1.35 | 2.70 | 4.05 | 5.40 |
| C | Any | .90-1.35 | 1.80-2.70 | 2.70-4.05 | 3.60-5.40 |
| D | Any | .45-0.68 | 0.90-1.35 | 1.35-2.02 | 1.80-2.70 |
| E | Any | .68-1.35 | 1.35-2.70 | 2.03-4.05 | 2.70-5.40 |

A = Offices, apartments, hotels, multistory buildings in general
B = Entrance halls or vestibules
C = Industrial buildings
D = Houses, all types, all rooms except vestibules
E = Public or institutional buildings

Table 3.5 HEAT LOSS FROM BUILDING BY INFILTRATION.
*Source: ASHRAE.*

can be done using dimensions from the plans.

7. Compute the heat transmissions for the floor, roof (both loss and gain) and ceiling if next to an unheated space.

8. Determine the equivalent temperature differentials for roof walls, glass and doors for summer heat gain. These tables are available in the 1972 ASHRAE *Handbook of Fundamentals*.

9. Estimate heat losses for winter heating, for each wall, ceiling, floor, glass and door by multiplying the Ufactor in each situation by the area of the surface in square feet and the temperature difference between the indoor and the outdoor or unheated space.

10. Estimate the indoor heat gain by occupants, machinery, lights, etc. for primarily cooling load calculations.

11. The total heating load is the sum of the transmission losses through the surrounding barriers (steps 7 & 9) and the heat equivalent of outdoor or unheated air entering by infiltration. The total heat gain is the result for cooling loads which may be designed by the unit ton. One ton of cooling load equals 12,000 BTU.

As defined by ASHRAE, the "cooling load is the rate at which heat must be removed from the space to maintain room air temperature at the constant value which was assumed when calculating heat gain." In addition to the heat gains, classification of sensible and latent heat could be grouped by any of the following smaller classifications:
-solar radiation
-conducted heat through adjacent exterior barriers
-conducted heat through interior surfaces
-heat generated within the space
-heat transferred by ventilation or infiltration from the outside and surrounding warmer spaces.

Much of the same information required for heat load calculations is needed for cooling load calculations. The following is a summary of the

| Kind of room or building | No. of air changes per hour |
|---|---|
| Rooms with no windows or exterior door | 1/2 |
| Rooms with windows or exterior doors on one side | 1 |
| Rooms with windows or exterior doors on two sides | 1-1/2 |
| Rooms with windows or exterior doors on three sides | 2 |
| Entrance halls | 2 |

TABLE 3.6   AIR CHANGES UNDER AVERAGE CONDITIONS IN RESIDENCES (not including for ventilation).  *Source: ASHRAE.*

necessary data needed for all cooling load calculations:

1. Characteristics of the building in terms of materials, component size, shape, orientation, location and amount of shading.
2. The design conditions for indoors and outdoors, wind direction and speed, indoor wet-bulb and dry-bulb temperature (psychometric chart) and ventilation rate.
3. Internal heat sources identified; people, machinery, lighting, etc.
4. Time of day, month and year for heat gain calculation.
5. The instantaneous heat gains such as from those sources previously mentioned-- solar radiation, adjacent spaces and surfaces, infiltration and ventilation.

FOOTNOTES:

1. Stein, Richard. "Architecture and Energy," *Architectural Forum*, July/August 1973, p. 47.

2. Vincent, Richard. "Oil Saving Invention Foils Energy Gobbler," *Catalyst*, vol. 4, no. 1, p. 13.

3. Berg, Charles A. "Energy Conservation through Effective Utilization," *Science*, July 13, 1973, p. 133.

4. Progressive Architecture. *Life Support System for a Dying Planet*, Reinhold Publishing Corp., Reprinted from *Progressive Architecture*, October 1971, p. 18.

5. *Op.cit.* Berg, Charles A.

6. *Ibid.*, p. 131.

7. Dubin, Fred. "A Wiser Use of Electricity and Energy Conservation through Building Design," *Building Systems Design*, January 1973, p. 9.

8. *Op.cit.* Stein, Richard, p. 48.

9. *Ibid.*, p. 49.

10. Fuchs, John. "A Realistic Approach to Conserving Energy," *Progressive Architecture*, September 1973, p. 99.

11. *Op.cit.* Berg, Charles A., p. 129.

12. *Ibid.*, p. 130.

13. Severns, W.H. and Fellows, J.R. *Air Conditioning and Refrigeration*, John Wiley and Sons, Inc., 1966.

14. Olgyay, Victor. *Design with Climate*, Princeton University Press, p. 118.

15. Chiang, R.N.S. *Lecture on Environmental Physics*, Virginia Polytechnic Institute and State University, College of Architecture 1969.

16. MacCurdy, David W. "Calculating Solar Heat Loads," *Progressive Architecture*, December 1962, p. 124.

17. *Op.cit.* Chiang, R.N.S.

REFERENCES:

Achenbach, P.R. and J.B. Cable. *Site Analysis for the Application of Total Energy Systems to Housing Developments*, National Bureau of Standards. Presented at the 17th Intersociety Energy Conservation Engineering Conference, San Diego, California. September 25-29, 1972.

Achenbach, P.R. and J.B. Cable. "A Round Table on Energy Conservation through Higher Quality Building," *Architectural Record*, January 1972.

Barham, R. *The Architecture of the Well Tempered Environment*, University of Chicago Press, 1969.

Berg, Charles A. "Energy Conservation through Effective Utilization," IAT/NBS, NBSIR 73-102, February 1973.

Dubin, Fred. "A Check-Off List on Energy Conservation with Regard to Power and Illumination," *Electrical Consultant*, vol. 89, no. 4, May 1973, p. 20.

Dubin, Fred S. "Energy for Architects," *Architecture Plus*, vol. 1, no. 6, July 1973, pp. 38-49.

Dubin, Fred S. "Energy Conservation through Design," *Professional Engineer*, October 1973, pp. 21-24.

Dubin, Fred S. "If You Want to Save Energy," *AIA Journal*, December 1972.

Dubin, Fred S. "Total Energy Systems and the Environment," *Actual Specifying Engineer*, October 1972.

Dubin, Fred S. "Total Energy Systems for Mass Housing-- Why It Makes Sense," *Actual Specifying Engineer*, February 1973.

Eccli, E. *Low Cost Energy-Efficient Shelter*, Rodde Press, Emmaus, Pa., 1975.

*Eleven Ways to Reduce Energy Consumption and Increase Conservation in Household Cooling.* U.S. Department of Commerce. NBS/IAT/BRO. Prepared in cooperation with the Office of Consumer Affairs.

Hammon, Bruce. "Options for Energy Conservation," Energy Research Group at the Center for Advanced Consumption in the University of Illinois. (NSF and EPP support)

Hittman Associates, Inc. "Residential Energy Consumption-- Single Family Housing --Final Report," Department of Housing and Urban Development #HUD-IIAI-2 with support from NSF/RANN (#HUD-PDR-29-2) March 1973.

Houghten, F.C. and C.P. Yaglou. "Determination of the Comfort Zone," *ASHRAE Transactions*, vol. 29, 1973, p. 361.

Large, David B. *Hidden Waste Potentials for Energy Conservation*, The Conservation Foundation, May 1973.

McGuinness, W.J. and B. Stein. *Mechanical and Electrical Equipment for Buildings*, 5th ed., John Wiley & Sons, New York, 1971.

Robinette, Gary O. *Plants, People and Environment Quality: a study of plants and their environmental functions*, Department of the Interior, National Park

Services, 1972.

Rogers, Tyler Stewart. *Thermal Design of Buildings,* New York, Wiley and Sons, Inc., 1964.

Seidet, Margins R.; Platkin, Steven M. and Robert O. Beck. "Energy Conservation Strategies, May 1973," Implementation Research Division, Office of Research and Monitoring, U.S. Environmental Protection Agency (EPA-R5-73-021).

"Seven Ways to Reduce Fuel Consumption in Household Heating-- through Energy Conservation," Ad Hoc Committee on Fuel Conservation, Office of Consumer Affairs and the U.S. Dept. of Commerce, NBS/IAT/CBT, December 1972.

Steadman, P. *Energy, Environment and Building,* Cambridge University Press, New York, 1975.

Stein, Richard G., FAIA. "Energy and Architecture," *Architectural Forum,* vol. 139, no. 1, July/August 1973, pp. 38-58.

*Technical Options for Energy Conservation in Buildings.*

National Bureau of Standards Technical Note 789, U.S. Government Printing Office, No. C13.46:789, July 1973.

The Conservation Foundation, 1717 Massachusetts Avenue, N.W., Washington, D.C. 20036.

Villecco, Marguerite, ed. *Energy Conservation Opportunities in Building Design,* A Report to the Ford Foundation Energy Policy Project, Washington, D.C., AIA Research Corp., October 1973.

**64 NOTES**

# 4. Natural Cooling and Ventilation

In most areas of the world, mechanical refrigeration is the resulting response to very poor designing. Since 1952, refrigerant air-cooling has been the quick-est and easiest answer to an overheated space. With basic knowledge of orien-tation, site planning and building structure the designer can avoid using over expensive (in material and fuel) energy draining mechanical systems. Granted there are parts of the world where certain kinds of me-chanical air conditioning are necessary, but those areas are also characterized by an abundance of solar radiation which can be transferred to cooling energy (Chapter 7). This chapter attempts to outline several natural methods of cooling from the most basic (insulation) to the more complicated (natural venti-lation). For further information, Chapters 3 and 7 have some appropriate data as well as the several references listed.

*4.1  Cooling Design Factors*

Physical comfort during hot months may be directly

related to metabolism and heat removal. Metabolism is the production of heat by the human body, which varies from 400 BTU per hour at rest to over 1400 BTU during physical activity.[1] As well as being proportional to physical activity it is also related to environmental conditions and increases with thermal stress, either hot or cold. When the metabolic rate is increased, more oxygen is needed and more heat must be dissipated into the surrounding environment. This places a stress on the process of cooling which is being employed. Other physiological aspects of metabolic heat rate involve heart rate, inner body temperature, sweat rate and skin temperature. The method of cooling utilized must be designed to respond to the various activities that will be performed in the building, so as not to place thermal stress on the human body.

When the ambient air temperature is 72° F, almost half of the total heat production is dissipated by evaporation.[2] Designers often assume this by in-

cluding 180 BTU of latent heat per person in their calculations. If the ambient air temperature assumes equilibrium with the skin temperature then neither radiation or convection can occur, which means the evaporation system must assume all the responsibility. When the wet-bulb temperature equals or exceeds the skin temperature then no evaporation takes place. What occurs is the 110 BTU normally dissipated[3] tend to raise the body temperature. When the body temperature is increased and stays at seven degrees above normal, death can result. In hot-humid areas, ventilation is most critical and must be a conscious design element. To say the least, humidity is also critical. As long as the relative humidity remains at 50% or less, evaporation takes place.[4] The humidity should remain below 50% when the air temperature climbs to 90° F. In most areas of the U.S. very simple concerns for thermal comfort will alleviate any need for mechanical air conditioning. Following these principles will also cut down on wasted energy.

## 4.2 Basic Cooling Design Responses

The most basic responses to solar radiation are orientation and shading. A more extensive discussion on orientation is found in section 2.6 and shading is briefly discussed in section 3.7. Table 2.4 gives regional orientation directions for a primary building surface for balanced heat distribution.

A basic principle is to shade all openings facing southwest, south, and southeast against penetration of solar radiation in the summer months and allowing its entrance in the winter. This shading can be done by overhangs and other forms of projections around a window, interior and exterior shades and vegetation in the form of ivy or large deciduous trees. Larger buildings should employ sunscreens, vertical projections or building form manipulation. Solar angles should be calculated (Appendix A) to find out the specifics needed in the design. It should be noted that certain kinds of overhangs and shading devices conflict with those

**66**

requirements of natural ventilation (4.5 and 4.6). If natural ventilation is to be used then physical elements should be chosen that can synthesize both shading and natural ventilation. As mentioned before (2.5) color can influence the amount of heat absorbed by the building surface that affects the internal temperature. If cooling is the predominant design factor, then a combination of light-colored surface and thermal resistant wall structure should be adopted.

Due to the high heat absorption of roofs, because of their exposure to summer solar radiation, insulation can increase cooling efficiency. In any area in the continental United States a black roof can reach 150° F during a clear summer day. Heavy insulation in the roof design can help alleviate the heat transmission, however, it also retards the expulsion of heat that does transfer in and takes longer to cool off. A roof vent that can allow heated air

to rise out would solve a lot of the problem.

The slant of the roof can offer a great deal to induced convective cooling. In house and small building design, the roof can be cooled by means of drawing in outside air and allowing it to rise through a vent to the outside.

A flat roof permits 50% more heat gain than a pitched roof on the same site.[5] Along with heavier insulation this can be very efficient. In winter this heavier insulation prevents heat loss through the roof. Reflective foil located just below the roof can be equivalent to 3" of mineral wool.[6] Reflective insulation can also reflect 90% of the radiation that would otherwise penetrate to the internal space.

When the external color of a roof is white, the effect of solar radiation is almost entirely prevented and long wave radiation to the sky is fully utilized. When the roof is dark, the underside temperature of the roof may be over 30° C above the outdoor level.[7] B. Givoni[8]

found that raising the ceiling height above 2.7 meters (9 feet) had little noticeable effect on indoor temperature. The little effect it did have is due to heat absorption by the roof, transferring to the ceiling and being radiated to the interior.

Induced thermal convection can be utilized for a very inexpensive means to cool structures. In large buildings a stack vent can be utilized. This form of cooling is arrived at by allowing the warmer air to rise out of the building,

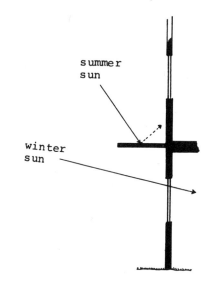

summer sun

winter sun

FIGURE 4.1 THE EFFECT OF AN OVERHANG ON SHADING.

drawing in cooler (possibly substructure) air from a basement, clay ducts in the earth, or from over a nearby vessel of water. The air could be drawn in from behind a fountain that would naturally cool the air during the daytime.

From this section natural cooling can be summarized into the following: orientation, surface color, shading by vegetation or other physical means, insulation and induced thermal convection.

### 4.3 Cooling Ponds

Water cooled roofs were first experimented with in the late 1930's. They were almost immediately successful, keeping out almost 80% of the solar radiation. At that time they were simply flooding a roof with 4" of water. This developed some problems in terms of algae and mosquitoes but by the mid-1940's, one might say the bugs had been worked out. Figure 4.2 shows the relative cooling effect of a roof pool or spray based on scientific tests. As dis-cussed earlier, the roof, when heated up, can act as a source of heat instead of a barrier against it. Placing the insulation above the ceiling and then ventilating the space between the roof and insulation helps, but water ponds tend to reduce the solar radiation penetration before it ever gets that far. One advantage roof ponds and sprays have is their easy adaptation to any flat roof, new or old. Water ponds act through reflection and evaporation to reduce the solar impact.

Life magazine performed an experiment on a small scale model house, one with roof ponds and the other dry. In the dry experiment, the indoor temperature jumped from 70° to 110° in a half hour under four infrared lamps. Under the same conditions but with water ponds the temperature only rose from 70° to 85°. The difference being 25° between experiments. In the 1942 ASHVE tests it was proven that a sprayed roof was 18 times as effective as a dry roof in excluding solar radiation.[9]

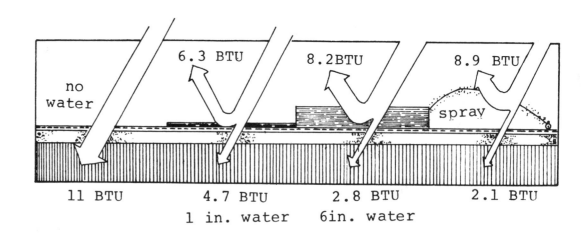

FIGURE 4.2 RELATIVE EFFECT OF A ROOF POND AND SPRAY.
*Source: Architectural Forum, June 1946.*

**68**

A roof spray can be installed on a pitched roof by running a perforated pipe along the ridge allowing the water to flow over the entire roof surface. This could be done at the hours of highest heat gain and then allow the roof to dry off later in the afternoon. The cooling affect on the roof also extends the life of the roof by minimizing expansion and contraction due to thermal stresses. This method of cooling is not without its drawbacks. Probably the biggest is the waste of water. Many places which need extensive cooling methods do not have the quantity of water available to distribute it freely to the atmosphere. In situations such as this means of collecting and storing the heated water may be the best answer (See Chapter 7).

The sky therm system, developed by Harold R. Hay and John I. Yellott is one of the more current processes of solar heating and cooling utilizing ceiling ponds with movable insulation.[10] Their testing offered very successful results for very hot, dry and hot, humid areas. The sky therm process utilizes six means of modulating the ambient temperature conditions: solar heating, heat capacity, nocturnal radiation, water evaporation, radiation, evaporation and fan-coil operation and fan-coil and pond blower use.

The first solarchitecture house designed by Hay is in Phoenix, Arizona (32°26'N). He is involved in the construction of another in Atascadero, California (35°N; 260 m.) which will provide a better test due to the different climatic conditions in Atascadero from those in Phoenix. Hay describes the structure of his first prototype in Phoenix as follows: "Corrugated metal sheets... form the ceiling between upward-extending roof beam supports. A black plastic film above the metal sheets was crossed over the beams to waterproof the structure. Six to seven inches of water in transparent plastic bags was laid on the lining between the beams. This amount of water provided the heat capacity effect of a foot of concrete with a weight equivalent of a 3" slab. Extruded aluminum trackings mounted atop the beams permitted insulation panels to be alternately positioned above the ponds or stacked two or three deep over a carport."[11] Figure 4.3 illustrates the roof plan and cross section.

For winter heating the ponds are exposed to solar radiation and at night covered by the insulating panels. The heat then radiates to the interior. The downward radiation kept the room at 66-73° F when the external temperature fell to the freezing point. The winter heating system is limited to snow-free regions that have strong solar radiation. Summer cooling was demonstrated by covering the ponds with the insulating panels during the day and allowing them to cool to minimum morning temperature by exposing them to the night air. The interior room temperature was between 74-77° F when the external maximum temperature was 100° F and the outside average was 83° F. By allowing nighttime evaporation of 1/8 to 1/4 inches

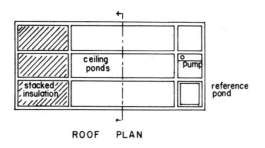

ROOF PLAN

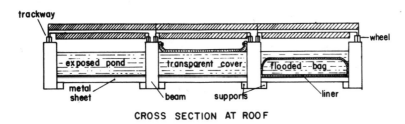

CROSS SECTION AT ROOF

FIGURE 4.3 CROSS-SECTION OF THE ROOF ON THE PHOENIX SOLARCHITECTURE HOUSE. *Source: Architectural Design, October 1973.*

of water, the ponds cooled to below the minimum morning air temperature. "The loss of only 1.37 gallons of pond water can produce the effect of a ton of refrigerant."[12] A fan coil, electrically operated, could be employed to remove the stratisfied room air to the cool overhead ponds to reduce temperatures.

Hay's solarchitecture house in California will be discussed in section 7.6 One of the more attractive aspects of this system is its ready adaptation to developing countries due to its low cost, low maintenance and no electricity required. The parts could easily be manufactured in industrialized nations if need be.

## 4.4 Natural Ventilation

Ventilation conditions inside a building have a direct influence on health, comfort and well-being of the occupants. The physiological aspect of man responds to air purity and motion, and the indirect influences of ventilation on temperature and humidity of the air and indoor surfaces. During hot periods natural ventilation, when properly used, can provide comfort by accelerating the conduction of heat and increasing the rate of evaporation around the occupants.

Although the welfare of the user is a primary concern, other factors should not be overlooked. Among the most significant is that the construction of a building may introduce particular phenomena to the micro-climate. For instance, the pattern of the wind may be uplifted and deflected. This can cause potential damage to vegetation as well as other buildings in the area.

Air flow through and within an internal space is stimulated by two means: the distribution of pressure gradients around a building and thermal forces caused by temperature gradients between indoor and outdoor air. The distribution of pressure zones is the result of wind being deflected around, within, and above the building. On the sides

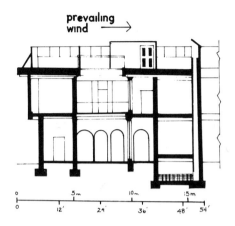

FIGURE 4.4 VENTILATION SHAFT IN PAKISTAN HOUSE. *Architectural Forum, July-August 1973.*

facing directly into the wind, high pressure zones are created. These areas are elevated above atmospheric pressure. Those areas where the velocity of the air is at its lowest, forming a suction effect, are called low pressure areas. The roof of a building is subject to suction in almost all cases. The difference in the high and low pressure zones determines the potential air flow velocity through the internal space. It is necessary for properly designed openings to be located in these areas.

Thermal force ventilation is caused by the different densities of air. The warmer or less dense air tends to rise by convection. This creates a vacuum, drawing in air to replace the rising air. If an opening is located at the bottom and top of an internal space, then convective natural ventilation is stimulated. However, in most hot, dry areas this ventilation is insufficient for giving thermal comfort.

Many of the drawings on the following pages are from research conducted by W.W. Caudill and Bill Reed at the Texas Engineering Experiment Station and research done at the Israel Institute of Technology by Dr. B. Givoni. The authors are indebted to them for their excellent work in this field.

4.5 *Three Functions of Ventilation*

Dr. B. Givoni[13] classifies ventilation into three distinct functions. These are: *health ventilation,* which maintains air quality in the building by replacing indoor air with fresh outdoor air; *thermal comfort ventilation,* whose purpose is to provide thermal comfort by facilitating the heat exchange from the body to the surrounding air; and *structural cooling ventilation,* which is a means by which the structure is cooled when the indoor temperature is higher than the outdoor temperature.

In buildings the quality of air is determined by the living processes (habits of cooking, keeping warm, etc.) and the activities occurring within it. The function of health ventilation is to provide the air quality necessary for the removal of odors, carbon monoxide, and any other by-product of the living processes.

Outdoor air, on the average, is composed of 21% oxygen, .03-.04% carbon dioxide, 78% nitrogen, 1% inert gases (primarily argon) and between 5 and 25 grams of water vapor per $M^3$ of air. Expired air contains about 16.3% oxygen, 4% carbon dioxide, 79.7% nitrogen and other gases, mainly ammonia and $459/m^3$ water vapor.[14] Bacteria and odor-producing

organic materials are given off by the body along with those effects that are a result of personal hygiene and diet (i.e., smoking). It should be remembered that oxygen requirements depend primarily on metabolic level of the individual and may directly affect other discharged gases from the body. In most cases the carbon dioxide and oxygen variations in buildings are rarely above 1%. The levels should not rise above 2-3% in carbon dioxide and 3-4% reduction in oxygen.

It is difficult to establish a requirement for dealing with odor levels. It should be assumed that the ventilation rate be adjusted for each activity occurring within a building so that any perceptable odor be eliminated. Spaces where cigarette smoking and cooking take place, as well as bathrooms and gymnasiums, require higher rates of air change than other places.

The perception of odor is directly related to air temperature. Researchers studied the effect of ventilation rate on odor level and found that a temperature reduction from 87 to 71° F caused a reduction in the perception of odor levels. This temperature difference was equivalent to an increase in air supply from 5 to 53 $ft^3$/min per person. Bacterial content was not affected by changes in ventilation rate from 1 to 53 $ft^3$/min per person.

Ventilation requirements need to be carefully determined for areas that have no direct outside connections such as windows.

As illustrated in Energy Cycle (fig. 1.1) carbon monoxide is the result of incomplete combustion of fossil fuels. This can also occur on the small scale in heating and cooling appliances. Carbon monoxide, when in contact with the bloodstream through breathing, has a reaction with the hemaglobin in the blood that deprives the body of oxygen, ultimately causing asphixiation. Ventilation requirements should be sufficient to eliminate any possibility of saturation of CO in the air. The best solution is to eliminate the need for fossil fuels in the first place. This would eliminate a "fix-it" approach to rectifying the problem.

The purpose of Thermal Comfort Ventilation is to remove the physiological and psychological discomforts due to high temperature, uncomfortable indoor conditions. In very few cases it is possible for natural ventilation to be distributed homogeneously throughout a space when high-velocity flow rates are involved. In terms of thermal comfort, the velocity of air flow, rather than the number of air changes, is important. It is important that a satisfactory number of air changes occur where odors are involved, but when rapid heat conductance is primary, a high velocity air flow is more important. Thermal Comfort Ventilation may also be employed during the cooler months. The purpose of this would be to force fresh air to the ceiling level where it can settle to the warmed floor. This can facilitate energy conservation. Thermal Comfort Ventilation is discussed

| External color | Point | Ventilation conditions | Concrete 12 cm | Concrete 22 cm | Hollow concrete blocks 20 cm | Young 12 cm | Young 22 cm | Ordinary curtain walls 7 cm | Insulated curtain walls 16 cm |
|---|---|---|---|---|---|---|---|---|---|
| Grey | Indoor Air | Without ventilation | 8.0 | 3.3 | 3.5 | 4.6 | 2.2 | 5.8 | 5.1 |
| | | Night ventilation | 7.2 | 1.9 | 1.7 | 3.4 | 0.2 | 4.8 | 3.7 |
| | | Permanent ventilation | 1.0 | -0.4 | -0.3 | 0.5 | -0.2 | 0.3 | 0.4 |
| | | Effect of night ventilation | -0.8 | -1.4 | -1.8 | -1.2 | -2.0 | -1.8 | -1.4 |
| | | Effect of permanent ventilation | -7.0 | -3.7 | -3.8 | -4.1 | -2.4 | -5.5 | -4.7 |
| White | Indoor Air | Without ventilation | -1.0 | -1.8 | -2.3 | -1.8 | -3.2 | -1.1 | -1.9 |
| | | Night ventilation | -2.7 | -2.5 | -2.8 | -2.7 | -4.8 | -0.5 | -3.1 |
| | | Permanent ventilation | -1.1 | -1.4 | -1.4 | -0.8 | -2.0 | 0.0 | -1.0 |
| | | Effect of night ventilation | -1.7 | -0.7 | -0.5 | -0.9 | -1.6 | 0.6 | -1.2 |
| | | Effect of permanent ventilation | -0.1 | 0.4 | 0.9 | 1.0 | 1.2 | 1.1 | 0.9 |

TABLE 4.1 EFFECTS OF VENTILATION ON INDOOR AIR TEMPERA-TURES. *Source: Man, Climate and Architecture.*

more thoroughly in the coming sections.

As discussed in the second chapter, air temperature is most directly affected by the heat absorption capabilities of the surrounding surfaces. This applies to indoor air temperatures also. Structural cooling ventilation deals primarily with reducing the temperature of the indoor surfaces. Those temperatures will fluctuate according to the average exterior surface temperatures. This, in turn, is the result of

external surface color, thermal resistance and orientation. Table 4.1 shows the results of tests conducted in Israel on the effects of ventilation on indoor air temperatures depending upon the type of ventilation and the color of the exterior surface. These temperatures are expressed as deviations from the maximum outdoor temperature. The results of the test indicate a relationship of ventilation and external color. The quantitative effect of ventilation varied with the material and its thickness,

especially when the exterior surface is gray. The cooling effect of permanent ventilation on the maximum temperature was greatest when the walls were thinner. It can be deduced that the gray painted concrete walls were more affected by ventilation than the lightweight concrete walls of the same thickness.

There are cases where ventilation may actually raise the temperatures on the inside due to a light exterior surface and thermal resistance of a wall retarding the absorption of solar radiation. The shading of windows and their size are important elements to consider. When the wall color is dark, ventilation reduces the daytime temperture of the internal surface, which affects the internal air temperature. This, of course, is relative to the thermal resistance of the wall and its thickness, and to the magnitude of change that ventilation can change.

Ventilation requirements vary with the general climatic and microclimatic conditions during different

seasons. The determination of those requirements should be done prior to the location of openings, mechanisms used in the openings and overall orientation of internal spaces. In the A.I.A. Bulletin from September 1949 to January 1952, form suggestions for 15 climatic regions are given.

In cold, dry regions where the importance is on minimizing the intrusion of outside air, humidified air is often desired. Ventilation is sometimes desired during the summer months. Humidity is undesirable at this time, so openings should be designed to provide cross ventilation along the NE-SW axis, consciously avoiding the south and west for humidity control. All windows should have two or three glazings for winter protection.

In areas where the winter months are very humid and not quite cold enough to require high thermal insulation, the rate of ventilation should be reduced so as not to lower the indoor temperature. In the temperate region of the U.S. openings should allow for summer breeze penetration (generally from the SW). Openings should be limited in the northern and western directions.

In hot areas, ventilation is important to remove moisture from the skin and aid in heat conduction. The velocity of the air is most critical, rather than the volumetric air flow. Natural ventilation is a very important element of design in these areas. In hot, humid areas the velocity should approach 400 ft/min during the hotter periods.[15] In a hot, dry climate, it is advisable to reduce the ventilation rate to a minimum during the daytime. Windows should be open during the night but during the day the velocity can even be lower than in cold climates. The open windows at night will allow ventilation to offset the increased temperatures on material walls and reduce the air temperature. The evening velocity may only be 200 ft/min.

The criteria for ventilation are determined by the exterior wall color and thermal resistance, the type of activity and the climate. The air velocity of natural ventilation is determined by temperature and humidity requirements. Ventilation effects may fluctuate within a space, necessitating an internal structuring of activities by the varying air velocities.

4.6 *Window Orientation, Size and Air Flow Patterns*

Air flow through a space is dependent upon the pressure distribution around the building, the orientation of the inlet, the sizes of the openings and the inertia of the outside air. This section will deal primarily with orientation and sizing of openings and their effects on inducing various air-flow patterns. The following section will focus on the location and type of openings.

Window orientation is very important to assure even distribution of air motion throughout the space. Quite often, with a direct axis between inlet and outlet, the flow of air will go

directly to the outlet if the inlet is perpendicular to the direction of the prevailing wind with little effect upon the other areas of the room. As Table 4.2 indicates, when windows are on opposite walls and the prevailing wind is oblique (45°) to the opening, higher velocities occur within the space when the inlet ratios are 1:1, 2:1, 2:2, 2:3, 3:2, 3:3. It will be shown later that it is not recommended to have the inlet larger than the outlet. The table also indicates that when the windows are located on adjacent walls the higher velocities occurred when the wind was perpendicular to the opening. The test was conducted by Givoni using a model that was square in plan. When tests were done on rectangular models it was found that wind shadows existed. Careful design of the openings and placement of internal walls can alleviate this. What occurs is that the inside flow enters (unless scooped such as by a casement window) and tends to follow its inertial direction until the pressure differ-

ence at the outlet causes it to change direction. This data is important for areas that have a westerly or easterly prevailing wind in the warmer months. Orientation requirements would conflict if the wind had to be perpendicular. Now the orientation direction can be towards the SE or SW and still facilitate natural ventilation. Aronin[16] tells of how the farmers of Quebec orient their houses on an east-west axis so the smallest areas bear the brunt of the winter prevailing wind. This orien-

tation facilitates an easy adaptation to Summer's prevailing wind.

Window size has a significant role in determining air flow velocity in cross-ventilated situations. In rooms where windows are only on one wall, there is little or no effect. In order for air to enter a room, it must be able to leave. Table 4.3 shows the average internal velocities that occurred in a model with a single window. In cross-ventilated situations the increased size of the openings has an influential

TABLE 4.2 EFFECT OF WINDOW SIZE IN ROOM WITH CROSS VENTILATION ON AVERAGE AIR VELOCITIES (% of external wind velocity)  Reprinted with permission from B. Givoni, *Man, Climate and Architecture.*

| Inlet width | Outlet width | Windows in opposite walls | | Windows in adjacent walls | |
|---|---|---|---|---|---|
| | | Wind perpend. | Wind oblique | Wind perpend. | Wind oblique |
| 1:3 | 1:3 | 35 | 42 | 45 | 37 |
| 1:3 | 2:3 | 39 | 40 | 39 | 40 |
| 2:3 | 1:3 | 34 | 43 | 51 | 36 |
| 2:3 | 2:3 | 37 | 51 | | |
| 1:3 | 3:3 | 44 | 44 | 51 | 45 |
| 3:3 | 1:3 | 32 | 41 | 50 | 37 |
| 2:3 | 3:3 | 35 | 59 | | |
| 3:3 | 2:3 | 36 | 62 | | |

TABLE 4.3  EFFECT OF WINDOW
LOCATION AND WIND DIRECTION
ON AVERAGE AIR VELOCITIES
(% of external velocity)

| Direction of wind | Width of Window | | |
|---|---|---|---|
| | 1/3 | 2/3 | 3/3 |
| Perpendicular to window | 13 | 13 | 16 |
| Oblique in front | 12 | 15 | 23 |
| Oblique from rear | 14 | 17 | 17 |

effect when both the inlet and the outlet are increased simultaneously.  It should be noted that the rate of velocity falls off as the windows get larger.  The average indoor velocity has a direct relationship to the size of the smaller opening but the maximum velocity is achieved through manipulation of the relative sizes of the inlet and outlet.

Most apartments and offices have only one external wall, with sometimes more than one window.  In this case, the ventilation must be induced by other means than that occurring in cross-ventilated rooms.  The air velocity inside these rooms is approximately 1/3 to 1/4 what it is in cross-ventilated rooms with the same total area of openings.[17] The rooms with only one external wall must have artificial pressure zones created.  This can be done by vertical projections from the wall.  Figure 4.6 indicates the results of tests done when an overhang was placed over the windows.  A slight increase in velocity is indicated.  Higher indoor velocities occurred when the wind was oblique to the window.  This can have important design implications in rooms with two windows and vertical projections between them.  Artificial high- and low-pressure zones were created, inducing the air to enter one window in the high pressure area and leave by the low pressure area.  Figure 4.5 illustrates the results.  If projections are located on both sides of the windows, the entire effect is lost.

Cross ventilation offers the optimum situation for natural ventilation.  Since cooling is the primary reason for using cross ventilation, the air flow should be directed to the level of human activity rather than toward the ceiling or above the head.  The location of the outlet, and the type of physical mechanism used in the inlet will determine the air flow pattern.  An important design consideration is that in most cases the maximum velocities occur in a room when the *outlet is larger than the inlet*.  Maximum air flow occurs when the outlet and inlet are the same size, but for cooling, maximum

velocity is more important. The average velocity is a direct function of the total area of the windows. In terms of orientation, higher indoor velocities occurred in a square test model when the wind was oblique to the inlet window.[18]

It has been shown that the inlet and outlet do not necessarily have to be located on opposite walls to induce air flow. Air flow pattern is directly determined by the design of the inlet and the horizontal location of the outlet. The inlet can act as a nozzle, directing up and down and determining the maximum cooling effect. Ceiling height does not directly affect the air flow pattern. If the ceiling is slanted, warm air rising can flow along the ceiling to an outlet which will draw in fresh air at an inlet. But this effect of thermal ventilation is not powerful enough to offer comfort during the warmer months. The depth of the room also has little effect[19] as long as a flow can occur between

inlet and outlet. In a design where a double-loaded corridor exists, the corridor may act as a plenum. The outlets can open onto it. If the corridor is a supplier of air, then sufficient obstructions must exist to distribute the air, yet not inhibit its flow.

When a small inlet tends to funnel the air and increase its velocity towards an outlet, it is called "venturi effect." This has both advantages and disadvantages. In rectangular rooms that are oriented so that the inlet and outlet are opposite each other on the smaller wall surfaces, the direct air flow will fill the entire room. In rooms that are square or where the inlet and outlet windows are on the larger wall surfaces then the effect will only cool the area located between the windows and do little for the surrounding surface area.

The rate of air flow can be determined from the equations given below.[20]

$Q = KAV$ (when cross ventilation is used)
$Q$ = rate of air flow, cu. ft/hr
$A$ = area of inlets, sq. ft.
$V$ = wind velocity, mph
$K$ = a value dependent upon the outlet to inlet relationship

| Area of Outlet / Area of Inlet | K |
|---|---|
| 1:1 | 3150 |
| 2:1 | 4000 |
| 3:1 | 4250 |
| 4:1 | 4350 |
| 5:1 | 4400 |
| 3:4 | 2700 |
| 1:2 | 2000 |
| 1:4 | 1100 |

$Q = KA\sqrt{H(t_i - t_o)}$ (when ventilation is by thermal differentialtion)[14]
$Q$ = rate of air flow, cu. ft/hr
$A$ = area of inlets, sq. ft.
$H$ = height between inlets and outlets, feet
$t_i$ = average temperature of indoor air at height H, °F
$t_o$ = temperature of indoor air, °F

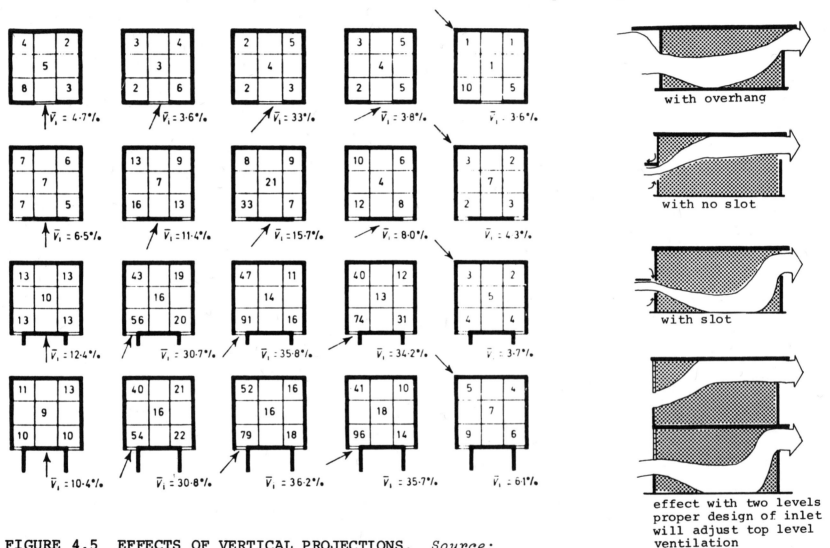

$\bar{V}_i = 4.7\%$ $\bar{V}_i = 3.6\%$ $\bar{V}_i = 33\%$ $\bar{V}_i = 3.8\%$ $\bar{V}_i = 3.6\%$

$\bar{V}_i = 6.5\%$ $\bar{V}_i = 11.4\%$ $\bar{V}_i = 15.7\%$ $\bar{V}_i = 8.0\%$ $\bar{V}_i = 4.3\%$

$\bar{V}_i = 12.4\%$ $\bar{V}_i = 30.7\%$ $\bar{V}_i = 35.8\%$ $\bar{V}_i = 34.2\%$ $\bar{V}_i = 3.7\%$

$\bar{V}_i = 10.4\%$ $\bar{V}_i = 30.8\%$ $\bar{V}_i = 36.2\%$ $\bar{V}_i = 35.7\%$ $\bar{V}_i = 6.1\%$

with overhang

with no slot

with slot

effect with two levels proper design of inlet will adjust top level ventilation

**FIGURE 4.5  EFFECTS OF VERTICAL PROJECTIONS.** *Source: Man, Climate and Architecture.*

**78**

FIGURE 4.6 continued

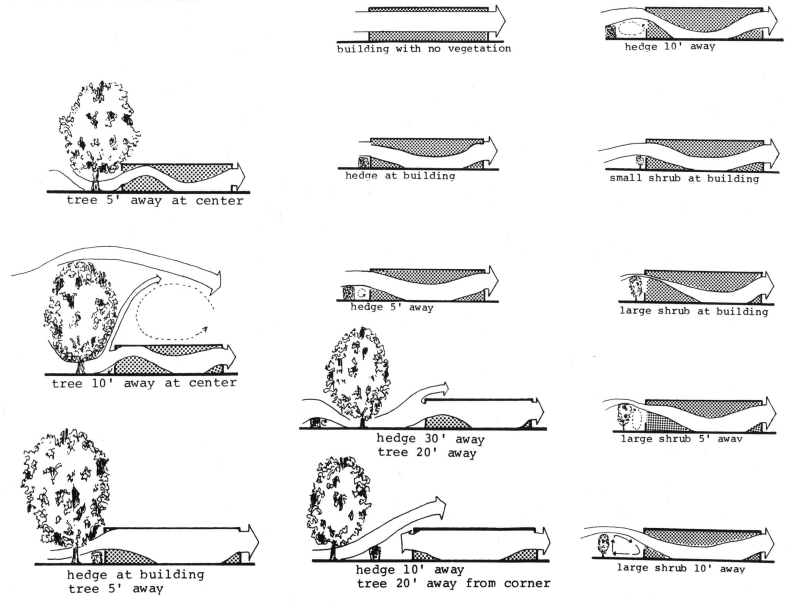

building with no vegetation

hedge 10' away

tree 5' away at center

hedge at building

small shrub at building

tree 10' away at center

hedge 5' away

large shrub at building

hedge at building
tree 5' away

hedge 30' away
tree 20' away

large shrub 5' away

hedge 10' away
tree 20' away from corner

large shrub 10' away

| Area of Outlet | K |
|---|---|
| Area of Inlet | |
| 5 | 745 |
| 4 | 740 |
| 3 | 720 |
| 2 | 680 |
| 1 | 540 |
| 3/4 | 455 |
| 1/2 | 340 |
| 1/4 | 185 |

The various drawings on the previous page exhibit the patterns of air flow under various conditions and the ratios of inlet to outlet. It can be seen that air flow energy is consumed when the initial direction is altered (figures 4.6 and 4.8).

*Summary No. 1*

- Depth of the room has little effect

- Ceiling height has little effect

- Vertical projections can induce ventilation when properly placed between two windows on the same external wall.

- When windows are located on adjacent walls having the inlet perpendicular to the prevailing wind is best.

- When the inlet and outlet are on opposite walls directly opposite each other, having the inlet oblique to the prevailing wind gives a more distributed affect.

- Maximum velocity occurs when the outlet is larger than the inlet.

- The inlet and the horizontal placement of the outlet determines the air flow pattern.

*4.7 Window Location and Type*

The vertical location and type of inlet is more critical to control than the respective characteristics of the outlet. The vertical location of the inlet has only a slight, if at all, effect on the air flow pattern. The vertical location of the inlet can control both the velocity and direction of the air flow. There is a drastic reduction in windspeed when the inlet is located below average windowsill level. When the inlet is located this low there can exist as much as a 25% reduction in velocity as compared with the main-stream velocity in a cross-ventilation situation. The average velocity, overall, is only affected slightly. As air strikes a vertical wall a force component is formed that tends to move parallel to the surface. When an opening is located in the wall, the amount of air entering that opening is dependent upon the pressure inside, the force component which varies with the surface area and the design of the inlet. As a result of this force component, the openings in a second or third story will generate completely different results than the first story. The force component will tend to flow up, or at times down, the faces of a large building. If the room has a window with an adjustable sash, the amount and direction of air can be regulated. This force component is an important consideration when designing overhangs or balconies for rooms also requiring natural ventilation.

In multistory buildings the force component splits up so that part flows down the face and part flows upward. Balconies and sun hoods over the inlet window directly affect the ventilation. Overhangs located well above the inlet tend to strengthen the downward force component giving a favorable direction to the incoming air when the wind was perpendicular. A sunshade with no slot tended to allow the upward component (even though it was small due to the limited surface area below the opening) to determine the direction of the entering air flow. When the sun hood had a sizable slot between it and the building surface, the downward component is allowed to influence the direction of the air flow.

In some cases when there are too many balconies or extended horizontal sun hoods, the force component breaks up before actually striking the surface of the inlets (when the wind is perpendicular) and the wind simply goes over the building. If the surface with all the balconies was oriented oblique to the wind, then possibly the wind would

be channeled underneath them, only to be caught by casement type windows. This is only theory, and a great deal of research is still necessary.

Different types of inlet windows produce different air flow patterns and affect the distribution of various velocities throughout the space. Strip windows, for instance, were found to give a more even distribution of air flow throughout a space than singular "punched in" type of windows.[21] Of course, even the strip windows require the proper kind of sash to direct the flow into the living zone. A study of various window types (fig. 4.7) was carried out by Holleman[22] at the Texas Engineering Experiment Station in 1951. He traced the wind patterns with smoke but no velocity recordings were made. The results of the test on the double hung type window indicated that the air flow came in on a horizontal level in each case studied: one sash open, both top and bottom open maximum and both open minimum. This

indicates that this type of window would have to be located at the level in which the effect was desired. With horizontal sliding windows, the same effect of the incoming air travels at a horizontal level occurred under all conditions. Again it should be located at the heighth where the air flow is desired. In the vertical

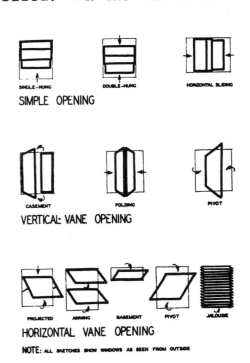

FIGURE 4.7 TYPES OF WINDOWS STUDIED. *Source: Air Flow through Conventional Window Openings by Theo R. Holleman.*

vane opening type windows tested (casement, folding, vertical pivot) the air could be adjusted to flow right or left but could not affect the vertical placement of the air flow, other than being located at the height where the air is desired. When the projected sash window was tested, it was found that the air was directed at a horizontal level when the sash was fully opened and directed upward when the sash was anything less than fully opened. The jalousie type produced a laminar effect as it flowed through the opening. Any upward angle could be adjusted and any downward angle to 'a maximum of 20°.

The awning and horizontal pivot type windows gave a horizontal direction to the air flow when opened all the way and an upward angle to any opening less than full. The basement window directed the air only upward. It appears that all the horizontal vane opening windows except possibly the jalousie type, need to be located below the level where the air is desired. With such few

types of windows existing that can satisfy the needs of natural ventilation, the need for more conscientious window designers is apparent.

The results indicate that to obtain desirable comfort conditions from natural ventilation, it is necessary:

*Summary No. 2*

- to have a movable sash which can adjust the breeze downward

- to properly slot sun hoods and permit downward forced air to flow into the space

- that the inlets should not be located below average window sill level

## 4.8 *Division of Interior Space*

Whenever an incoming air flow is forced to change direction within a space, the energy inherent in the inertia of the flow is appreciably depleted. This occurs when the width of a building is greater than the depth of its rooms. It is necessary that each room

must be ventilated with respect to the other rooms. With the proper location of interior partitions, a greater area of space can be exposed to the effect of natural ventilation with only moderate reduction in velocity. The larger the internal opening between spaces, the less the reduction in velocity. It should also be noted that from the results shown in figures 4.6 and 4.8 that the closer the internal partition can be to the outlet, the more satisfactory the ventilation will be. It is preferable for the upwind room to be larger. Furniture, equipment and shades or curtains can affect the air flow. It should be remembered that the main airstream can often be eight times as powerful as the cartwheeling eddies.

## 4.9 *Influence of Landscape*

Depending upon the height, width and density characteristics of landscape elements, the air movement

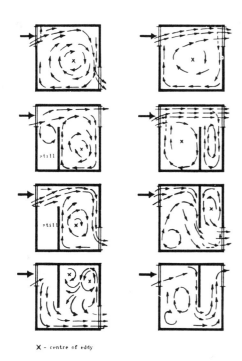

FIGURE 4.8  FLOW PATTERNS
WITH INTERNAL DIVISIONS.
*Source:  Man, Climate and
Architecture.*

within a structure can be
proportionally influenced.
Studies done at the Texas
Engineering Experimental
Station by Robert F. White[23]
indicated that the foliage
mass of a tree serves as a
direct block to the passage
of air and that the air
velocity underneath a tree
is measurably increased with
respect to surrounding flow
velocities.  Planting was
found to cause change of
direction of air flow into
the building.  Figure 4.6
illustrates the results of
White's testing with the
effects of a hedge.  Figure
4.6 further shows how
shrubbery tends to give air
flow a diminishing downward
appearance and an eddy is
created behind the shrub.
Also illustrated is the
effect of a tree 30' high,
with a 25' spread starting
at 5' off the ground, on the
air flow pattern, and how a
tree hedge combination
causes a reversed air flow
within the structure.

*4.9a   Summary of Town
        Planning Principles*

The potential influence of
ventilation on a building
is greatly influenced by the

location, distance, size
and shape of nearby con-
structions.  Givoni summar-
izes the main elements of
town planning affecting
ventilation as follows:

- direction and effective
  width of the main and
  secondary streets with
  respect to wind

- distance between buildings
  along the streets

- general height of buildings

- presence of high-rise
  buildings among lower
  buildings

Steamlines of air are pushed
above the level of building
tops causing eddies behind
the building, relative to its
size and height.  Any building located in an eddy is
dependent upon its velocity,
which is generally very low.
Air flow along streets is an
important consideration.
Where thermal convection from
the air layer closest to the
building surface is to used
for natural ventilation, the
amount of solar radiation on
the surface is important (to
heat up the air so it will
rise).  Surrounding buildings
may shade these surfaces if

orientation is not carefully decided. Care should be taken to analyze the wind patterns of the surroundings either by building a model and testing with smoke tracings in a wind chamber or on site anemometer readings. Predictions could then be made as to the effects on and created by the new structure. A new structure should be built with considerations for the other elements of both the natural and built environment.

*4.9b   Summary of Natural Ventilation*

- the ventilation conditions within a building have a direct effect on the human body through air purity temperature and heat dissipation capabilities

- ventilation serves three functions: to maintain the air quality, as in *health* ventilation; to increase thermal comfort by aiding heat conduction from the body as in *thermal comfort ventilation;* and to cool the indoor surface temperature by *structural cooling ventilation*

- air flow through a building is dependent upon the wind pressure forces creating high and low zones; when openings are placed in each of the two areas, air flow is induced

- it is impossible to induce air flow in rooms with openings only on the windward side by creating artificial pressure zones by vertical projections

- air flow patterns are the result of inlet location and design and external building elements

- more than one space within a room may be ventilated with the smaller space closer to the outlet

- landscape can alter or aid air flow through a building

FOOTNOTES:

1. Emerick, R.H. "Comfort Factors Affecting Cooling Design," *Progressive Architecture*, December 1951, p. 97.

2. *Ibid.*

3. *Ibid.*

4. *Ibid.*

5. Kern, Ken. *Owner Built Home*, Ken Kern Drafting, Sierra Route, Oakhurst, Co.

6. Givoni, B. *Man, Climate and Architecture*, Elsevier Publishers, New York and London, 1969, p. 150.

7. *Ibid.*, p. 191.

8. *Ibid.*

9. "Water Cooled Roofs," *Architectural Forum*, June 1946, p. 167.

10. Yellott, J.I. and Hay, H.R. "Thermal Analysis of a Building with Natural Air Conditioning," *ASHRAE*, Semiannual Meeting, Chicago, January 1969, Paper #2103.

11. Hay, Harold, as quoted in "Solar Energy in Housing"

by C. Moorcraft. *Architectural Design*, October 1973, p. 654.

12. *Ibid*.

13. *Op.cit.* **Givoni**, p. 230.

14. *Ibid*., p. 231.

15. *Ibid*., p. 249.

16. Aronin, J.E. *Climate and Architecture*, Reinhold, New York, 1953, p. 206.

17. Givoni, B. *Ventilation Problems in Hot Countries*, Ford Foundation Research Report, Haifa, Israel, May 1968, p. 8.

18. Givoni, B. "Laboratory Study of the Effect of Window Size and Location on Indoor Air Motion," *Architectural Science Review*, June 1965, p. 44.

19. Olgyay, V. *Design with Climate*, Princeton University Press, Princeton, New Jersey, 1963, p. 112.

20. *Ibid*.

21. Holloman, T.R. *Air Flow through Conventional Windows*, Research Report No. 33, Texas Engineering Experimental Station, November 1951.

REFERENCES:

*ASHRAE Guide and Data Book*, 1963, pp. 438-441.

Caudill, W.W. "Classroom Comfort through Natural Ventilation," *A.I.A. Bulletin*, May 1952, p. 22-24.

Dick, J.B. "The Fundamentals of Natural Ventilation of Houses," *Journal of the Institution of Heating and Ventilating Engineers*, June 1953, pp. 123-134.

Hay, Harold. "New Roofs for Hot, Dry Regions," *Ekistics*, No. 183, February 1971, pp. 158-164.

Hay, H.R. and Yellott, J.I. "International Aspects of Air Conditioning with Movable Insulation," *Solar Energy*, Vol. 12, pp. 427-438.

Texas Engineering Experimental Station, *Research Reports Nos. 21, 22, 26, 36, 59*.

"Ventilation," *Architectural Forum*, May 1951, pp. 174-177.

"Well-Ventilated Schoolrooms," *Architectural Forum*, January 1952, pp. 150-157.

Yellott, J.I. and Hay, H.R. "Natural Air Conditioning with Roof Ponds and Movable Insulation," *ASHRAE*, Semiannual Meeting, Chicago, 1968, Research Paper #2102.

**86 NOTES**

# 5. Water Power

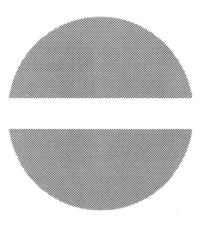

Water power is discussed
only briefly here because
its applications are almost
totally isolated to rural
situations. As the reali-
zation that water is a
viable source of power
grows, imaginative applications may develop which will
encourage further explora-
tion of its potentials.
The bulk of this information
is derived from the five-
part series published in
*Popular Science Monthly*
beginning in April 1947, and
"Power from Small Streams"
by C.A. Crowley in *Popular
Mechanics*, September 1940.

## 5.1 Water Power

The power is not isolated to
large streams: small
streams can also generate
a surprising amount of
energy. There are, however,
at least three questions
that need to be answered
before undertaking plans to
build a water powerhouse.
These are (1) Does water
flow the year around,
including late summer
months? (2) Does enough
water flow to make the
economical investment wise?
(3) What is the least amount
of power worth developing?
The first question can be

answered through observation; the second through measurement techniques which will be discussed later. The third question can simply be answered by others' experiences. It has been found that if 500 watts is not generated dependably, then the undertaking may not be worthwhile.[1] Half a kilowatt will generate electricity for five 100-watt bulbs or supply 2/3 (horsepower) to a deep-well pump. To aid in the determination of what the specific power needs are, Table D.2 is provided in the appendix.

The power available where a water wheel is located (not including wheel and generator inefficiencies) is:

$$Hp = \frac{62.4 \times Q \times H}{33,000}$$

Q = cubic feet per minute of water passing through the wheel

H = the head, which can be defined as the vertical distance in feet that the water falls

62.4 = the weight in pounds of 1 cu.ft. of water

33,000 = the number of foot-pounds (ft.-lbs.) per min. in 1 hp.

To be able to determine the measurements, it is first necessary to locate the dam.

## 5.2   Dam Location and Flow Measurement

Dam location is generally determined by (1) where the greatest head is obtainable at a place where the stream is smallest and (2) where the stream can be smallest but also retard the greatest amount of water. Obviously the dam will create a small pond, so the valley walls should be considered also. The height of the dam is dependent on the height of the valley walls, the materials used, the equipment available and economics. The higher the dam, the greater the head and the larger the pond. A guess at the available head can now be made, but accurate measurements will have to be made later. The pond water or "pondage" is principally for peak demand. It allows for heavy usage of the water at the time of day required without limiting one to using just the flow of the stream. If the wheel runs 16 hours a day, then the pond can fill up 8 hours a day.

If a small waterfall is along the stream, it offers a good opportunity for the creation of a large head through the construction of a small, inexpensive dam. Swampy meadows indicate a natural reservoir, so placing the dam at the narrowest point where the stream leaves the area would be a good location.

The powerhouse may be located at the dam where only the artificial head is used, or it may be located with the wheel below the dam, thus adding the natural

head to the artificial one. The latter requires a pipe to the wheel of the system. Both methods have advantages and disadvantages. The powerhouse at the dam is easier and simpler to build, but an adequate spillway must be designed to protect it during times of high water. When the wheel is located right at the dam, only the artificial head can be used.

Once a tentative site has been located, it is necessary to derive the pertinent data. There are basically three methods of measurement to determine the cubic feet per minute of flow. These are (1) the direct method, (2) the floating method, and (3) the weir method. The direct method is the simplest, but can only be used where the flow is small (usually under 10 gallons per minute). It involves a small temporary dam with a pipe that allows water to flow into a small pail. One cu.ft. of water is approximately equal to 7-1/2 gallons. Simply time the water flowing into a pail of a given capacity.

The float method is for a very large stream, too large for a weir. This requires measuring the velocity of a float (a bottle with a weight and a cork; or simply, a block of wood) over a given distance. Figure 5.1 illustrates a typical setup. The following formula can be used:[2]

$$Q = A \times V \times 60$$

Q=cu.ft./min of flowing water
A=cross-sectional area of the stream in sq.ft.
V=the average velocity of the stream at the point where the cross-section is determined.

The site must be a place where the sides of the stream are approximately parallel, basically straight and unobstructed by large rocks, for at least 100'. At two points along the stream, 100' apart, two lengths of taut string or wire are stretched across the stream. The float is then timed (preferably with a stop-watch) as it passes between the lengths of wire. A series of runs should be timed, and an average derived. Inasmuch as the water flows most rapidly

at the top and at the center, the value derived should be multiplied by .83 to give a more accurate velocity. The cross-section should be taken in the middle of the course. This can be done by stretching a taut wire or string that is marked off into 10 sections, across the stream. A measurement is taken at each point and an average depth is determined. The cross-sectional area, A, is the measurement of the

FIGURE 5.1  MEASURING FLOW WITH THE FLOAT METHOD. *Source: Popular Science.*

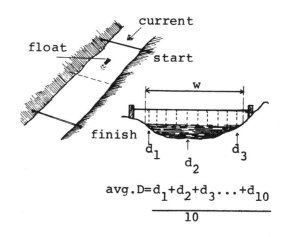

$$\text{avg.D} = \frac{d_1 + d_2 + d_3 \ldots + d_{10}}{10}$$

width of the stream in inches, multiplied by the average depth in inches and divided by 144 to get the answer in square feet.

The weir method is more complex, but much more accurate. A temporary dam is erected. The rectangular opening has a flat edge of at least 1/8" width in the upstream direction, and the remaining width is beveled. Figure 5.2 illustrates this. The flow of water through this opening should be free of turbulance, and there should be no leakage around or under the weir. The height of the weir should equal the depth of the stream at the point to be dammed. The length of the weir should not be less than three times its height. It is necessary that the dam be perpendicular to the flow of water. The weir is located in the center of the temporary dam with its lower edge not less than 1' above the surface of the water below the dam.

A stake is driven not less than 5 ft. upstream. The top of the stake should be perfectly level with the bottom of the weir. As the water flows over the weir the depth of the water is measured from the stake with a ruler. Using Table 5.1 the cubic feet per minute can be determined.

If a dam is already present on the site, a temporary weir can be fitted to it and measurements determined. Again, the same degree of accuracy should be employed.

Using this temporary dam, an accurate measurement of the head can be made. It should be noted that the head is measured as the vertical difference between

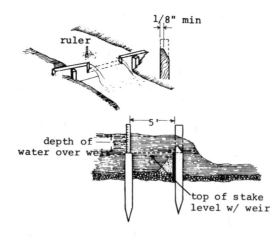

FIGURE 5.2  MEASURING FLOW WITH THE WEIR METHOD.
*Source:  Popular Science.*

| Inches Depth over Stake, D | | 1/8 in. | 1/4 in. | 3/8 in. |
|---|---|---|---|---|
| 1 inch | .40 | .47 | .55 | .65 |
| 2 " | 1.14 | 1.24 | 2.36 | 1.47 |
| 3 " | 2.09 | 2.23 | 2.36 | 2.50 |
| 4 " | 3.22 | 3.37 | 3.52 | 3.68 |
| 5 " | 4.50 | 4.67 | 4.84 | 5.01 |
| 6 " | 5.90 | 6.09 | 6.28 | 6.47 |
| 7 " | 7.44 | 7.64 | 7.84 | 8.05 |
| 8 " | 9.10 | 9.31 | 9.52 | 9.74 |
| 9 " | 10.86 | 11.08 | 11.31 | 11.54 |
| 10 " | 12.71 | 12.95 | 13.19 | 13.43 |
| 11 " | 14.67 | 14.92 | 15.18 | 15.43 |
| 12 " | 16.73 | 16.99 | 17.26 | 17.52 |
| 13 " | 18.87 | 19.14 | 19.42 | 19.69 |
| 14 " | 21.09 | 21.37 | 21.65 | 21.94 |
| 15 " | 23.38 | 23.67 | 23.97 | 24.26 |
| 16 " | 25.76 | 26.06 | 26.36 | 26.66 |
| 17 " | 28.20 | 28.51 | 28.82 | 29.14 |
| 18 " | 30.70 | 31.02 | 31.34 | 31.66 |
| 19 " | 33.29 | 33.61 | 33.94 | 34.27 |
| 20 " | 35.94 | 36.27 | 36.60 | 36.94 |
| 21 " | 38.65 | 39.00 | 39.34 | 39.69 |
| 22 " | 41.43 | 41.78 | 42.13 | 42.49 |
| 23 " | 44.28 | 44.64 | 45.00 | 45.38 |
| 24 " | 47.18 | 47.55 | 47.91 | 48.28 |

| Inches Depth over Stake, D | 1/2 in. | 5/8 in. | 3/4 in. | 7/8 in. |
|---|---|---|---|---|
| 1 inch | .74 | .83 | .93 | 1.03 |
| 2 " | 1.59 | 1.71 | 1.83 | 1.96 |
| 3 " | 2.63 | 2.78 | 2.92 | 3.07 |
| 4 " | 3.83 | 3.99 | 4.16 | 4.32 |
| 5 " | 5.18 | 5.36 | 5.54 | 5.72 |
| 6 " | 6.65 | 6.85 | 7.05 | 7.25 |
| 7 " | 8.25 | 8.45 | 8.66 | 8.86 |
| 8 " | 9.96 | 10.18 | 10.40 | 10.62 |
| 9 " | 11.77 | 12.00 | 12.23 | 12.47 |
| 10 " | 13.67 | 13.93 | 14.16 | 14.42 |
| 11 " | 15.67 | 15.96 | 16.20 | 16.46 |
| 12 " | 17.78 | 18.05 | 18.32 | 18.58 |
| 13 " | 19.97 | 20.24 | 20.52 | 20.80 |
| 14 " | 22.22 | 22.51 | 22.70 | 23.08 |
| 15 " | 24.56 | 24.86 | 25.16 | 25.46 |
| 16 " | 26.97 | 27.27 | 27.58 | 27.89 |
| 17 " | 29.45 | 29.76 | 30.08 | 30.39 |
| 18 " | 31.98 | 32.31 | 32.63 | 32.96 |
| 19 " | 34.60 | 34.94 | 35.27 | 35.60 |
| 20 " | 37.28 | 37.62 | 37.96 | 38.31 |
| 21 " | 40.04 | 40.39 | 40.73 | 41.09 |
| 22 " | 42.84 | 43.20 | 43.56 | 32.92 |
| 23 " | 45.71 | 46.08 | 46.43 | 46.81 |
| 24 " | 48.65 | 49.02 | 49.39 | 49.76 |

*Table indicates cfm for each inch of notch width. The depth D is a combination of the left and right columns, multiply the result by the width of the notch in inches.*
TABLE 5.1  AMOUNT OF WATER OVER A WEIR. *Source: Popular Science*

the surface of the water behind the dam and the surface of the stream below the dam. The measurement can be easily determined with a transit and a surveyor's pole. If these are not available, it may be done with a carpenter's level; a folding rule or tape measure; a 1" x 2" x 6' board with two edges planed parallel, two wooden pegs, a stake and a C clamp. Figure 5.3 illustrates the method. With these accurate measurements, the actual available horsepower can be determined by the equation (1).

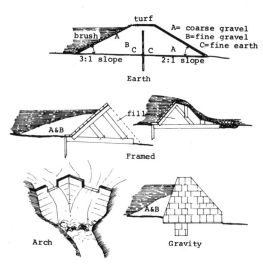

FIGURE 5.4  TYPES OF DAMS.
*Source: Popular Science.*

5.3  *Dam Type and Construction*

Prior to construction of a dam, it is recommended that the State specifications (should there be any) be checked. Many areas have either strict or relaxed laws concerning dam construction, and the laws may be able to offer additional information regarding the particular type of construction to be used. Figures 5.4 and 5.5 show several types: the earth type, the gravity type (concrete, cinder block, rock, etc.), the wood-framed and an arch type.

A cofferdam can be built to divert the stream from its usual channel while a permanent dam is being constructed. This dam and a necessary diversion ditch will keep the construction site free of water. The diversion ditch is dug at a small angle to the stream for easy redirection of the flow. Then pilings are sunk, and planks are nailed to the pilings. Chicken wire is then attached across the pilings, and sandbags are banked on both sides.

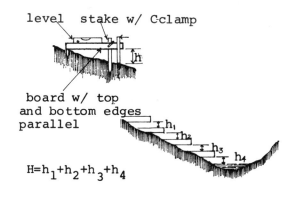

$$H = h_1 + h_2 + h_3 + h_4$$

FIGURE 5.3  MEASURING THE HEAD. *Source: Popular Science.*

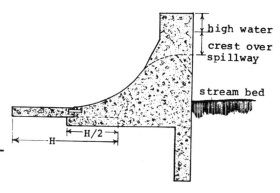

FIGURE 5.5  CONCRETE DAM.
*Source: Popular Mechanics.*

**91**

The height of the dam may be determined by adding together the maximum depth of water at the dam (including the high-water level) plus 2-1/2'. That includes 1' for the height above high water-level and 18" for a suitable foundation. Table 5.2 provides additional information. Drain pipes should be included in large dams to aid in evacuating excess water at flood or very high water-level periods. The entrances to the drain pipes should be capable of being opened and closed.

Depending upon what type of dam is used, the spillway should be large enough to carry off the maximum overflow of water, while still allowing the water level to stay within 1' of the top of the dam. On earth dams, it is necessary to increase the width of the spillway to prevent erosion of the earth in the dam. Where a pipe is to extend from the dam to the powerhouse, the spillway dimension should take into account the amount of water not going over the spillway during the operating time of the water wheel. The

| HEIGHT (H) | | BASE (B) | | DEPTH OF CORE WALL | | DEPTH OF WATER AT HEAD OF DAM | |
|---|---|---|---|---|---|---|---|
| FT. | IN. | FT. | IN. | FT. | IN. | FT. | IN. |
| 5 | - | 4 | 4-1/2 | 2 | 6 | 2 | 6 |
| 6 | - | 5 | 1-1/2 | 3 | - | 3 | 6 |
| 7 | - | 5 | 10-1/2 | 3 | 6 | 4 | 6 |
| 8 | - | 6 | 7-1/2 | 4 | - | 5 | 6 |
| 9 | - | 7 | 4-1/2 | 4 | 6 | 6 | 6 |
| 10 | - | 8 | 1-1/2 | 5 | - | 7 | 6 |

TABLE 5.2 DAM DIMENSIONS.
*Source: Popular Mechanics.*

spillway may curve downstream so as to follow the natural curve of the water and prevent unnecessary erosion. If a curved spillway is not going to be used, then large rocks should be placed at the point where the water falls to avoid erosion. Table 5.3 gives the dimensions for a spillway.

To help prevent the breeding of mosquitoes, all vegetation should be cleared in the dam and flood area. Any trees which must be removed should be cut close to the

ground. It may be possible to use the cut trees in the construction of the dam.

The earth is constructed using various types of soil. The fill should be deposited in layers, and with even tampering. Matted woven brush on the slope against the water aids in preventing erosion. Grass planted on the supporting slope helps to hold the earth also. The spillway in an earth dam should be of some resistant material, such as masonry or wood, and, as mentioned earlier, the sides should

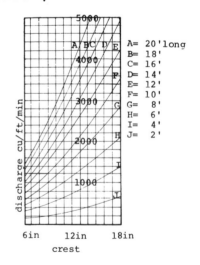

TABLE 5.3 SPILLWAY DIMENSIONS FOR A 6" TO 18" CREST.
*Source: Popular Mechanics.*

**92**

be stepped or also of re-
sistant material to avoid
erosion.

The framed dam consists
basically of a joist with
one or more struts against
planking. The planking
seals should extend below
the foundation. A footing
can also be applied between
the base of the joist and
the base of the strut.

Gravity dams can be con-
structed of concrete,
concrete block or rock.
Small concrete dams can be
cast in one piece, but
larger dams should be cast
in sections. The end
sections should extend well
into the valley walls to
ensure tightness and
stability. A suitable
foundation should be ex-
cavated also. If a forebay
is to be used, such as when
the powerhouse is downstream
from the dam, then this
should also be a part of the
dam construction.

*5.4   The Wheel*

Only four of the more popular
wheels are discussed here:
the overshot wheel, the
undershot wheel, the turbine

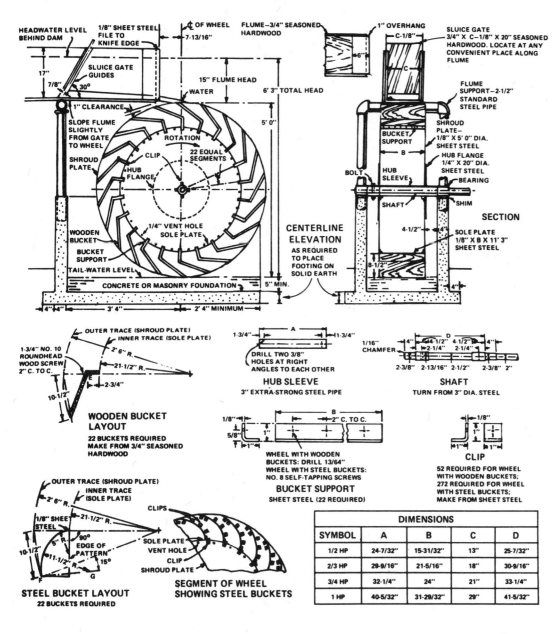

| DIMENSIONS | | | | |
|---|---|---|---|---|
| SYMBOL | A | B | C | D |
| 1/2 HP | 24-7/32" | 15-31/32" | 13" | 25-7/32" |
| 2/3 HP | 29-9/16" | 21-5/16" | 18" | 30-9/16" |
| 3/4 HP | 32-1/4" | 24" | 21" | 33-1/4" |
| 1 HP | 40-5/32" | 31-29/32" | 29" | 41-5/32" |

**FIGURE 5.6  OVERSHOT WHEEL.** *Reprinted Courtesy of Popular Science ©1947 Popular Science Publ. Co. Inc.*

and the Pelton or impulse wheel.

Figures 5.6 and 5.7 illustrate the overshot and undershot wheels. The overshot and undershot wheels are characterized by small-capacity output. The amount of power is dependent on the weight of water that the buckets hold and the diameter of the wheel which is the height or head that the water actually falls. For maximum wheel efficiency, the buckets should not loose any water until they reach tail water. The wheel in figure 5.6 was designed for a head of about 6'3" and the actual wheel is about 5'. The flume is about 15." The horsepower is variable according to the width. In other words, the larger the width, the greater the horsepower. For example, a wheel that is 15-31/32" wide generates 1/2 hp, but when the wheel width is increased to 31-29/32" the wheel generates.[3]

The over or under shot wheel is located off to one side of the dam or downstream, where a sluice or pipe carries the water to the

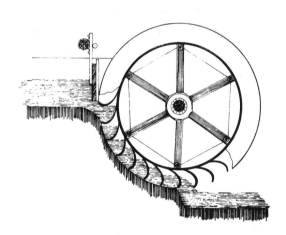

FIGURE 5.7 OVERSHOT AND UNDERSHOT WHEELS. *Source: Survival Scrapbook #3 Energy.*

wheel. When it is down-stream, both the natural and the artificial head can be used.

Construction of this wheel is not as critical a factor as it is in the case of the impulse wheel. The wheel rotates generally slowly enough so that critical balancing is not that important. The buckets are the most important compo-nent. They should be formed so that the water enters smoothly and remains until each reaches the bottom. Sheet metal or wood can be used, but wood is not recommended in cold climates where freezing and thawing may take place. The sluice gate should also be carefully designed because it is actually the governing mechanism of the wheel. It should be in-stalled at an angle to hold back the pressure of the water. It should be adjusted to allow water to fill the buckets only one quarter full. This pre-vents spilling before the tail water. The "mill race" and the sluice gate should be made of durable materials, such as spruce, pine, or oak.

The turbine is a much more efficient means of getting power from a stream. But, of course, it lacks the peculiar beauty of an over or undershot wheel. Table 5.4 will help in determining turbine size. Turbines are still manufactured by Leffel and Co., Springfield, Ohio 45501, according to the Volunteers for International Technical Assistance (VITA) manual, "Low-Cost Develop-ment of Small Water Power Sites." This manual is an excellent reference and worthy of purchasing. The address is provided in the

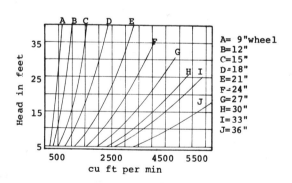

TABLE 5.4 TURBINE SIZE. *Source: Popular Mechanics.*

**95**

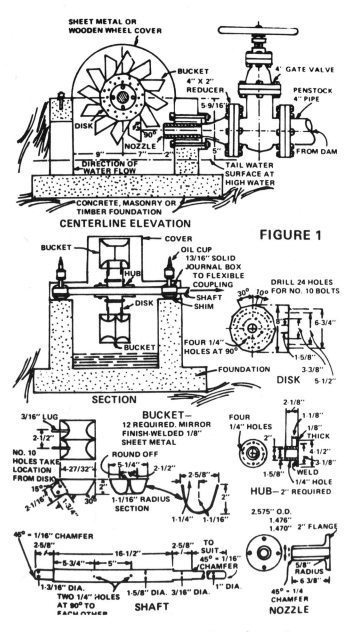

**CENTERLINE ELEVATION**

**FIGURE 1**

**SECTION**

**DISK**

**BUCKET—**
12 REQUIRED. MIRROR FINISH-WELDED 1/8" SHEET METAL

**HUB—** 2" REQUIRED

**SHAFT**

**NOZZLE**

FIGURE 5.8   THE IMPULSE WHEEL.   *Reprinted Courtesy of Popular Science* ©*1947 Popular Science Publ. Co. Inc.*

references at the end of this chapter. VITA recommends using a centrifugal pump as a cheap turbine (as much as one-fiftieth as expensive). The efficiency is not as high as a turbine, but neither is the cost.

Figure 5.8 shows the Pelton or impulse wheel setup. Basically, this wheel operates on impulses produced when water strikes revolving blades or buckets. This wheel must be carefully designed and built because it generally operates at high revolutions per minute, thus requiring accurate balancing. The wheel was developed by Lestor Pelton who substituted a cup-shaped, divided bucket for vanes. The 16" wheel illustrated can deliver the following horsepower, depending upon the head:

| Head | Flow | R.P.M. | Hp. |
|------|------|--------|------|
| 25' | .43 | 350 | 1.0 |
| 30' | .51 | 390 | 1.3 |
| 40' | .59 | 450 | 2.0 |
| 50' | .66 | 500 | 2.8 |
| 60' | .73 | 550 | 3.75 |

The primary elements are the wheel, the buckets and the nozzel. Both the inside diameter and the location

of the nozzel with respect to the wheel are important. The water leaving the nozzel must be split evenly by the ridge between the cups of each bucket.

Just as with the overshot wheel, the buckets are very important. They should be of a mirror finish on the inside, and even the back should be very smooth to prevent spraying. The buckets should be uniform and well-balanced. The foundation of the penstock (the housing that holds the equipment, just below the dam) should be firm enough to hold the nozzel

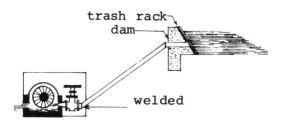

FIGURE 5.9  THE BASIC LAYOUT OF THE IMPULSE WHEEL. *Source: Popular Science.*

and wheel in a correct position. Each piece of machinery should be easily accessible for cleaning and maintenance.

The gate-valve is also a very important component. Its function is the same as the sluice gate on the overshot wheel: it regulates the amount of water striking the buckets. A tachometer or revolution counter should be used with the gate-valve to ensure accurate adjustments in securing the optimum speed and horsepower for the stream load.

The calculation for the head should be adjusted approximately 5" (depending upon the size wheel) because the impulse wheel is not located at tail water, the usual boundary of the head measurement.

5.5  *The Hydraulic Ram*

The hydraulic ram is essentially a pump which operates on nothing but water pressure and air. No additional fuel is required. It is applicable to the small-scale farm and to the

community/village. Prior to the rural electrification program, the ram was used extensively. In Japan, the ram still supplies water to villages from the mountains. VITA has published an excellent pamphlet, "A Hydraulic Ram for Village Use." This document explains how to make a ram for as little as $20.

Figure 5.10 illustrates the basic layout with a detail of the ram itself. The primary source for the following information is Don Marier's article in *Alternative Sources of Energy*, No. 1, July 1971.

The process goes as follows. Water rushes down the drive pipe, escaping through the waste valve, until enough pressure is determined by the amount of fall. When the waste valve closes, water is forced through the check valve into the air chamber. The air is compressed by the force of the water and pushes back like a piston. This reaction closes the check valve, and the water is forced up the delivery pipe. When the check valve closes, the water in the drive pipe is halted, and a small vacuum is created. This vacuum forces the waste valve open, and any excess water which was not forced up the delivery pipe goes out the waste valve. Now, the water going out the waste valve is not necessarily wasted: it can be caught and used for any desirable purpose. The partial vacuum that is created by the closing of the check valve also draws air into the ram through the air valve. As the waste valve closes, the air is forced into the air chamber, and the process repeats itself. This cycle is repeated anywhere between 25 to 100 times a minute. The slower the ram operates, the more water it will pump. The speed is related to the tension placed on the waste valve spring. Simple screws allow for adjustment of the tension.

The amount that the ram can pump can be calculated from the following equation:

$$D = \frac{S \times F}{L} \times \frac{2}{3}$$

D=amount of water delivered in gpm
S=amount of water supplied

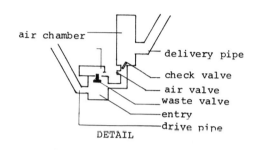

air chamber
delivery pipe
check valve
air valve
waste valve
entry
drive pipe

DETAIL

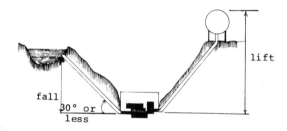

lift

fall

30° or less

FIGURE 5.10   THE BASIC LAYOUT OF THE HYDRAULIC RAM. *Source: Alternative Sources of Energy Newsletter No. 1.*

to the ram in gpm
F=the fall or vertical
   difference in height
   between the ram and the
   storage tank
L=lift or vertical distance
   from the ram to the
   storage tank
2/3=the efficiency

The minimum fall with which a ram will operate is 18". Pipe friction prevents pumping the water to an indefinite height, so large pipes with a minimum of bends help prevent frictional loss.

The drive pipe should be between five and ten times the height of the fall and should not be greater than 30° from the horizontal. The delivery pipe should not be over 20 times the lift height in length.[4] A small structure should be put around the ram to keep it from freezing and a trash rack should be placed over the intake pipe.

One company still manufactures rams at about $180 and up. They are the Rife Hydraulic Engine Manufacturing Company, Box 367, Millburn, New Jersey, 07041.

FOOTNOTES

1. Bassett, C.D. "Your Own Water-Power Plant," Part 1, *Popular Science Monthly*, April 1947, p. 186.

2. *Ibid.*, p. 188.

3. Bassett, C.D. "Building an Overshot Wheel," Part 5, *Popular Science Monthly*, August 1947, p. 193.

4. Anderson, E.P. *Domestic Water Supply and Sewage Disposal Guide*, Theodore Audel & Co., New York, 1967.


REFERENCES

Access Catalog. *The Owner-Built Hydroelectric Plant*, Vol. 1, No. 7, pp. 12-15.

Bassett, C.D. "Putting Water to Work," Part 2, *Popular Science Monthly*, May 1947, pp. 180-184.

"Dams Turn Water into Kilowatts," Part 3, *Popular Science Monthly*, June 1947, pp. 200-203.

"Water Wheel Delivers over 3 Hp.," Part 4, *Popular Science Monthly*, July 1947, pp. 194-197.

Crowley, C.A. "Power from Small Streams," Part 1, *Popular Mechanics*, Sept. 1940, pp. 466-473, Part 2, October 1940, pp. 626-630.

Daniels, A.M. *Power for the Farm from Small Streams*, U.S. Dept. of Agriculture, Washington, D.C., 1925.

*Design of Small Dams*, U.S. Dept. of the Interior, Bureau of Reclamation, U.S. Gov't. Printing Office, Washington, D.C.

Kaufman, A.W. "Hydraulic Ram Forces Water to Pump Itself," *Popular Science Monthly*, October 1948, pp. 231-233.

Marier, Don. "Measuring Water Flow," A.S.E., No. 1, July 1971, pp. 8-10.

Mother Earth News, *Handbook of Homemade Power*, Bantam Book, New York, May 1974.

Reynolds, John. *Windmills and Watermills*, Praeger Publishers, New York, 1970.

Rife Hydraulic Engine Mfg. Co., *Manual of Information: Rife Hydraulic Water Rams*, Box 367, Millburn, New Jersey, 07041, 1968.

Szczelkun, Stefan A. *Survival Scrapbook #3 Energy*, Schocken Books, New York, 1973.

Vallentine, H.R. *Water in the Service of Man*, Penguin Books, Baltimore, 1967.

VITA, *A Hydraulic Ram for Village Use*, by Ersal W. Kindel, 3706 Rhode Island Ave., Mt. Rainier, Maryland, 20822.

VITA, *Low Cost Development of Small Water-Power Sites*, Hans W. Hamm, 1967.

VITA, *Village Technology Handbook*.

VITA, *Savonius Rotor for Water Pumping*, Pub. No. 11132.1.

## 6. Wind Power

Throughout time, man has tried to utilize the wind's kinetic energy to augment his own physical power. His earliest use of wind was for transportation: he used it to propel sailing ships. Man later harnessed the wind to grind his corn and pump his water. He used wind as virtually his only source of power (excluding water) until the advent of the steam engine toward the end of the 18th century.

Our complex wind system is the result of unequal distribution of radiation between the poles and tropics; unequal temperature of land masses, the sea and the effects of the earth's rotation.

To be more specific, there are three main forces that act on the atmosphere to produce winds. The first is the *pressure gradient force* which is directed from high to low pressure. This is the force that makes air rush in to fill a vacuum. The second important force influencing air motion is the *coriolis force*. The coriolis force is directed

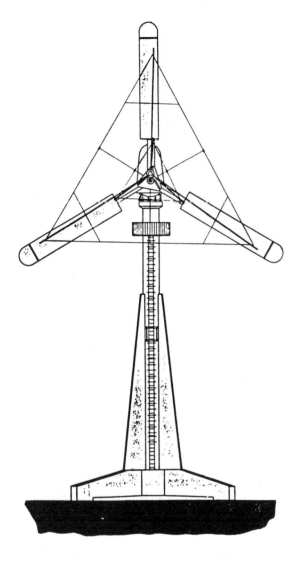

to the right of the direction of the motion of air in the northern hemisphere and to the left of the direction of motion in the southern hemisphere. The coriolis force is only a deflecting force. It acts on air by changing its directional motion but never its speed. The third force, *friction*, only acts on air already in motion. It always acts to slow the wind's speed, and its effect is strongest in the layers of the atmosphere nearest the ground.

Records of the use of windmills go back to about 250 B.C. (Watermills were used even earlier.) Windmills of the sail type were commonly used in western European countries for grinding corn and pumping water. The rotors in these slow-running windmills consisted of from four to eight or more sails, usually made by stretching cloth over a wooden framework or by constructing hinged wooden slats that could be opened or closed to control the relative power output of the mill.

Only recently has there been a renewed interest in the generation of power from wind energy. Wind energy as a power source is attractive because it is continuously regenerated in the atmosphere under the influence of radiant energy from the sun. Wind energy does not impose an extra heat burden on the environment as does energy extracted from fossil and nuclear fuels. Unlike hydropower and tidal power, which also represent the entrapment of solar energy, wind is available everywhere, thus obviating the necessity for a complex network to bring the energy to the power plant. And finally, wind power is not likely to have any detrimental effect on the environment.

The disadvantages encountered with wind are equally obvious. The uncertainty and capricious nature of wind and the uncertainty of the availability of wind at any given time and place pose severe restraints. To harness the wind effectively one must be able to store the energy captured when the wind blows and release it

more or less continuously.

## 6.1 Power Available from the Wind

Primarily, wind is regarded as a column of air mass moving horizontally. The power in the wind is proportional to the cross section area of the air-mass column and to the cube of the wind's speed. Basically, these are the same factors used to determine the amount of energy that can be extracted from the wind by a given facility. (See Appendix D for application.)

Ideally, a windmill extracts 59.3% of an airstream's energy. This is the theoretical maximum based on momentum and blade element theory. Modern windmills generally extract only 70% of the theoretical maximum. How much of the 59.3% can be extracted by a wind generator is dependent on the wind-velocity gradient due to ground effect, the aerodynamic efficiency of the rotor minus friction loss in gearing, the power transmission, and other factors.

## 6.2 Wind Velocities on Site

As stated previously, the actual power available from the wind is proportional to the cube of the wind speed; in other words, if the wind speed is doubled, there will be an 8 times increase in power. Because this relationship exists, the optimum placement of the wind plant becomes of fundamental importance. If a location with a wind speed of 2 miles per hour faster can be found, a tremendous output in gain over a period of time can be expected.

There are basically two forms of data which will give an indication of the wind profile for a specific site. The first are wind records that are available from the nearest National Weather Bureau Meterological Station. These records deal with data concerning:

a. Areas of highest wind speed
b. Direction of prevailing winds
c. Measure of consistency and variability of the year to year wind speed
d. Indication of annual wind regime
e. Maximum speeds and duration of calm spells

A computer print-out concerning wind tabulation, percentage frequency of wind direction and wind speed is available from the National Climatic Center, Ashville, North Carolina. If the annual mean wind speed indicated by this record is less than 6 miles per hour, it is probably pointless to pursue the matter further unless there are periodically much higher wind speeds than the average indicated by the record or unless there is an acceleration by topographic profile.[1] It is important to note that any data given by the National Weather Bureau is only useful for design approximations. The accuracy that is lacking exists because of the topographic differences between meteorological stations and perspective wind generator sites.

The second form of data, onsite wind measurements, provides the only accurate means of producing consistent wind-speed readings. These wind-speed readings

should be taken over a two-year period. Readings should be taken from different topographical locations and at different altitudes on the site. (Wind velocity increases with height because airflow is less retarded by ground-level friction.) Wind-speed readings taken at different altitudes provide an indicator of the constancy of the wind. The greater the variation of readings from different heights, the greater the wind variability and turbulence, and the less suitable the site is for a wind generator installation.

An analysis should be made to determine whether wind speed is accelerated by certain onsite topographical forms and whether any built form would augment or deter the velocity of the wind. A detailed site model could be built and analyzed with the help of a wind tunnel.

In the selection of a site for a wind generator installation, it has been found that a smoothly-shaped hill gives good results when it is well exposed and is not

obstructed by high ground within 3 to 4 miles. The elevated site selected should be one upon which the wind does not break as it accelerates up the slope. Breaking of the wind gives rise to turbulent effects which should be avoided. Isolated hills are preferred to long ridges. Wind can accelerate over the top of a hill from any direction, however, this accelerating effect occurs only on a ridge when the wind blows

in one particular direction. The site should be free of trees and precipitous outcrops of rocks, both of which cause turbulent flow.[2]

Vegetation can also provide an accurate indicator of long term wind velocities. In one particular case, balsam-firs indicated wind velocity by a progressive deformity. At an annual mean wind velocity of 17 mph, the fir showed some flagging, a condition in which the branches extend downwind. As the mean annual velocity increased, the deformity passed through four more distinct stages. The last stage, at 27 miles per hour, produced carpeting, a condition in which growth is limited to a carpet of branches no more than 6" off the ground. This sensitive ecological indicator defined the path of mountain windstreams that varied sharply in mean annual speed even within distances of 100 yards.[3]

Henry Clews, in his booklet *Electric Power from the Wind*, suggests an interpolation method for securing longterm wind data over a

short period of time. Clews suggests taking daily onsite wind data for a 1-month period. All readings taken should correspond to one time throughout the day. This data should then be compared with the wind data taken at the meteorological station closest to the site. Upon comparison of the two sets of figures, it should become apparent that a correlation factor exists between them. This correlation factor should help establish a relationship that will allow the application of long term wind data collected by the weather bureau over many years to your particular location.

## 6.3 Components of a Wind-Generated Power Plant

All wind generator power plants have the following in common:

a. A wind-driven rotor which extracts a certain percentage of energy from the moving air mass. (This can take many forms.)

b. A tower which allows the collector to take advantage of greater wind velocities that exist at higher elevations. The collector may be incorporated into a building design so that the built form can be used to accelerate the wind velocity.

c. Some form of mechanism to protect the wind generator plant from excessive wind speeds.

d. The power-producing component (generator), and battery storage and power conversion systems.

e. Alternate methods of wind energy storage.

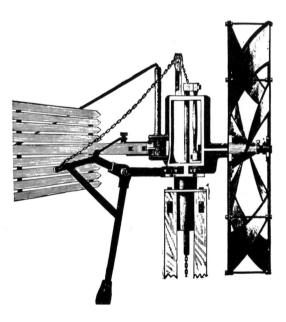

## 6.3a Collection Devices

A wind-driven collector should be designed so that wind striking against it causes the wind to loose some of its kinetic energy. The collection device passes the collected energy on to a power-generating machine.

There are two broad classifications of rotors that can be found in wind power plants: those with a vertical axis and those with a horizontal axis. These classifications are somewhat generalized and can be broken down further to:

Classification

6.3a-1 Airfoil Collectors (propeller shaped)
6.3a-2 Drag Collectors (savonious rotor)
6.3a-3 Airfoil/Drag Collectors (catenary rotor)
6.3a-4 Concentrating Collectors (venturi shroud design)

For the sake of comparative analysis between different collector types, the power

coefficient (efficiency index) $C_p$ has been referred to throughout the text. The following will be a clarification as to its meaning and implications.

The potential energy in a windstream (Es) is equal to 1/2 the density of the air (slugs per cu. ft.) times the cross sectional area swept by the propeller blades (sq. ft.) times the wind velocity (ft. per sec.). How much of this potential energy that can be extracted by a windmill is limited to 0.593. (This figure is derived from momentum blade theory.) This figure is also a theoretical maximum and cannot be attained, only approached, due to aerodynamic and mechanical losses of the windmill. The percentage of power that can be extracted from the theoretical maximum (.593) is known as the coefficient of power. Modern airfoils can extract 70% of the theoretical maximum (.593) indicating a coefficient of power of 42%.

6.3a-1  Airfoil Collectors

Todate, the airfoil has been the commonly used collection device in wind generator plants. A collection device represents an aerodynamic propeller but in actuality it is an "impeller," that is, propeller driven by the wind. It is seldom realized that the force which the wind exerts is composed of two distinct parts, pressure and suction. For example, a sailboat which seems to be pushed along by the wind is actually deriving most of its propulsion from the suction on the lee side of the sail. Consequently, the blades of the impeller must be so shaped that this suction force can aid them in turning. High efficiency airfoils that utilize this negative pressure gradient are created with high lift-to-drag ratios. The same considerations are necessary in the creation of glider airfoils. As a matter of fact, high efficiency airfoil rotors are designed around glider airfoils such as the Wortman FX150B glider airfoil and the Wortman FX72-MS-150B airfoil. In effect, the high efficiency airfoils will result in a higher useful power output at lower wind speeds.

Aerodynamic efficiencies and airfoil design for wind generator application are expressed in another form which is the tip-speed ratio, a comparison between the velocity of the blade tips and the wind speed. Tip-speed ratios between 5:1 and 8:1 are not un-common for efficient high-speed mills. Ratios between 1:1 and 3:1 are typical for the slower running multiblade water pumping machines. High tip-speed ratios from five to eight are desirable for windmills used to generate electricity. The higher the tip-speed ratio, the higher the propeller's rpm. In effect, less gearing is needed to drive the generator. For optimum output (or high tip-speed ratios), the blades should be designed to have a "twist" so that their surface presents an increasing angle to the wind at increasing distances outward from the hub.

All modern electric wind-generating plants use either two or three aerodynamically shaped blades. There are certain advantages and disadvantages to both.

For onsite locations where wind speed is low, the 3-blade design will extract the most power. For onsite locations where the wind velocities are high and where high rotational speed (rather than a high torque) is desired, the two-blade design will run more efficiently because there is less interference between blade wakes. A three-blade propeller operates more smoothly than a one- or two-blade design which has trouble with balance and vibration as loads increase. Under gusty wind conditions, the two-blade propeller undergoes jerky movements as it orients itself.

Most rotor assemblies are designed to face the wind with the aid of a tail vane or fantail; however, the rotor assembly can be designed to operate downwind. The advantage of the latter design is that the assembly is self-orienting without the need of a tail vane. The main drawback is the turbulent or shadow effect caused by the tower. As each blade passes behind the tower, it is removed from the pressure of the wind by the screening effect of the tower, and experiences a severe shock due to the rapid changes in wind conditions during this passage. Designing the rotor to run upwind of the tower presents vibration as a potential source of trouble which can, however, be minimized.[4]  (See figure 6.1)

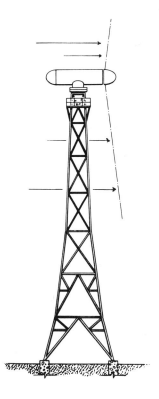

The materials used in blade construction may be such that the blades are strong, yet light in weight and resistant to effects of severe weather conditions. Blade materials previously used range from wood, steel, and aluminum, to plastic, fiberglass and paper honey-

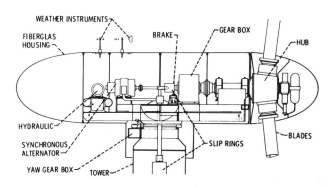

Figure 1. - 100 kW wind turbine drive train assembly

FIGURE 6.1 DOWNWIND ROTOR. *Source: NASA Lewis Research Center.*

comb laminates. The paper honeycomb laminate blade is made from paper hexcel, coated with fiberglass. In its compressed state, the hexcel is cut to the desired airfoil shape. The hexcel is then stretched to the correct length with an aluminum rod that is run through the center of the blade. The surface of the blade is covered with a fine grade glass fabric. The entire assembly is covered with an epoxy resin that is waterproof, erosion resistant and impervious to ultraviolet rays.

The sailwing (see figure 6.2) represents a different approach to the design and construction of an airfoil collector. The sailwing was developed by Thomas Sweeny of Princeton University's Flight Concepts Laboratory. The original sailwing consists of a two-blade design, 10' in diameter. The top and bottom surfaces of the propeller are dacron. When at rest, the fabric surfaces are stretched flat. As the blades rotate, the flat surfaces assume an airfoil contour that is an optimum shape

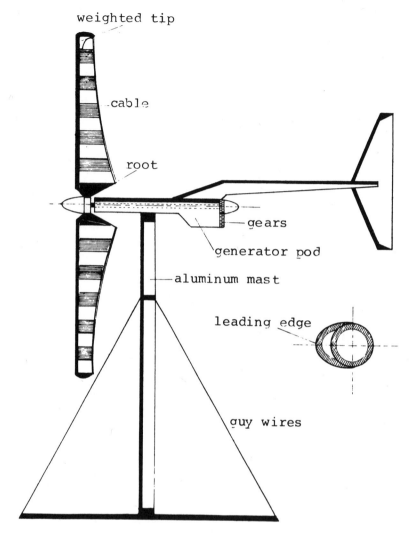

FIGURE 6.2  PRINCETON SAILWING.

for this rotational speed. The sailwing attacks two major stumbling blocks in windmill development: excessive weight and mechanical complexity. A 25'-diameter sailwing weighs only 44 lbs. or a little more than 1/2 lb. per square foot.

## 6.3a-2 Drag Collectors

Drag collectors fall under the classification of the vertical axis type. An example of a drag collector is the cup anaemometer in which the rotor moves in a horizontal plane or in a direction that is parallel to the wind.

Of the drag-collector type, the more common device used for wind power generation is the savonious rotor or S-rotor. The savonious rotor is a simple device in which a cylinder is equally split through its length. The halves are offset by a distance equal to the radius of the original core (See figure 6.3) Offsetting the two halves creates an air passage in the middle of the rotor. The wind striking the cup of one vane flows through the central gap into the other vane causing the unit to rotate. One or more S-rotor units may be stacked, one on top of another, 60° out of phase with each other. This allows the unit to run more smoothly under gusty conditions.

As with any other wind-gen-erating system, the S-rotor has its advantages and dis-advantages. As previously stated, the maximum theore-tical power coefficient for an airfoil collector (pro-peller type) is 59%. The S-rotor is limited to a theoretical power coefficient of 33% which is approximately one-third that of the air-foil collector. It is important to remember that the theoretical power coefficient is determined through wind tunnel tests. In actual onsite applica-tions, the S-rotor might perform better than the airfoil collector due to certain factors. The air-foil-type of windmill looses much power through changes in the direction of the wind, but the S-rotor does not lose power at all under such directional changes. The S-rotor does not orient itself because it is always facing the wind. The S-rotor can instantly utilize any increase in the wind's speed without having to lose time getting into the correct position. Wind gusts occur from directions other than that of the main air flow. A nonorienting collector, such as the S-rotor, can readily extract wind-gust

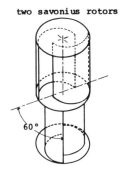

two savonius rotors

A. S-rotor
B. main bearings
C. S-rotor gear
D. end thrust plate
E. fixed shaft

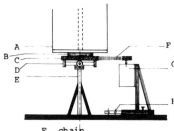

F. chain
G. alternator
H. chain tensioning bar

Detail At Base

FIGURE 6.3 SAVONIOUS ROTOR AND POWER TRANSMISSION. *Source: Earthmind.*

energy which would normally be lost by an airfoil collec-tor. Rotational energy is stored in the mass of the rotor. Even when the wind speed decreases, the rota-tional speed is maintained for a considerable amount of time, causing more pronounced symmetry in the airflow and

allowing the rotor to utilize more than its strict share of the weaker wind following a gust. With all aspects considered, the S-rotor is much simpler in construction than the airfoil collector. It does not require close tolerance aerodynamic shape needed by the airfoil collector. The spinning propeller of the airfoil collector represents a gyroscopic action at high velocities and results in resistance to wind tracking plus heavy forces upon support structure and airfoil blades.

The maximum rotational speed for an S-rotor is the velocity of the wind. Therefore, there must be a gearing step up to utilize this slow rotational force to drive the electrical conversion device.

### 6.3a-3  Airfoil/Drag Collectors

An airfoil/drag collector is actually a combination of the airfoil rotor and the drag rotor (See figure 6.4). The darrieus, or

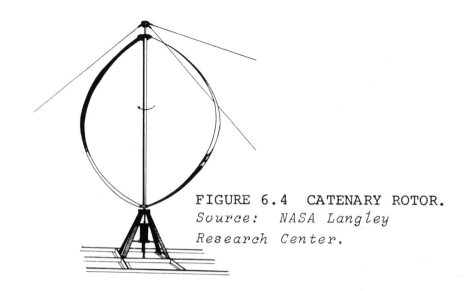

FIGURE 6.4  CATENARY ROTOR. *Source:  NASA Langley Research Center.*

catenary type, possesses the advantages of an airfoil and the ease of orientation of the S-rotor.

Two or three long narrow strips with an airfoil shape are draped from the top of an axis and brought together at the bottom to resemble an egg beater. The blades or airfoils are somewhat flexible and assume a natural curve in response to wind loads and centrifugal force. A high-speed rotor with straight rigid blades parallel to its axis of rotation would be subjected to high bending moments

from centrifugal forces and would require extensive bracing. It is for this reason that a flexible blade is used. Under centrifugal and aerodynamic forces, a flexible blade will conform to a shape in which the only stresses are tensile. The resultant shape of the blade would approximate a catenary. (A catenary is actually the curve taken by a free-hanging flexible cable supported at its ends.)

The strongest advantages of the cantenary windmill are its simplicity and its ability to accept wind from

any direction and transfer the power to ground level for use in conversion devices. The catenary or vertical axis meets the criteria of design simplicity and ease of orientation at high aerodynamic efficiency.

The output of the rotor in terms of the maximum power coefficient is approximately .65 which compares favorably with the airfoil's power coefficient of .70.

### 6.3a-4   Concentrating Collectors

A concentrating collector converges diffuse horizontally moving air masses. Concentrating the air flow into a confined area not only smoothes the airflow, but also increases the velocity through the collector.

One means of accelerating the wind speed is the use of a venturi section. To adapt such a section to a windmill would require that a shroud be built around the propeller airfoil. The inside surface of the shroud would have the shape of a

venturi tube with an airfoil blade located at the throat of it (See figure 6.5)

Through the use of the venturi, the velocity of an airstream can be increased up to 100%. Inasmuch as power in the wind is proportional to the cube of the velocity, doubling the velocity gives eight times the power.

Concentrating collectors with venturi sections can be designed into built structures (such as build-

ings) to take advantage of a constant directional airflow.

### 6.3b   Supporting Structures

Fundamentally, the only requirements of the supporting structure are that it must be tall enough to lift the windmill rotor well off the ground and strong enough to withstand both the various forces likely to occur from wind pressure in exposed positions and the vibrational effects transmitted from the rotating part of the generator.

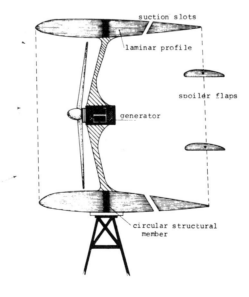

FIGURE 6.5   VENTURI SHROUD DESIGN. *Source: Hans Meyer Domebook 2.*

A tall tower will intercept a stronger windstream because of the reduction of frictional loss at higher altitudes. Over flat ground the wind speed increases with height approximately in proportion to the 1/7 power of this height. This relationship does not exist on hilltop sites and the only height requirement of the tower is to provide safe clearance over the ground, which equals to the length of one blade plus 15 or 20'.

The tower can be a single tube, pole, or mast, resting on a prepared foundation and supported in a vertical position by guys.

An easily constructed free-standing tower for light-weight installations can be built from 1" conduit fabricated into six octo-hedron modules. The conduit is bolted at its end after being bent from 4° to 24°. The tower may be held fast with footings of concrete or a steel anchor buried in the ground.

The tower should be designed so that a minimum amount of surface area is exposed to the wind. The less wind resistance, the less air turbulence and screening effect of the tower. This is particularly important if a downwind rotor is to be used.

The wind power plant should be located on the tower at least 30' above ground and 10' above surrounding objects within a 500' radius. The wind plant installation should not be located more than 1000' from the point of usage because of electrical transmission losses.

*6.3c  Controlling Mechanisms and Power Transmission*

Another important factor to be considered is the protection of the power-generating plant from excessive winds such as severe storms, hurricanes, or tornadoes. Provisions must be made for feathering the windmill blades, i.e., changing the attitude of the propeller so that the wind hits the ends and edges instead of the airfoil surfaces or applying some sort of brake or aerodynamic spoiler.

The centrifugal force on the airfoil blades during excessive winds can be enough to destroy them. Most wind generating plants are designed to feather the blades after some wind speed, usually 20-24 mph.

In order for the blades to be feathered, they must be either rotated about their axis, or moved out in a helical motion along the axis. If the blades rotate about their axis, they must be moved by a type of fly-ball governor or by spring-restrained

weights which move outward as centrifugal force increases. If the motion is helical, the blades themselves can act as their own centrifugal weights. The blades are restrained by a spring, the tension of which equals the centrifugal force required for feathering. It is the centrifugal force on the blades which is used to feather them, not the force of the wind on the blade surface.[5]

In multiple-blade designs, it is important to have some mechanism to ensure that the blades move in precisely the same motion. If one blade feathers before the other, great instability and damage results.

An additional device which prevents propeller overspeed was first used on prairie windmills. The device, a pilot vane, is placed at right angles to the main vane. A pilot vane is generally 50-70% as large as the total cross sectional area of the main tail and its arm length is the radius of the propeller in use.

When the wind velocity approaches a critical design speed, the pilot vane counteracts the main tail vane, working against spring tension which pushes the propeller out of the wind.

The pilot vane can also be designed so that, when a given wind speed is reached, it will disengage a set of stops, allowing the main tail vane spring to contract, pulling the main tail vane along side the pilot vane, and thus turning the windmill out of the wind until the main tail vane is reset via a rope on the ground.

The primary requirement of most wind generators is that the relatively slow rotation of the windmill propeller be geared to the higher speeds required to spin the generator rotors efficiently. A windmill may, for example, turn at 150 rpm, while a generator may operate at 600 rpm. This means that one must either find a special low-speed generator (which is large and expensive) or resort to some form of stepping up the speed of the generator using belts and gears. A positive drive system such as a chain drive should be used to prevent slippages that are the result of severe accelerations and decelerations encountered in wind plants.
A bevel gear can be used to transform the rotation of the rotor about a horizontal axis into rotation about a vertical axis. The drive is carried to ground level by means of a drive shaft passing down through the tower. This allows the generator or other power-producing component to be located on the ground for easy access.

## 6.3d Power-Producing Component (Generator), Battery Storage and Power Conversion System (Inverter)

Power from the wind can be converted into mechanical or electrical power. This section will be dealing with the electrical conversion of wind energy, its storage and transformation into electrical energy that is compatible with present-day electrical equipment.

There has been much discussion as to which type of power generator is more suited for wind generation, the alternator or the generator. An alternator is an alternating current generator with its cycle unregulated and its output rectified through a diode bridge so that the unit yields full-wave direct current (D.C.). Generators produce direct current without the intervention of power conversion. D.C. generators can be designed to give maximum output at the same speed the propeller is turning. Allowing the use of a direct drive from the propeller without any intervening gears. To get maximum output at low speed requires that the generator be large in diameter. The advantage of a direct drive is that the low speed of the generator results in long bearing life and eliminates the need for gears.

In the past, alternators have been used in low-cost wind generator design because of their inexpensiveness, availability, and the belief that they produce usable current at lower rpm's than generators do. The performance of an automotive alternator at low wind speeds can be improved through modification of the windings of the alternator's stator. This modification also allows for a reduction in gear ratios, thereby reducing gear losses.

Another factor that must be considered in using an alternator is that it creates electrical energy by inducing a field current into the rotating field of an armature. An alternator will generate power as long as the armature spins and cuts across the field current line of electromagnetic force. If the field current is left on while the armature is at rest, the unit will slowly drain any batteries to which it is connected. Jim Sencenbaugh, in his wind generator design, uses a device which turns the alternator on only when the wind is blowing strong enough to generate power.[6] His design utilizes a vane dampened with a spring to operate a relay that is capable of switching the alternator's field current on and off.

If a D.C. generator is to be used, some provision must be made to prevent it from motoring. A D.C. generator will act as an electric motor if the current is reversed. Without any anti-motor device, the electricity from the batteries will motor the generator when the wind is not blowing. The inclusion of a diode connected between the generator and the batteries prevents the generator from running on reverse current from the batteries.

Recent developments in wind generator design have produced a unique means of creating electricity with-

out complex gearing mechanisms. A generator built on the Island of Sylt on the German North Sea to supply power for five homes features two five-blade rotors that contra-rotate. One of the rotors drives the strator, the other the armature of the alternator, thereby eliminating the need for gears and simultaneously achieving the high velocity needed to produce power. Inasmuch as each contra-rotating rotor turns at 71.4 rpm, the 42-pole generator turns at a relative speed of 142.8 rpm's. The rotating parts of the generator move past each other at a high speed to generate power, and, at the same time, minimize blade speed to reduce centrifugal loads.

Power storage is the key to a successful wind generator power plant. The following will deal with battery storage because it represents the least costly and most practical energy storage system presently available to the individual user.

Battery storage represents a large portion of the ini-tial cost of a generating plant. The expense for battery storage may, in fact, range from one quarter to one half of the total cost. The actual capacity requirement of the battery, expressed in amphere hours depends upon the expected duration of the load period in calm spells. (See Appendix D for Battery Sizing.) A wind generator installation should provide battery storage capacity sufficient to meet normal electrical needs for a period of at least 3-4 days. In extreme windless situations, battery storage capacity should provide power for at least six days. It is at this point that consideration must be given to the initial cost of the batteries versus the cost of an alternative backup system such as a gasoline-powered generator.

Batteries used in wind storage systems are specially designed for repeated cycling; that is, charging and discharging over a period of many years. Another plus factor of batteries is that they are easily modularized and can be added or subtracted to bring the system to the desired voltage and storage capacity.

If lead-acid batteries are to be used, some provisions must be made to include a regulator between the generating and storage units. The regulator prevents the batteries from being over-charged. Overcharging lead-acid batteries can warp their plates, making them worthless. Other disadvantages with the lead-acid storage batteries are that they can lose up to 50% of their capacity in cold or freezing weather; they do not dissipate heat well when under high-current stress; they contain acid that can violently burn flesh, and they are large and bulky. Lead-acid batteries also give off hydrogen gas so they should not be located near a spark or a flame.

Even with these drawbacks lead-acid batteries still represent a cost-effective means of energy storage. If care is exercised in their location and use, they can also be safe. For care and maintenance of lead-acid

batteries, only distilled water should be used in them and the charge of each should be checked periodically with a hydrometer. The hydrometer measures the specific gravity of the electrolyte. The float inside the hydrometer rises to a point determined by the specific gravity of the electrolyte, indicating the charge of the battery. Some of the more expensive batteries have built-in hydrometers.

Nickel-cadmium (Ni-cads) batteries are far better electrical storage battery units than lead-acid batteries, but they are very expensive. Ni-cad batteries are smaller and lighter and do not lose their capacity in cold weather. Ni-cads can also be charged faster and high currents can be drawn from them without damaging them. Inasmuch as ni-cads cannot be overcharged, they do not require a voltage regulator. If ni-cad batteries are used with an alternator, the alternator will charge only the load indicated by the batteries. If a ni-cad battery is fully charged, the alternator will produce

just a minimum amount of current which will not damage a nickel-cadmium battery unit.

At this point, wind energy is stored in the form of D.C. electrical energy in the battery. Direct current can be used to operate light bulbs, heating elements, and most brush motors. Other electrical appliances require alternating current at the

frequency of 60 cycles per second. There are presently two methods by which direct current can be changed into alternating current at 60 cycles per second. One is called dynamic conversion in which a D.C. motor turns at a steady speed and is connected to an A.C. generator. This type of energy conversion has an efficiency on the order of 60%. The other method involves the use of a static or solid state inverter which converts

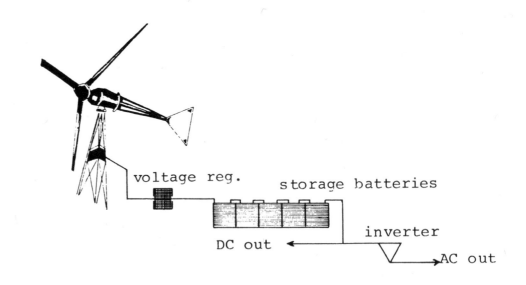

FIGURE 6.6  SCHEMATIC OF ON-SITE 2-5KW WIND GENERATING UNIT WITH BATTERY STORAGE.

**116**

the D.C. current to 60 cycle A.C. through electronic means. Its efficiency is on the order of 80%.

In a wind generating system, there is a tendency toward using both alternating and direct current. The installation would include receptacles having both A.C. and D.C. The direct current would be used for light bulbs, heating elements, power tools, and other appliances with universal A.C.-D.C. motors. (See figure 6.6)

Recently, an alternator has been designed to deliver 60-cycle A.C. current independent of the rotation shaft speed of the propeller. This alternator, unlike standard generators, does not have a fixed number of poles. The alternator has a unique outer housing called the rotor, with a continuous layer of magnetizable material lining the bore. The stator has a special coil or exciter head that continuously "writes" the proper pole position on the magnetic material.

6.3e  *Alternate Methods of*

| Eff.(%) | STORAGE DEVICE | CAPACITY (BTU/lb) | COST(BTU/$) |
|---|---|---|---|
| 70 | Battery | 18-35* | 25 |
| 35 | Flywheel | 20-90 | 35 |
| 67 | Compressed Air | 100 | 25 |
| 50 | Fuel Cell | 90 | 35 |
| 67 | Water Reservoir | 0.25(100' head) | 18 |
| 67 | Mass Reservoir | 0.25(100' head) | 18 |

*Future estimation for battery capacity is 350 BTU/lb.

TABLE 6.9  ENERGY STORAGE CAPACITY FOR DIFFERENT STORAGE DEVICES. *Source: NSF/NASA, December 1973, Wind Energy Conversion Systems.*

*Wind Energy Storage*

Because of the capricious nature of the wind, storage capabilities are a vital part of a wind energy system. Because of their complexity and intermediate detail, storage systems are costly. For a comparison of different storage devices, their capacity and cost, consult Table 6.9.

There is one method which eliminates the need for storage facilities, but requires connection to a power line. A wind generating plant that could be directly paralleled into a main power line would provide a constant frequency power. Reversible meters could be installed to register a credit for the amount of energy supplied to the power grid from the wind generator. (See figure 6.7)

Wind generated electricity can be used to power electrolysis units which convert water into its two components, hydrogen and oxygen. (See figure 6.8) This approach would, in essence, convert wind energy into chemical energy in the

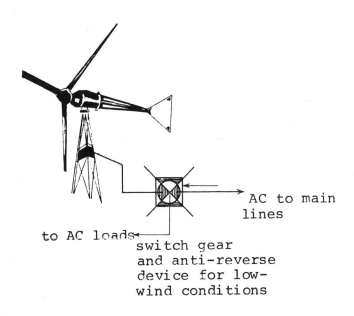

to AC loads

switch gear
and anti-reverse
device for low-
wind conditions

AC to main
lines

FIGURE 6.7  SCHEMATIC OF WIND GENERATING UNIT WITHOUT STOR-AGE FACILITIES.

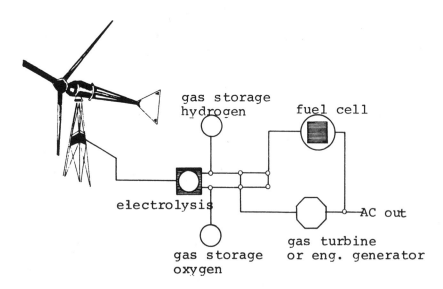

gas storage
hydrogen

fuel cell

electrolysis

gas storage
oxygen

gas turbine
or eng. generator

AC out

FIGURE 6.8  WIND INSTALLATION UTILIZING ELECTROLYSIS UNITS/FUEL CELLS.

form of hydrogen.  The hydrogen could be stored as a compressed gas, metal hydride, or as a cryogenic liquid.  Gas storage is presently the most economical method, and hydrides offer promise.  Cryogenic (cold liquid storage) systems offer extremely high energy densities (approximately 17 kw hours per pound), but involve proportionately high costs at this time.

Hydrogen could be used on a massive scale for conventional industrial needs.  Hydrogen can be used as a fuel in its own right in combustion processes to supplement or to replace natural gas. Hydrogen can be utilized in fuel cells (not commercially available yet).

Pumped water storage or pumped hydroelectric storage becomes another means in which wind energy can be retained for later distribution.  Water is pumped to a high reservoir during periods of excessive power production and then released to generate electricity when the wind source is not available.  For small scale installations, water could be stored in

tanks, whereas for larger scale operations, water would require storage at appropriate sites such as mountainous or hilly areas. Another point worth noting is that when the main purpose is pumping water, it is more efficient to use a wind-driven electric generator located on the most favorable site available and transmitting its power output to an electrical pump, than it is to use a mechanical pumping windmill which must be located immediately above the well.

Compressed air storage is yet another means by which wind energy can be mechanically converted. Compressed air can be easily stored in receivers to meet short term high energy demands powering electrical generators along with pneumatic tools. (For storage capacity and efficiency see Table 6.9)

Finally, there are fly wheel storage systems which are still largely in the experimental stage. A fly wheel storage capacity is determined by how much energy can be supplied before centrifugal force destroys the fly

wheel. What determines the capacity is the strength of the material used to make the fly wheel. Recent research has provided materials that are particularly strong in one direction; that is, the outward direction of the stress which seeks to destroy a fast-spinning fly wheel. Some of the materials used have been radial filaments of high strength music wire, graphite, boron fibers, or crystals imbeded in a matrix of plastic or metal.

The use of new materials in the construction of fly wheels provides for lighter and more compact energy storage devices. Engineers have projected fly wheel storage capacity per pound of weight to be about 4 times as much as a conventional lead-acid acid storage battery.

The fly wheel would be housed in a vacuum less than 1/100 of an atmosphere. The fly wheel is supported on a frictionless magnetic suspension. The motor/generator is coupled to the fly wheel with a magnetic coupler that

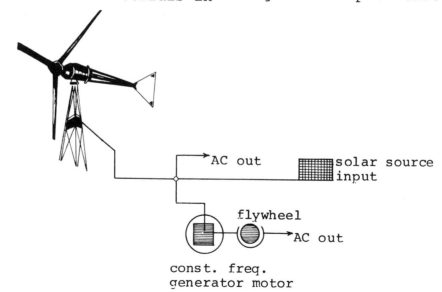

FIGURE 6.10   WIND INSTALLATION UTILIZING MECHANICAL STORAGE (FLYWHEEL).

requires no direct connection through the vacuum container.

To spin the fly wheel, a wind generator could provide power to the combination motor/generator. (See figure 6.10) When there is a lull in wind energy production, the fly wheel would spin the generator, producing electrical energy. (For storage capacity and efficiency see Table 6.9)

Some of the components and storage systems discussed represent exotic, costly, and high technology developments, but they demonstrate research taking place to develop an efficient and cost-effective means of storing energy.

FOOTNOTES:

1. Wind Power United Nations Publications. "New Sources of Energy," Proceedings of Conference, Rome, August 1961, Vol. 7, p. 238.

2. "Wind-Generated Electricity-Prototype 100KW Plant," *Engineering*, Vol. 179, No. 4652, March 1955, p. 374.

3. McCaull, Julian. "Windmills," *Environment*, Vol. 15, January/February 1973, p. 11.

4. *Op.cit.* "New Sources of Energy," p. 230.

5. Marier, Don. "Some Notes on Windmills," *Alternative Sources of Energy*, No. 12, October/November 1973, p. 3.

6. Sencenbaugh, Jim. "I Built a Wind Generator for $400," *Handbook of Homemade Power*, Bantam Books, Inc., 1974, p. 186.

REFERENCES:

Abbott, I.H. *Theory of Wing Sections*, Dover Publications, 1959.

Baumeister, T. and L.S. Marks. *Standard Handbook for Mechanical Engineers*, McGraw-Hill, New York, 1974.

Boyle, G. and P. Harper, ed. *Radical Technology*, Pantheon Press, New York, 1976.

Benson, Arnold. *Plans for the Construction of a Small Wind Electric Plant*. Publ. No. 33, Oklahoma State Univ., Stillwater, Oklahoma 74079.

Bossel, Helmut. "Low-Cost Windmill for Developing Nations," *V.I.T.A. Handbook*, VITA College, Schenectady, New York 12308.

Betz, Albert. *Introduction to the Theory of Flow Machines*, Pergamon Press, 1966.

Clews, Henry. *Electric Power from the Wind*, Solar Wind Co., East Holden, Maine, 04429, 1973.

*Climatic Atlas of the United States*, U.S. Department of Commerce, 1968.

Coonley, Doug. *Design with Wind*, Master's thesis, College of Architecture, Massachusetts Institute of Technology, Cambridge, Massachusetts, 1974.

*Energy from the Wind*. World Meteorological Organization, Geneva, 1954.

Fales, E.N. "Windmills," *Mechanical Engineers Handbook*, Lionel S. Marks, McGraw-Hill, 5th edition.

Golding, E.W. *The Generation of Electricity by Wind Power*, E. and F.N. Spon Ltd., 22 Henrietta St., London, 1955.

Hackleman, Michael A. *Wind and Windspinners*, Earthmind, 26510 Josel Drive, Saugus, California, 81350, 1974.

Hidy, George. *The Winds*, Van Nostrand Co., 1967.

Leckie, J., et.al. *Other Homes and Garbage*, Sierra Club Books, San Francisco, 1975.

Marier, Don, ed. *Alternative Sources of Energy, No. 14*, May 1974.

Merrill, R., et.al. *Energy Primer*, Portola Institute, Menlo Park, California, 1975.

Meyer, Hans. "Wind Generators: here's an advanced design you can build," *Popular Science*, November 1972, pp. 103-105.

The Mother Earth News. *Handbook of Homemade Power*, Bantam Books, New York, 1974.

Putnam, P.C. *Power from the Wind*, Van Nostrand Co., New York, 1948.

Reynolds, John. *Windmills and Watermills*, Prager Publishers, 1970.

Savonious, S.J. "The S-Rotor and Its Application," *Mechanical Engineering*, vol. 53, no. 5, May 1931.

Syverson, C.D. and J.G. Symens. *Wind Power*, Wind Power, P.O. Box 233, Mankato, Minnesota 56001.

V.I.T.A. *Village Technology Handbook*, 3706 Rhode Island Ave., Mount Rainier, Md., 20822.

Wind Works. *Wind Energy Bibliography*, Box 329, Rt. 3, Mukwonago, Wisconsin, 53149, 1973.

"Windmill Manufacturers," University of Cambridge, Department of Architecture, Technical Research Division, 1 Scroop Terrace, Cambridge CB2 1PX, England, 1974.

**122 NOTES**

# 7. Solar Energy

Excluding the surface of the earth, the total amount of solar energy received by a surface over a period of time can be readily calculated. This solar constant is 442 BTU/hr-sq.ft., and only varies with the distance between the earth and sun and the angle of incidence between the sun's rays and the surface under consideration.

## 7.1 The Availability of Solar Energy for Solar Heating and Cooling

However, the amount of solar energy that reaches the earth's surface is dependent on many variables. As solar radiation passes through the earth's atmosphere, it is absorbed and scattered by the various components, such as water vapor, molecules, ozone, carbon dioxide, and particulate matter. It is because of these variables that the intensity of solar radiation on the earth's surface at a particular point in time is difficult to calculate. The availability of such solar radiation can only be described statistically on a long term basis.

The U.S. Weather Bureau, also known as the National Oceanographic and Atmospheric Administration (NOAA), publishes information concerning monthly and annual values of percentage of possible sunshine, total hours of sunshine, mean solar radiation, mean sky cover, wind speed and wind direction. This data can be found in one convenient source, *The Climatic Atlas of the U.S.* (U.S. Govt. Printing Office, Washington, D.C.). Appendix A includes tables showing daily values of direct solar radiation computed for selected angles, aspects and days at varying latitudes. These values are useful for design approximations.

For more information concerning qualitative and quantitative aspects of the solar energy component, see ASHRAE *1974 Applications Handbook*, Chapter 59, "Solar Energy Utilization for Heating and Cooling," and the Appendix A - A-4

## 7.2 Solar Energy Subsystems

There are three basic forms of conversion in which solar energy can be utilized. They are heliochemical, helioelectrical and heliothermal. In this section, we will be specifically dealing with the latter, heliothermal conversion. Heliothermal conversion, at the present time, is the most technically developed, and the most cost-effective means of providing space heating and cooling and domestic water heating.

## 7.2a Collectors

There are three basic categories of collectors: flat-plate, focusing or concentrating, and photovoltaic. Their basic function is to convert incoming solar radiation into heat or electrical energy at a prescribed rate and temperature.

## 7.2a-1 Flat-Plate Collectors

A flat-plate collector

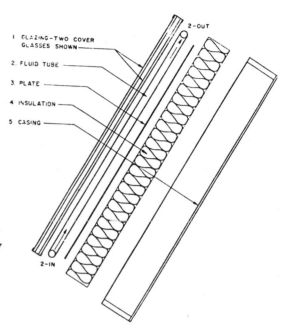

1 GLAZING-TWO COVER GLASSES SHOWN
2. FLUID TUBE
3 PLATE
4 INSULATION
5 CASING
2-OUT
2-IN

FIGURE 7.1  FIVE BASIC PARTS OF A FLAT-PLATE COLLECTOR. *Source: ASHRAE 1974 Applications Handbook.*

consists of five basic parts. (See figure 7.1.)

1. Transparent cover plate (glazing) which may be one or more sheets of glass or plastic.

2. Absorber plate, generally

a highly conductive material such as copper or aluminum, coated with a blackened or selective surface.

3. Tubes or fins that circulate heat transfer fluid to carry heat away from the collector's surface. They can be either fastened to the plate or integral to the collection surface.

4. Insulation which prevents downward heat loss from the collector plate.

5. A container which protects the entire assembly from the environment and from heat loss due to convection. This may be integral to the structure of the building.

The overall operation of the flat-plate collector is essentially simple. Sunlight is transmitted through the transparent cover and absorbed by the blackened cover plate. As the temperature of the cover plate rises, the black surface re-radiates long wave or infrared radiation. The cover plate tends to be opaque to the infrared radiation, thus trapping most of the heat. (This is commonly known as the "greenhouse effect.") Heat

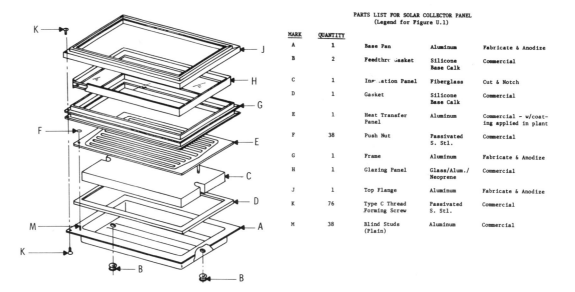

PARTS LIST FOR SOLAR COLLECTOR PANEL
(Legend for Figure U.1)

| MARK | QUANTITY | | | |
|---|---|---|---|---|
| A | 1 | Base Pan | Aluminum | Fabricate & Anodize |
| B | 2 | Feedthru Gasket | Silicone Base Calk | Commercial |
| C | 1 | Insulation Panel | Fiberglass | Cut & Notch |
| D | 1 | Gasket | Silicone Base Calk | Commercial |
| E | 1 | Heat Transfer Panel | Aluminum | Commercial – w/coating applied in plant |
| F | 38 | Push Nut | Passivated S. Stl. | Commercial |
| G | 1 | Frame | Aluminum | Fabricate & Anodize |
| H | 1 | Glazing Panel | Glass/Alum./ Neoprene | Commercial |
| J | 1 | Top Flange | Aluminum | Fabricate & Anodize |
| K | 76 | Type C Thread Forming Screw | Passivated S. Stl. | Commercial |
| M | 38 | Blind Studs (Plain) | Aluminum | Commercial |

FIGURE 7.1a  MODULAR SOLAR COLLECTOR. *Source: Westinghouse, Solar Heating and Cooling of Buildings, Vol. 3.*

may be carried away from the flat-plate collector by a stream of air or water led under, through, and over the plate. This warm fluid may then be used directly for heating purposes or heat may be extracted from it and stored.

Because the temperature range required for space heating and cooling is quite moderate even for absorption refrigeration, it can be obtained with the use of a carefully designed flat-plate collector which produces

temperatures in excess of 150°F above ambient.

A significant advantage of the use of a flat-plate to produce energy is that it is responsive to both the direct and diffuse solar energy components; that is, a flat-plate collector will provide useful heat energy even when there is no direct sunshine.

*7.2a-2  Concentrating Collectors*

If higher temperatures are desired, the sunlight must

be concentrated on to the collecting surface. By concentrating direct solar radiation, temperatures in excess of 300°F can be attained. These higher temperatures are advantageous in operating air-conditioning equipment, electrical power generators, and industrial and agricultural dryers.

Most concentrating collectors employ a reflective parabolic or parabodial surface to concentrate the sun's energy on one point. In order to concentrate the sun's direct radiation, the collector must be constantly oriented toward the sun. For this reason and their high cost, concentrating collectors are seldom considered to have housing applications.

There has been a great deal of research undertaken to try to reduce the expenses and engineering difficulties associated with the orientation of concentrating collectors. There have been two general approaches: one, to perfect a simple automatic steering mechanism; and the other, to develop concentrators with fixed

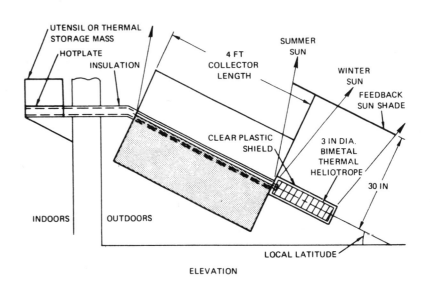

FIGURE 7.2  A PROTOTYPE SOLAR KITCHEN. *Source: C.J. Swet, Johns Hopkins University.*

mirrors and movable heat collectors. One example of a solar energy device which utilizes a simple automatic steering mechanism is found in a solar kitchen developed by C. J. Swet of Johns Hopkins University. The device consists of a parabolic trough concentrator which is oriented by a thermal heliotrope made up of a single bimetallic coil with thermal coatings and a feedback sunshade. (See figure 7.2.) One end of the helix is fastened to a stationary support. The other end is fastened to the trough with

its feedback shade. The reference shade controls the amount of solar radiation falling on the surface of the helix and thus controls the rotation of the helix and the orientation of the trough. A bimetallic helix consists of a highly active thermal metal whose surface changes with the amount of solar radiation falling upon it.

The second approach in eliminating orientation problems of concentrating collectors, to fix the reflector and allow the heat collecting element to move,

allows the collector to be
integrated more readily
with a building design.
This concept is based on
optical principles which
indicate that-- regardless
of the sun's location--
a fixed spherical mirror
can focus most of the
incoming solar radiation
on to a line close to the
mirror's surface. Although
the focal line moves as the
sun moves, it is not
necessary to move the
mirror; only a small
cylindrical absorber which
collects and concentrates
a high percentage of the
incoming solar radiation

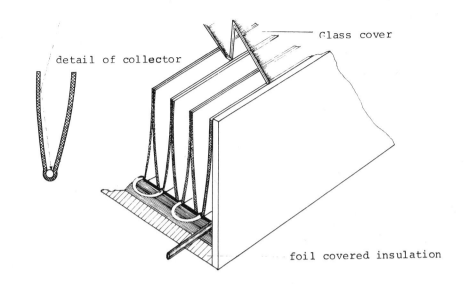

FIGURE 7.4   WINSTON COLLECTOR. *Source: Argonne National Laboratory.*

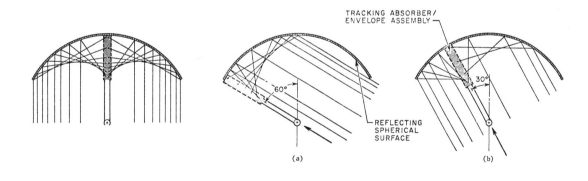

FIGURE 7.3   THE STATIONARY REFLECTOR/TRACKING ABSORBER
SOLAR CONCENTRATOR. *Source: Environmental Consulting Services.*

need be moved. (See
figure 7.3.)

A new development in the
field of stationary con-
centrating collectors is
the Winston Collector.
This collector consists of
a series of curved cones
positioned in troughlike
arrays. Each cone concen-
trates the light at its
narrow end in which a
copper heat-absorbing pipe
is located. The basic
advantages of such a
collector are that it does
not require diurinal tracking of the sun and that it's
capable of utilizing some

**127**

diffuse radiation in addition to direct beam radiation.[1] (See figure 7.4.)

### 7.2a-3  Photovoltaics

A photovoltaic cell is a self-generating semi-conductive device which when struck by light converts light energy into electrical energy. The solar cell, in spite of its remarkable conversion process, has not moved into serious contention as a source of large amounts of electrical power because of its relatively high cost. Extensive research is being done to lower the cost and raise the conversion efficiency through large volume production and the use of new materials.

Photovoltaic cells can be combined with a flat-plate collector so that the radiant energy not converted into electric power is collected as heat and used to supply hot water, space heating, absorption refrigeration, and air-conditioning. A system similar to this was developed by the University of Delaware Institute of Energy

FIGURE 7.5  CROSS SECTION OF FLAT-PLATE COLLECTOR CONTAINING SOLAR CELLS. *Reprinted with permission from University of Delaware Solar House Project, Karl W. Boer.*

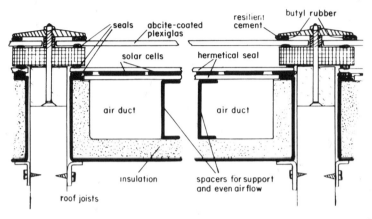

FIGURE 7.5a  SCHEMATIC OF A SOLAR TOTAL ENERGY SYSTEM FOR A BUILDING USING A COMBINED FLAT-PLATE COLLECTOR WITH SOLAR CELLS. *Source: NSF/NASA Solar Energy Panel (University of Maryland, 1972).*

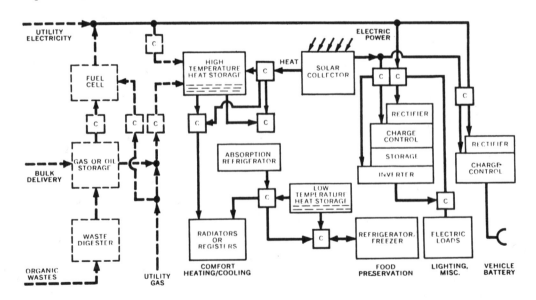

Conversion. In "Solar One," the Institute's experimental house, cadmium sulfide cells are mounted on 4 X 8' roof panels. Behind these panels are heat-transport channels that keep the solar cells from overheating and provide hot air for space heating. (See figure 7.5.)

Another system combining the thermal flat-plate and solar cells entails using electricity produced by the solar cells to power an electric heat pump. (See section 7.3c-1.) During the winter, the thermal collector provides hot water and a thermal input to the heat pump. During the summer, it provides only hot water heating, while the cells operate the heat pump in a refrigeration cycle.

## 7.2b Analysis of Flat-Plate Collectors

The following sections provide a detailed analysis of the flat-plate collector and concentrate on its integration in home heating and cooling systems. The reasons flat-plate collectors were chosen over concentrating collectors are as follows:

1. Concentrating collectors are not available for low-cost quantity manufacture.
2. Their design and application at this time is too complex to expect high reliability at low cost.
3. The high temperatures produced by concentrating collectors are not required for present heating and cooling operations.
4. The high temperature and high pressure output of concentrating collectors produce installation difficulties.
5. Concentrating collectors are not as responsive to the diffuse solar radiation component as flat-plate collectors are.
6. The reflectance of the mirror surfaces of concentrating collectors may diminish with time, thereby reducing collector efficiency.

The above statements are not intended to suggest that flat-plate collectors are without difficulties; however, it is felt that such collectors do offer adaptable, dependable, and cost-effective means for solar energy thermal conversion.

In order to better understand the operation of a flat-plate collector and the variables that influence it, the following simplified formula for determining the performance of a flat-plate collector can prove helpful.

Where: $I\tau\alpha = q_l + q_s + q_u$

$I$ = normal incidence solar radiation on the plane of the collector
$\tau$ = transmissivity of any glazing covering the collector surface
$\alpha$ = absorptivity of the collector plate to solar radiation. This is a property of the surface, and it varies both as a function of wavelength and incidence angle.
$q_l$ = rate at which heat is lost from the collector plate from convection, conduction, and radiation; $BTU/hr/ft^2$
$q_s$ = rate at which heat is stored within the collector; $BTU/hr/ft^2$
$q_u$ = rate at which useful heat can be withdrawn from the collector; $BTU/hr/ft^2$

Optimization of the collector's performance can be clarified through comprehension of the above equation and it's components.

The left side of the equation deals with the incoming rate of heat. This rate can be maximized by:

A. maintaining high values of incident solar radiation (I) through optimal orientation of the collector.[2]

If the only parameter governing collector orientation were total irradiation intensity, the collector would need to be placed facing due south, and tilted at exactly the angle of latitude. However, inasmuch as the amount of solar absorption is generally more critical in the mid-winter when the sun is low in the sky, a solar collector is often tilted at the angle of latitude plus 12-15° so that its surface is perpendicular to the sun's radiation at the coldest period. This steeper tilt produces fewer snow, rain and dust problems. If summer collection is desired solely for space cooling, the collector orientation becomes minus 10 to 15° the latitude of the area. When collector efficiency is the most important parameter, the collector should be oriented about 10° west of due south to take advantage of the higher afternoon temperatures. While a southerly orientation is optimum from the point of view of total radiation collection, a collector oriented as much as 45° off due south will still perform fairly well.

When the collector is used only in the winter and summer insolation is intense and unwanted, tilting the collector at 90° in a southerly direction might be most appropriate. Winter absorption at this angle of tilt is good, and summer absorption is largely decreased.

B. The rate of heat produced by the flat-plate collector can also be maximized by maintaining a high value of transmissivity ($\tau$) in the optical path of the transmission of sunlight.

Transmissivity is the property which allows solar radiation to pass through a collector without being absorbed. The transmissivity of glass or plastic covers have a marked effect on collector performance. Glass of low iron content has a relatively high transmittance (approximately 0.85 - 0.90 at normal incidence for the solar spectrum from 0.30 - 3.0 microns). The purpose of the glazing is to admit as much solar radiation as possible and to reduce the upward heat loss to a minimum. High transmissivity can also be achieved by using thin optical material over the collector to create short light paths. If glass is to be used, the application of an anti-reflection coating to one side will improve transmissivity by 5%.

C. The rate of heat produced by the flat-plate collector can also be maximized by increasing the absorptivity of the collector plate. ($\alpha$)

The absorptivity of the collector's surface for short wave radiation is

determined by the nature and color of its coating. The objective in applying a *selective coating* is to produce a surface that has a high solar absorptivity and low (infrared) emissivity. For example, selective nickel-black surfaces produced by Honeywell have an absorptivity of 0.94 and an emissivity of 0.07. On the other hand, a black-painted surface (3M Company No. 101-C10 Black Velvet) could be expected to have an absorptivity of 0.95 and emissivity of 0.95.

There are four basic means of producing a selective surface:[3]

1. Thin films. The collector plate, a highly reflective metallic surface, is covered by a thin film opaque to infrared light. The film thickness is approximately one visible wave length (0.5 microns). This thickness is sufficient to absorb visible light effectively, but insufficient to absorb infrared wave length thermal radiation. The latter is reflected by the base because the film thickness is a small fraction of an infrared wave length and is therefore radiated extremely inefficiently.

2. Geometric trappings. A metallic surface is polished on the scale of 5 micron wave lengths but pitted or scratched on the scale of 0.5 micron, so that it absorbs visible light. In addition, a base is covered by a layer of finely divided metal, such as gold, where the particle size is such that for visible light, the layer is virtually black, but at longer wave lengths, the true reflective character of the metal is dominant.

3. Interference filter. By vacuum deposition of several layers of material of suitable thickness (on the order of one-half wave length) and with different indecies of refraction, it is possible to achieve high infrared reflectance and low visible light reflectance.

4. Semiconductors. A semiconductor, which is intrinsically opaque to photons having energies higher than the band gap energy, but transparent to photons having energies lower than the band gap energy, is deposited on a polished metal base. The semiconductor's opacity dominates at visible wave lengths (higher energies), whereas the polished base reflectivity dominates at infrared wave lengths (lower energies).

Special precautions must be taken to avoid deterioration of the optical and/or thermal properties of the surface resulting from oxidation, chemical changes, etc.

Special geometry of the collector itself can be designed to enhance absorptivity and/or reduce effective emissivity.

The Vee-corrugated absorber, as a solar air heater, allows an incoming solar ray to undergo multiple reflections which increase the effective solar absorptivity; however, this process also increases the effective emissivity of the surface. For example, a 30° Vee made from a surface having an absorptivity of 0.8 and emissivity of 0.05 would possess an effective

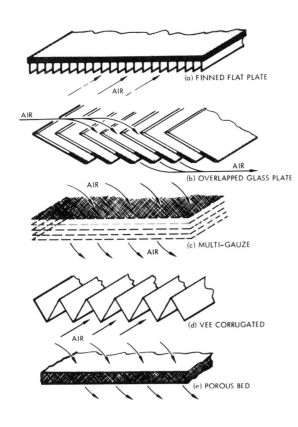

FIGURE 7.6 SOLAR ABSORBERS USED WITH AIR. *Source: TRW Solar Heating and Cooling of Buildings, Vol. II.*

absorptivity of 0.99 and an emittance of 0.18.[14] (See figure 7.6d)

Honeycombs offer yet another way to enhance absorptivity and reduce effective emissivity. The honeycomb cell is an array of aluminized, clear, resin-overcoated paper in a rectangular shape. The honeycomb is placed between the absorber plate and cover plate. (See figure 7.7.)

Trapping geometries, such as honeycombs or vee-corrugations, are less effective traps when the sun is a few degrees from normal incidence. The angle of interception is determined by the geometry; therefore, some of these designs require that the collector be mobile in order to provide optimal orientation to the sun.

The rate of heat produced by the flat-plate collector can also be maximized by:

D. increasing the rate at which useful heat ($q_u$) can be withdrawn from the collector. The most effective means of increasing this rate is to

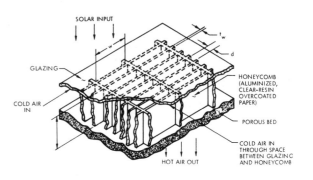

FIGURE 7.7 HONEYCOMB SECTION. *Source: TRW Solar Heating and Cooling of Buildings, Vol. III.*

reduce heat loss resulting from conduction, convection, and radiation. This can be accomplished using the following methods.

1. Multiple glazing (cover plates). Convection loss rates to the ambient air, primarily through natural convection and force convection (wind), are minimized by covering the collector plate with one or more optically transparent sheets. The sheets are spaced roughly a half inch apart in order to lessen internally generated

FIGURE 7.8 GUIDE TO THE SE-
LECTION AND NUMBER OF TRANS-
PARENT PLATES. *Source: TRW
Solar Heating and Cooling
of Buildings, Vol. II.*

| Collection Temperature Above Ambient Air | Typical Application | Number of Cover Plates | |
|---|---|---|---|
| | | Black Painted Absorber ϵ=0.9, 0.95 | Selective Absorber ϵ=0.2 |
| -10 to 10°F | Heat source for heat pump. Air heating for drying Service hot water boosting. | none | none |
| 10 to 60°F | Summer water heating Air heating for drying Space heating in non-freezing climates | 1 | 1 |
| 60 to 100°F | Winter water heating Winter space heating | 2 | 1 |
| 100 to 150°F | Summer air conditioning Refrigeration Cooking by boiling Steam production | 3 | 2 |

convection between either
the plate and cover or
between pairs of covers.
The number of sheets needed
depends upon the degree to
which the collector temperature exceeds the temperature of the ambient air.[4]
A convenient guide to the
number of covers to use for
various applications is
given in Table 7.8.

2. Insulation. Conductive
losses through the back of
the collector can be
minimized with the use of
foil-covered fiberglass
insulation.

3. Honeycombs or cells.
Honeycombs such as those
discussed in the last section can also be useful in
the reduction of convection
losses. The configuration
of the cell unit should be
made narrow (to prevent
convection) and long (to
reduce conduction).

4. Evacuation. (See figure
7.9.) Convection can be
reduced by evacuating the
air space between the
absorber plate and glazing.
At pressures in the range
of $10^{-2}$ to $10^{-4}$ atmospheres,
convection is suppressed.
An evacuated glass cylinder

containing a selective
absorber plate is one configuration that can be used.
It is important to note
that highly selective surfaces with emissivities of
not less than 0.4 must be
utilized or the collector's
performance may be no better
than that of one with two or
three glass plates and no
evacuation.[5]

5. Counterflow exchange.
The concept of counterflow
exchange is employed to
reduce convection losses in
some air heating collectors.
Incoming (cooler) air is
forced in a downward or

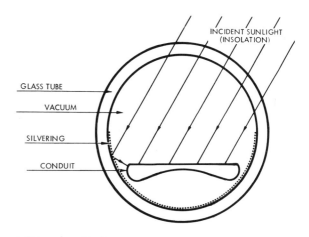

FIGURE 7.9 EVACUATED TUBE
SOLAR COLLECTOR. *Source:
TRW Solar Heating and Cooling
of Buildings, Vol. III.*

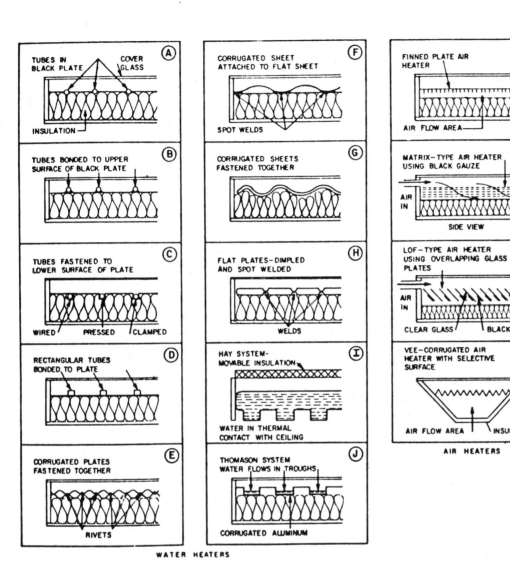

FIGURE 7.10 VARIATIONS OF SOLAR WATER AND AIR HEATERS.
*Reprinted from ASHRAE Handbook of Fundamentals (1972), by permission of the American Society of Heating, Refrigerating and Air Conditioning Engineers, Inc.*

transverse direction so that heated air does not reach the collector cover. In a sense, the heated air may preheat the incoming air. In any event, the collector can be designed so that air flow reduces the upward convective heat transfer.

### 7.2b-1  Fluid Heat Transfer

This section deals with the transfer of heat from the absorber plate to the fluid entering the collector. There are two broad categories of absorber designs: those which utilize a liquid as a heat transfer medium, and those which use air as a transfer fluid.

### 7.2b-1a  Water Heating Absorbers

Most water heating collectors (see figure 7.10) excluding types I and J, vary in the configuration of the tube-in-plate absorbing surface. As the collector plate absorbs solar radiation, it conducts the heat to a liquid contained in tubes attached to the collector plate surface or in tubes integral to the

collector plate. If the tubes are to be located above or beneath the collector's surface (figure 7.10b-c), they must be attached to the plate with a good thermal bond. Good bond conductance can be provided by securely soldering the collection tubes to the absorber plate. Plates with tubes that are integral to the absorber plate offer the best thermal bond. Rectangular tubing attached to the collector plate offers more contact surface for a thermal bond (figure 7.10d). Figures e, f, and g show different ways corrugated galvanized sheeting can be fastened together to make watertight fluid passages. Parallel sheets of copper (figure 7.10h) can be substituted for the galvanized sheeting. Parallel sheets can be either spot welded or riveted to provide individual fluid passages. All the non-tubular designs (figure 7.10e, f, g, and h) are limited by the water pressures they can sustain, and, in general, they are not suited for use with the high line pressures found in the U.S.[6] Figure 7.10i shows the roof pond collector used in the Skytherm process developed by Harold Hay. Water is contained in transparent plastic bags supported by a metal ceiling. Heat is absorbed by the water, transferred to the metal ceiling, which, in turn, transfers it to the living space. Movable horizontal insulation is placed above the surface of the water at night to prevent the water from losing its heat to the outside air. In the summer, the process is reversed: the insulating panels are closed during the day; the water bags cool the room by convection at night; the insulating panels are opened and heat is dissipated from the roof pond to the cool night sky. (For further discussion, see 7.6). The Thomason Collector, shown in figure 10j, utilizes a corrugated aluminum panel, painted black. Water is allowed to trickle over the absorber's surface, thus collecing heat.

In terms of overall collector performance, a high plate-to-fluid temperature difference implies lower collector efficiency, because radiation and conduction/convection losses increase with increasing plate temperature. In contrast, systems efficiency, in general, increases with higher fluid temperature, which necessarily implies a higher average plate temperature. Therefore, the collector must be designed to minimize plate-to-fluid temperature differences, and the system must be designed to optimize overall performance in terms of collector operating temperature. These considerations do not produce serious problems in water heating collectors because the operating temperature of the collector can be controlled by simply adjusting the rate of fluid flowing over the collector's surface.[7]

### 7.3b-1b Air Heating Collectors

Inasmuch as the heat transfer coefficient between air and metal is low compared to that of metal and water, some method should be employed to increase the

transfer of heat from the collector's surface to the air. This can be accomplished by increasing the heat transfer surface area, increasing the air turbulence within the collector, and allowing the air to make multiple passes. Figures 7.10k, l, and m and figure 7.6 show how a large contact area can be provided between the absorbing material and air.

7.2b-2 *Special Considerations in Flat-Plate Collector Design*[8]

Several problems, not directly affecting calculated performance, are listed and discussed below. While most of these problems are not so important when considering performance concepts, their effect on final collector and system designs are very significant.

**Freezing and Boiling in Water Heater Collectors:**

A collector can be drained at night to prevent freezing, but this aggravates corrosion problems, and sometimes causes problems in completely and automatically refilling all tubes to assure even flow. The fluid can be charged with an antifreeze (ethylene glycol is most commonly mentioned) solutions, but this requires a separate heat exchange loop to storage if the system is using water storage. It has been suggested that slow circulation from storage could be used to prevent freezing, but it has not yet been shown what effect on system performance this might have (additionally, a pump failure could then have disastrous effects on the collector). Boiling causes problems in a tightly sealed system, yet it is desirable to have a sealed system from the corrosion standpoint. One may have to design the system to withstand the pressures attending the highest temperature the collector can reach. For 300°F this is about 59 psia, with no safety factor. Over-temperature relief systems such as steam release, increased convection cooling, shading, etc., should probably be designed into a collector because designing

and building the collector to hold the required pressure could cause safety hazards.

Corrosion:

Copper tubing may be used to prevent corrosion in a water collector, but copper is expensive. Aluminum and steel are the next choices, and both of these materials are subject to corrosion. Suitable inhibitors may be used to prevent corrosion, but at present the inhibitors are somewhat less satisfactory for aluminum. The corrosion problem is aggravated by draining, since the metals are then exposed to oxygen in the air.

Damage by Heating:

Materials in contact with the absorber surface need to withstand temperatures (perhaps 200°C) which might be encountered as a consequence of lost fluid circulation. High temperatures can also cause degradation of selective absorbing surfaces.

Damage by Hail:

Since nearly all collectors considered to date (and likely to be considered in the near term) have glass covers, glass breakage could be an important consideration in some locations. Double strength glass can be used to resist breakage, but this glass is, of course, more expensive. Even so, it is important to construct the collector so that the glass can be easily replaced, and so it is well supported and not in too large sections. Architectural standards would apply here.

Contamination in Air Collectors:

Dust, moisture, and pollutants will circulate through an air heating collector and can conceivably cause surface deterioration, clogging of small passages, etc. This, of course, becomes serious if an air heating collector makes use of a selective surface, since selective surfaces are often delicate to begin with.

Deterioration of Paints

and Other Materials:

Since the collector in a system will involve a high capital investment, it is desirable to design for at least 20 year life. The relatively high temperature environment inside the collector poses special problems in materials. A black paint (which might be used to avoid instabilities of a selective surface) might become faded, cracked, etc. in the long term. Therefore, special materials must be used, or simple maintenance procedures must be provided.

Heat Transfer Fluids:

Air and water have been mentioned as the most suitable heat transfer fluids. Water must be protected from freezing, and as a result the heat carrying capacity is reduced 10 to 20 percent. Other liquids could be considered for heat transport from the collector. Any of them would have a lower specific heat than water, often half or less, but some have higher boiling points (lower vapor pressures) and may also have lower freezing

temperature. With liquids other than water, the freezing is not likely to damage the collector, anyway, because they shrink when freezing.

*7.2c Heat Energy Storage*

Heat energy storage is a means of translating an intermittant thermal source, such as solar radiation, to a consistant one. The success of any system is a measure of the regularity with which it can supply the thermal needs of a living space. In a solar energy thermal storage system (TES), this regularity is dependent upon the storage capacity. Creation of the optimum energy storage system requires consideration of numerous factors: climate, insulation, and cost of thermal storage material and local fuel. A study of system cost and energy storage capacity was done by Tybout and Löf. Their findings show that the minimum average operating cost occurs when about 10-15 lb. of water storage per square foot of collector area is used. This is equivalent

of 1 to 3 days of winter heat delivery.[9]

There are two basic ways in which thermal energy can be stored: sensible heat storage and latent heat storage. In sensible heat storage, solar energy is used to raise the temperature of the storage medium without changing the phase of the material. In latent storage, solar energy causes the storage material to undergo a physical phase change. The following deals with the two forms of heat storage.

### 7.2c-1 Sensible Heat Storage

The formula which defines the quantity of heat which can be stored in a medium due to a change in its temperature is:

$$Q = mct \qquad \text{where:}$$

Q = thermal heat energy
m = mass of material
c = thermal capacity
t = change in temperature

Water and stones have been the most widely used forms

| Material | Specific Heat | Heat Capacity | | Density | |
|---|---|---|---|---|---|
| | | Btu/ft$^3$/°F | kJ/m$^3$°C | lb/ft$^3$ | kg/m$^3$ |
| Water | 1.00 | 62.5 | 4,190 | 62.5 | 1,000 |
| Water-Ethylene Glycol Mixture (30-70% by weight), at 230°F | 0.80 | 51.2 | 3,440 | 64.1 | 1,025 |
| Concrete | 0.156 | 22.4 | 1,490 | 144 | 2,310 |
| Scrap Iron | 0.12 | 54.0 | 3,630 | 450 | 7,230 |
| Rocks (crushed) | 0.20 | 20.0 | 3,350 | 100 | 1,601 |
| Marble (solid) | 0.21 | 34.2 | 2,280 | 162 | 2,600 |
| Rock Salt | 0.219 | 29.6 | 1,985 | 136 | 2,180 |
| Sand | 0.191 | 18.1 | 1,215 | 94.6 | 1,533 |
| Stone (quarried) | 0.20 | 19.0 | 1,275 | 95 | 1,540 |

TABLE 7.11  THERMAL CAPACITY OF STORAGE MATERIAL. *Source: TRW Solar Heating and Cooling of Buildings, Vol. II.*

of thermal storage in house heating and cooling operations. Water has the highest heat capacity per weight, volume, and dollar, of any material that is commonly available. Water can be easily stored and pumped through heat exchangers. All these factors point to water as an attractive material for thermal energy storage. The unit heat capacity of water is 62 BTU/cu.ft./°F. (See Table 7.11.) Therefore, a cubic foot of water raised 1° will return 62 BTU's of heat when it is cooled to its original temperature.

Rock or pebble storage is only about 30-40% as efficient per unit volume as water storage is because the specific heat of rock is about 0.2. Therefore, a larger storage capacity must be provided for rocks than for water. Very crudely put, 1 cubic foot of rock is required in storage for every square foot of collector area, while 1 cubic foot of water is required for every 3 square feet of collector. In a rock storage bed, a blower is necessary to transport heated air to the living

space. The blower capacity depends upon the resistance to air flow which is contingent upon the size of the pebbles. A convenient size for storing heat is 2" diameter gravel, crushed rock, or brick.

An airloop rock storage convective system developed by Zomeworks (See figure 7.12) utilizes a bin of cobble-sized rocks for heat storage. The air is circulated by natural convection from the air solar heater to the rock bins. When heat is needed in the house, a vent is opened, and the warm air rises into the room. The same system can be operated for cooling by allowing the rock bed to draw in cool night air, thus lowering its temperature. The vent is opened to allow the cool air into the house during the day.

The incorporation of a rock storage system into a building is easier than the incorporation of a water storage system because the former does not require a waterproof container. Furthermore, such a container made of fiberglas insulated steel can be expensive

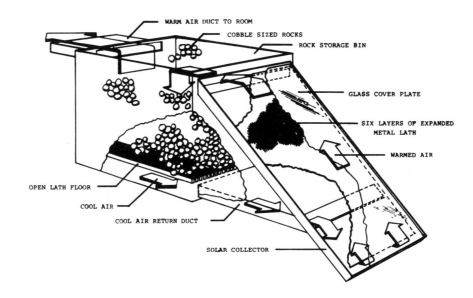

FIGURE 7.12   AN AIR-LOOP ROCK STORAGE CONVECTIVE SOLAR HEATER. *Reprinted by permission from Zomeworks, Inc.*

(for a 10,000 gal. tank capacity, the cost in 1959 was $1,300).

Heat loss considerations make adequate insulation of the heat storage unit a necessity. Furthermore, the storage unit should be located so that the heat losses from the storage go into portions of the living space. The storage system should be integral to the living space, and, for greatest efficiency, the system should be located as close to the collector as possible.

The storage system should be designed so that the fluid supplied to the collector is at the lowest possible temperature and the heat taken from the collector enters the hottest portion of the storage tank. The tank should be positioned vertically to encourage stratification and to allow only a minimum amount of mixing of the fluid.

The amount of heat or the heat of fusion that can be stored or released by a material when it changes state from a solid to a liquid is given by the relationship:

$$Q = mL \quad \text{where:}$$

Q = amount of heat stored (or removed)

m = mass of the material

L = latent heat of fusion

Because of their high heat storage capacities per unit of volume, phase change material can store more heat in less volume.

There are two major categories of materials which show promise as mediums for thermal energy storage. They are salt hydrates and paraffin. (See Table 7.13.)

Sodium sulfate, decahydrate (glaubers salt) has been considered one of the most promising low-cost materials for storage of thermal energy, especially for use with solar heating and cooling systems. The salt

| Materials | Melting Point | | Heat of Fusion | | Heat Capacity | |
|---|---|---|---|---|---|---|
| | °F | °C | Btu/lb | kj/kg | Btu/ft$^3$ | kj/m$^3$ |
| **a) Salt Hydrates** | | | | | | |
| $Na_2SO_4 \cdot 1/2NH_4Cl \cdot 1/2NaCl \cdot 10H_2O$ | 55 | 12.8 | 78 | 181 | 7200 | 268,265 |
| $K_2HPO_4 \cdot 6H_2O$ | 52-56 | 11.1-13.3 | 47 | 109 | 4900 | 182,570 |
| $Ca(NO_3)_2 \cdot 4H_2O$ | 117 | 47.2 | 66 | 154 | 7650 | 285,032 |
| $Na_2S_2O_3 \cdot 5H_2O$ | 113-120 | 45.0-48.9 | 90 | 209 | 9200 | 342,784 |
| $Na_2SO_4 \cdot 10H_2O$ (Glauber Salt) | 90 | 32.2 | 108 | 251 | 9900 | 368,865 |
| $MgCl_2 \cdot 6H_2$) | 239 | 115 | 71 | 165 | 6940 | 258,578 |
| **b) Waxes** | | | | | | |
| C14-C16 Paraffin | 35-45 | 1.7-7.2 | 65.4 | 152 | 3185 | 118,670 |
| C15-C16 Paraffin | 40-50 | 4.4-10.0 | 65.7 | 153 | 3200 | 119,229 |
| 1 - Decanol | 40-45 | 4.4-7.2 | 88.6 | 206 | 4590 | 171,019 |
| C14 Paraffin | 35-40 | 1.7-4.4 | 71.1 | 165 | 3420 | 127,426 |
| C16 Paraffin | 58-65 | 14.4-18.3 | 86.2 | 200 | 4190 | 156,116 |
| P116 Paraffin | 116 | 46.7 | 90 | 209 | 4380 | 163,195 |
| **c) Plastics** | | | | | | |
| High Density Polyethylene | 230-255 | 110-123.9 | 108 | 251 | 7200 | 268,266 |

TABLE 7.13 PHASE CHANGE THERMAL ENERGY STORAGE MATERIAL. *Source: TRW Solar Heating and Cooling of Buildings, Vol. II.*

has a large heat storage capacity, 9,900 BTU/cu.ft., (Table 7.13) and melts at 90°F making it ideal for heat storage and house-heating applications. With the addition of other salts, (NACL and $NH_4CL$), the material can be made to melt between 64 and 45°F, implying possibilities for air conditioning applications. Some disadvantages which plague latent heat storage systems are described below.[10]

1. Instability of solution under cycling.

2. Tendency to supercool, making the addition of nu-

cleating agents a necessity.

3. Low thermal conductivity of solid phase, reducing the heat transfer.

4. Shrinkage of solid phase away from the walls of the containing vessel, further reducing heat transfer.

5. High cost of containment vessel, tanks, and materials.

### 7.2c-3  Heat Retrieval from Storage Unit

In order for the stored thermal energy in the storage tank to become useful, there must be a means of retrieving it. The transfer of heat from the thermal energy storage unit to the living space can take place through a water loop (baseboard heater) or an airloop. Heat can be retrieved from a storage unit by having water circulate directly through radiators in the building or through pipes imbedded in the floor, or the heated water may be transferred to a heat exchanger which air is blown across. The warm air is then circulated through ducts to condition the air of the living space. The water loop heat exchanger (baseboard heater) is the simplest and least expensive means for the transfer of heat; the only drawback is that it is not adaptable to air conditioning use.

In systems using air as a transfer fluid and rock beds as a storage unit, the simplest method for retrieving heat is to have air blown through the storage unit, then circulated through the living space. The benefit in using an airloop heat exchanger is that the same loop can be used for air conditioning, and possibly, humidity control.

A more detailed description of solar heating and air conditioning equipment follows:

### 7.3  Subsystem Integration/ House Heating and Cooling

For ease of discussion, the descriptions of the selected systems providing space heating and/or cooling will be broken down into the following divisions:

7.3a   Space Heating
7.3a-1 Direct Heat Exchangers
7.3a-1a System Operation
7.3b Space Cooling
7.3b-1 Solar Absorption
        Cooling Systems
7.3b-1a System Operation
7.3b-2 Stirling Cycle Air
        Conditioning
7.3b-2a System Operation
7.3c Combined Systems Capable
        of Heating and Cooling
7.3c-1 Heat Pumps
7.3c-1a Solar-Assisted Heat
        Pumps
7.3c-1b Rankine Cycle Powered
        Heat Pumps

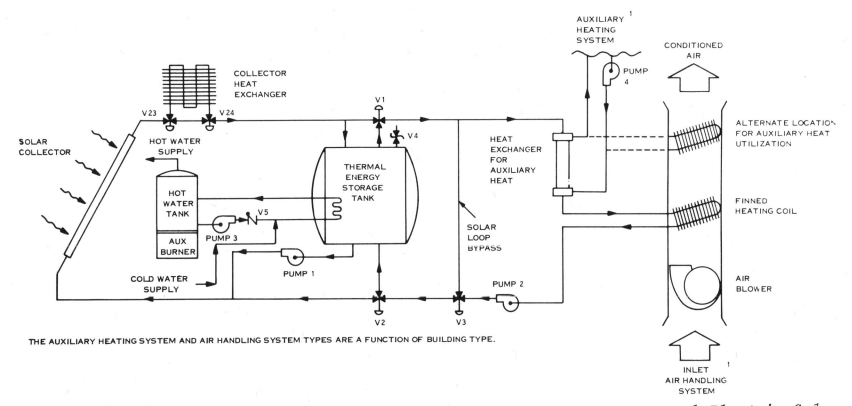

FIGURE 7.14  DIRECT HEAT EXCHANGE SOLAR HEATING SYSTEM. *Source: General Electric Solar Heating and Cooling of Buildings, Vol. II.*

*7.3a-1  Space Heating/Direct Heat Exchangers*

To date, direct exchange systems are the most widely used for space heating, largely because of their simplicity and efficiency in converting solar energy into space heat.

*7.3a-1a  System Operation (See figure 7.14.)*

Pump No. 1 is an electrically driven centrifugal hot water pump which circulates fluid at low flow rates (approximately 1 gal/hr/sq. ft. of absorber plate) from the thermal energy storage tank (TES tank), through the flat-plate absorber where it is heated and then returned

to the upper section of the TES tank. The size of the flat-plate absorber is determined by the amount of floor space to be heated, the type of insulation used in the building, the amount of infiltration anticipated, and other parameters that would contribute to heat loss from the building. When the flat-plate collector is located below and near the TES tank, a pump is not

**142**

| Control Mode | Description | Valve Flow Direction | | | Pumps | | | |
|---|---|---|---|---|---|---|---|---|
| | | V1 | V2 | V3 | P1 | P2 | P3 | P4 |
| 1 | Heat TES from Collectors | 3-2 | 1-3 | 1-2 | On | Off | Off | Off |
| 2 | Provide Heat to Space Air. TES > 35°C | 3-2 | 1-3 | 1-2 | Off | On | Off | Off |
| 3 | Provide Heat to Space Air. TES > 35°C or Thermostat Lower Set Point is Activated | 3-2 | 1-3 | 1-3 | Off | On | Off | On |
| 4 | HW Tank Temp. < TES Temp. | - | - | - | Off | Off | On | Off |
| * | | | | | | | | |

\* Combinations of modes 1, 4 and 2 or 3 are possible. Valve and pump settings follow individual mode settings.

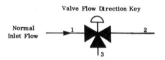

Valve Flow Direction Key

Normal Inlet Flow → 1    2
3

TABLE 7.15   PUMP AND VALVE SETTINGS FOR DIRECT HEAT EX-CHANGER OPERATING IN DIFFERENT MODES. *Source: General Electric Solar Heating and Cooling of Buildings, Vol. II.*

needed because of the thermo-syphon effect. Water flow through the collector is automatically controlled by the thermal gradient (the temperature differential between the cold water supplied to the collector and the warm water supplied to the TES tank). The major disadvantages of a thermo-syphon effect are that no manual control over the flow rate exists and severe design constraints are imposed because the TES tank must be located close to and above the flat-plate collector.

To prevent damage to the solar collector, the thermal energy transfer loop between the solar collector and the TES tank must constitute a closed loop system if the outside air reaches freezing temperatures. In such a case, a solution of ethylene glycol would be a necessary addition to the transfer fluid. Heat exchange between the solar collector and the TES tank would be accomplished with a liquid-to-liquid heat exchanger. This whole system could be

eliminated by incorporating an automatic dump cycle in which fluid from the collector would be allowed to drain back to the TES tank when the ambient air temperature approached freezing.

The energy transfer from the TES tank is accomplished through a liquid-to-liquid heat exchanger in the TES tank to a finned heating coil located in the air handling and distribution system.

If and when the temperature in the TES tank reaches a minimum usable temperature (95°F), the fluid within it is diverted through a solar loop bypass to an auxiliary heating unit.

Domestic hot water can be provided by thermally connecting a hot water tank and the TES tank with a heat exchange coil. The operation of the hot water tank is the same as that of a conventional hot water heater, with an auxiliary heating unit providing supplemental heat should the temperature from the TES tank be insufficient.

For a further description of system operation, valve positions, and pump conditions for the various operating modes, consult Table 7.15.

### 7.3b-1 Space Cooling/Solar Absorption Cooling System

The same components used to produce space heating for a house can also be used to power an absorption air conditioner. Solar absorption cooling systems lend themselves to the scale of residential heating units. For cooling capacities of 25 tons and greater, the solar absorption system is impractical.

At the present time, there is only one small (3-ton) gas absorption cooling unit that is compatible with solar cooling systems. This is the Arkla Model 501 which uses lithium bromide-water (Li-Br) as the working fluid.

### 7.3b-1a System Operation/ Gas Absorption Refrigeration Cycle (See figure 7.16 and 7.17)

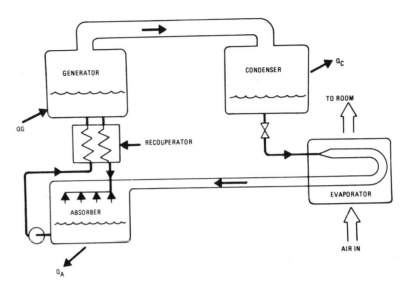

FIGURE 7.16  BASIC VAPOR ABSORPTION REFRIGERATION SYSTEM. *Source: Westinghouse Solar Heating and Cooling of Buildings, Vol. II.*

In Li-Br water units, water is the refrigerant and Li-Br is the absorber. An Li-Br water solution containing on the order of 50-60% Li-Br is heated to approximately 170°F in the generator which is supplied heat by a flat-plate collector, and the water boils off. The enriched Li-Br water solution returns to the absorber, while the water vapor flows to the condenser where it is condensed, giving up heat. Then the condensed water flows through an expansion valve to the evaporator which is at a much lower pressure than the condenser, and the water evaporates at approximately 40°F, taking in heat and performing the refrigeration function. The cool water vapor flows to the absorber where it is mixed with a concentrated Li-Br solution. The water is absorbed by the Li-Br, giving up heat in the process. The Li-Br solution is then pumped up to the generator, heated, and water is evaporated again to repeat the cycle.[11]

144

The relatively high temperatures (180°F - 210°F) that have to be provided for the operation of the absorption cooling system impose stringent design constraints on the collector.  It is important to note that the cooling capacity of the gas absorption machine is dependent not only on the temperature of the fluid supplied to the generator, but also on the temperature difference between the fluid supplied to the generator and the cooling water supplied to the heat exchanger. For example, the normal operating temperatures for the 3-ton Arkla machine are 210°F for the generator and 85°F for the cooling water inlet.  If the operating temperature were dropped to 180°F, the cooling water inlet temperature would have to be 65°F to obtain the same cooling capacity.  (For every 3° decrease in the generator temperature, the cooling water temperature must be lowered 2°.)  Therefore, the cooler the water provided by a cooling tower or any other cold water source, the lower the temperature required by the flat-plate collector to operate the solar absorption

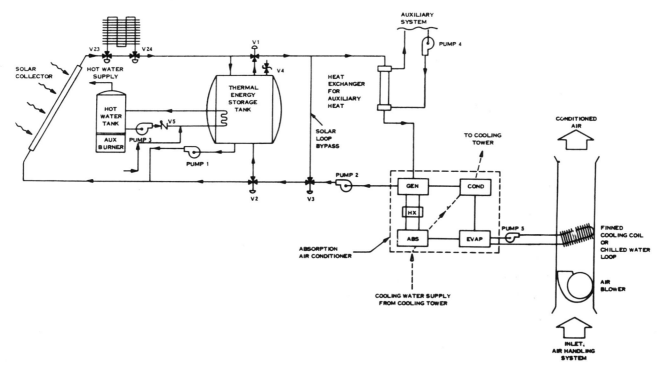

FIGURE 7.17  SOLAR ABSORPTION COOLING SYSTEM.  *Source:  General Electric, Solar Heating and Cooling of Buildings, Vol. II.*

cycle.

For space cooling, the subsystem's operation is similar to those described in figure 7.14 with the addition of an absorption air-conditioning unit and cooling tower (figure 7.17).

Pump No. 2 forces hot fluid (180°F) from the TES tank to the generator of the absorption air-conditioner. The absorption air-conditioner supplies chilled water from the evaporator, and pumps it through a finned cooling coil, which acts as a liquid-air heat exchanger in centrally located air handling units. The air is then distributed throughout the building by forced air ducts.

### 7.3b-2   Space Cooling/ Stirling Cycle Air- Conditioning[12]

The temperatures needed to operate a stirling cycle are easily attained using a concentrating collector. If a flat-plate collector is used to produce adequate temperatures, some modification, such as optical concentration, will be needed to increase its heat output. (See section 7.4a-3.)

The free piston Stirling Cycle air-conditioner described here was developed at Ohio University by Professor William Beale and Stephen A. Lewis. The advantages of their design over conventional motor/compressor air-conditioners are as follows:

1. Extreme simplicity: the engine has two moving parts and the compressor has one.
2. High energy efficiency.
3. Largely maintenance-free/long life.
4. Very low cost.

A conventional stirling cycle uses solar energy to heat an expandable gas, working against a power piston. The gas, normally helium or hydrogen, is under pressure in the sealed engine and is heated through the walls of the working cylinder. At the opposite end of the piston stroke, a cooling medium (usually water) takes away waste heat. A second piston, a displacer, working out of phase with the power piston, squeezes the working gas from one end to the other so that is is cooled and reheated to again expand against the piston. The power is delivered in the form of a rotary motion. It is on this point that Beale and Lewis's design differs. The Stirling Cycle they developed produces a reciprocating motion that operates an inertia air-conditioning compressor.

### 7.3b-2a   System Operation

(The sequence of their Stirling Cycle engine is as follows. (See figures 7.18 and 7.19.)

1-2 Working gas heated by solar energy expands,driving the displacer up.
2-3 The bounce gas (helium) in the pressure vessel is compressed. Because the pressure of the bounce gas is greater than that of the working gas, the displacer is forced down, moving the working gas into the heat exchanger and giving off heat.
3-4 The cold working gas is compressed by the momentum of the displacer.
4-5 The working gas is compressed by the piston

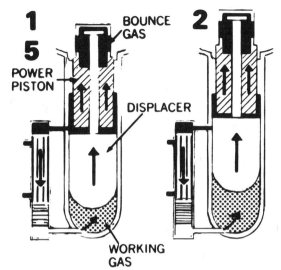

1
5
POWER PISTON
BOUNCE GAS
2
DISPLACER
WORKING GAS

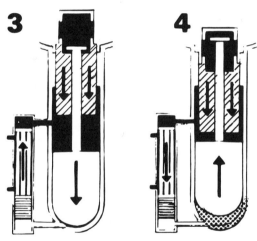

3
4

FIGURE 7.18 and 7.19 RECIPROCATING FREE PISTON STIRLING CYCLE AIR CONDITIONER. *Reprinted with permisson from Times Mirror Magazine, Inc., 1974.*

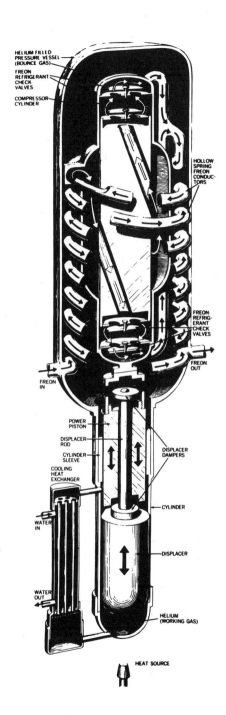

HELIUM FILLED PRESSURE VESSEL (BOUNCE GAS)
FREON REFRIGERANT CHECK VALVES
COMPRESSOR CYLINDER
HOLLOW SPRING FREON CONDUCTORS
FREON REFRIGERANT CHECK VALVES
FREON OUT
FREON IN
POWER PISTON
DISPLACER ROD
CYLINDER SLEEVE
COOLING HEAT EXCHANGER
DISPLACER DAMPERS
CYLINDER
WATER IN
DISPLACER
WATER OUT
HELIUM (WORKING GAS)
HEAT SOURCE

momentum driving the displacer up, and shuttling cold gas to the hot space.

The sequence of the inertia air-conditioning compressor is as follows:

The compressor operates from the reciprocating motion produced by the displacer. The compressor cylinder is connected to the displacer. Freon tubes follow cylinder movement with a springlike action. Inertial mass, too heavy to follow movement, remains fixed. Freon alternately passes through top and bottom check valves and is compressed between the ends of the inertial mass and the cylinder. The pressure forces freon through the tubing.

*7.3c-1   Combined Systems Capable of Heating and Cooling/Heat Pumps*

A heat pump is a device which transfers heat from one temperature level to another by means of an electrically driven compressor. There is really no difference between a heat

pump and a conventional vapor compression refrigeration cycle except that the heat pump can be operated as an air cooling unit or reversed and operated as a heating unit. When the heat pump takes heat of a relatively low temperature level and transfers it to a higher level, it is said to be operating in the heating mode. When it removes heat from a relatively high temperature source and discharges it elsewhere at still higher temperatures, it is said to be operating in the cooling mode.

In the standard vapor compression cycle, a mechanical compressor is used to pump the refrigerant vapor from the evaporator to the condenser. During the heating cycle the external heat exchanger operates as the evaporator, picking up heat from the outside air and discharging it into the house. During the cooling operation, the refrigerant flow is reversed by a four-way valve. See figures 7.20 and 7.21 for the heating and cooling modes of the heat pump.

FIGURE 7.21 COOLING MODE.

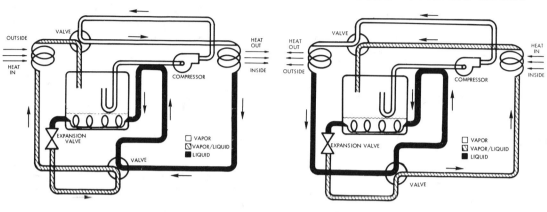

FIGURE 7.20 HEAT PUMP IN HEATING MODE.

*Source: TRW, Solar Heating and Cooling of Buildings, Vol. II.*

The heat pump offers a very flexible and versatile means for heating and cooling. The heat pump is also the most economical device now available for converting electricity into heat. The coefficient of performance (or the indicator of the efficiency with which the heat pump can convert electricity into heat) ranges from 3-4 when the heat pump is under optimum conditions. This means that for every unit of electrical energy supplied to the compressor, 3-4 units of heating or cooling energy is delivered to the house.

In the heating operation, solar energy enhances the performance of the heat pump by providing higher grade energy than the cold environment, thereby lowering the amount of electric energy required by the heat pump. The heat pump cannot use the sun's energy directly for cooling unless a solar-powered engine (Rankine) is used to operate the compressor. (See section 7.3c-1b.)

148

FIGURE 7.22 SOLAR ASSISTED HEAT PUMP SYSTEM HEATING MODE. *Source: General Electric, Solar Heating and Cooling of Buildings, Vol. II.*

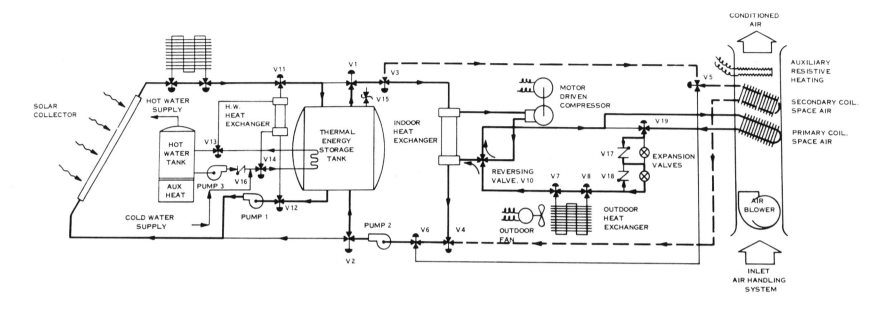

*7.3c-1a Combined Systems Capable of Heating and Cooling/Solar Assisted Heat Pump Operation/Heating Mode (See figure 7.22.)*

Solar energy is collected by a flat-plate collector and transferred to the TES tank. The energy transfer loop between the TES tank and the heat pump consists of

pump no. 2, the indoor heat exchanger, and the directional valves V-1 through V-6. The indoor heat exchanger is a liquid-to-liquid configuration that performs the function of an evaporator for the heat pump whenever the TES fluid is either the energy source for heating or the sink for cooling.

The heat pump circuit con-

tains an electrically-driven reciprocal compressor and an outdoor finned heat exchanger with a motor-driven fan. With an air-to-air heat pump, the air-handling system consists of a single air blower and forced air duct distribution system. If the ambient air temperature is greater than the temperature in the TES tank, the ambient air or any low-grade source of

**149**

heat can be used for the heat pump operation.

In the cooling mode, the heat pump operates as a standard vapor compression refrigeration system, using the TES tank to store excess cooling. In this operation, the heat pump does not use solar heat. The heat pump can be operated during off-peak cooling load hours and off-peak electric rate hours to satisfy immediate cooling load needs while storing excess cooling in the TES tank.

*7.3c-1b Combined Systems Capable of Heating and Cooling/ Rankine-Cycle Powered Heat Pump*

This system uses heat collected from a flat-plate collector to power a Rankine-Cycle engine. This engine, in turn, powers the compressor of a convention- al heat pump. One of the main advantages of this system is that the Rankine- Cycle engine can be coupled to a generator to produce electrical power when excess solar heat is

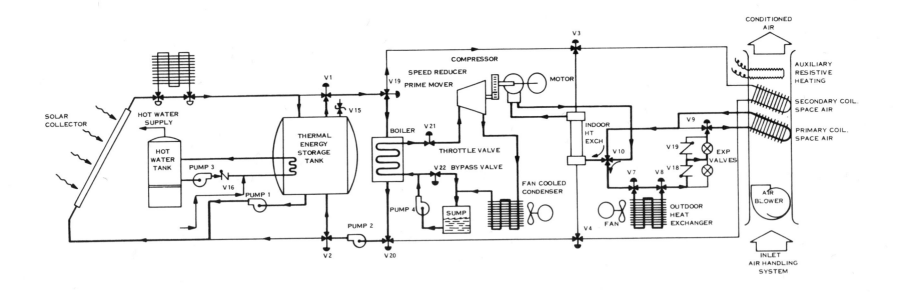

**FIGURE 7.23** SOLAR RANKINE COOLING SYSTEM. *Source: Proceedings of the "Solar Heating and Cooling for Buildings Workshop," Washington, D.C., 1973.*

available. The same generator can be reversed, and, by applying electrical power from an external source, used as a motor to power the compressor or used as a motor operated at part-power to aid the Rankine Engine.

The solar Rankine cooling system is similar to the solar-assisted heat pump except that in the Rankine system an engine loop is inserted between the TES unit and the heat pump circuit. Inasmuch as the heating mode of the solar Rankine system is identical to that of the heat pump, only the cooling mode will be described. *Cooling Mode:* See figure 7.23.

The solar Rankine cooling system can operate in either of two modes: Using solar energy, the Rankine can drive the heat pump compressor or a back up auxiliary motor can be used to drive the compressor in a conventional manner. The output shaft of the Rankine engine is connected to the heat pump compressor through a clutch so that the compressor can operate in the latter mode.

The operation of the collector, the hot water loop, and the air handling unit, are similar to that described in the direct heat exchange system and the direct solar-assisted heat pump system.

## 7.4 Interface of Subsystems and Structures (Architectural Implications)

The basic envelope consideration, when using solar energy to provide heating and cooling is the provision of a space that is optimized for energy reduction. Generally, the present attitude toward solar heating and/or cooling systems is one of regarding them as comparable to traditional energy systems rather than viewing them on the basis of their own unique parameters. What is needed is the development of careful techniques in building design-- techniques that are more sensitive to natural processes-- so that the whole fabric of the building is shaped to respond, without the aid of mechanical devices, to the positive and negative

effects of temperature, humidity, winds and radiation. Only when this is done should the integration of solar energy systems take place.

## 7.4a Architectural Component Considerations/The Collector

The collector is a dominant element because of its sheer size and its orientation characteristics. Two basic options exist: to incorporate the collector into the roof structure or to place it on the ground.

## 7.4a-1 Roof Placement

Roof placement of the collector partially eliminates the cost of a collector because it allows for a reduction in the cost of roofing material. If the flat-plate collector is to be built integrally with the roof, the roof pitch and orientation will necessarily be dictated by the requirements of the collector. As previously stated,

the optimum angle and orientation for the flat-plate collector (see section 7.2b) is the angle of latitude plus 12-15° and 10° west of due south to take advantage of the higher afternoon temperatures. Designing a structure incorporating the "optimum" angle and orientation commits every structure to an unbroken monotony. There is, however, an acceptable area of variance surrounding these optimum values which will allow the solar space heating and cooling system to function normally, thus suggesting greater freedom in building design. In other words, while a southerly orientation is optimum from the point of view of total radiation that can be collected, a collector oriented as much as 45° off of south will still perform fairly well, allowing considerable choice in building orientation.

### 7.4a-2  Ground Placement

Separating the collector from the living space can permit greater flexibility in house design than can incorporating the collector within the structure. The collector cannot, however, provide the dual function of shelter-plus-collector discussed above. Ground placement of the collector results in large heat losses through the back of the collector, whereas roof placement allows the backward heat loss to facilitate space heating. An increase in the length of the mechanical run between a collector and the living space is necessary when the two are separated, resulting in greater heat loss and greater cost. If glass is to be used as a transparent layer of the collector, consideration must be given to the elimination of damage due to ground traffic.

### 7.4a-3  Collector Size and Reduction

Inasmuch as the sheer mass and size of the collector create severe design constraints, methods of reducing the overall size should be investigated thoroughly.

For each 2 square feet of floor area of a house, 1 square foot of collector surface is required. This is a generalized statement and is included to give an idea of the physical size needed. For the specific sizing of a collector, see section 7.5.

One method of reducing the overall collector size is to use reflective optics to focus the sun's energy on a standard flat-plate collector. Wormser Scientific Corporation in Stamford, Connecticut has developed a solar heating system employing a reflective pyramid optic system mounted in the attic space of a residence. The pyramid, or the concentrating portion, is made of up the inside roof rafters, the ceiling joists, and two inclined vertical side panels, all of which are covered by aluminized mylar. At the truncated apex of this pyramid is situated a standard flat-plate collector. (See figure 7.24.)

The mouth of the pyramid is a hinged, vertical, movable panel which forms the south

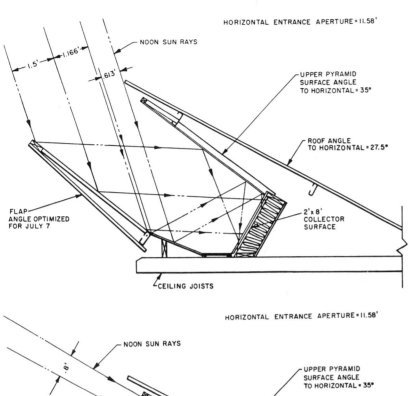

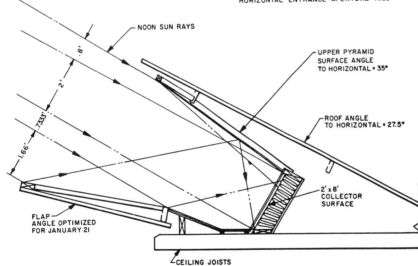

FIGURE 7.24 CONSTRUCTION DETAIL FOR PYRAMIDAL OPTICAL CONCENTRATOR. *Reprinted with permission from Wormser Scientific.*

side of the roof. This panel is adjustable, so it can be placed at the optimum angle to the sun's seasonal elevation. (See figure 7.24.)

Some of the advantages of this system are:[13]

1. The area, and hence, the overall size, weight, and cost of the flat-plate collector is reduced in proportion to the optical gain of the pyramidal reflector from a minimum of a factor of 2X to a maximum in excess of 6X.

2. Because the temperature of a flat-plate collector is proportional to the energy incident per unit area which is a function of the net optical gain of the system, the increased temperatures of a collector **are more** conducive for use in absorptive air-conditioning systems.

3. Heat losses from the collector plate due to conduction will be minimized as a result of the reduction in size of the collector assembly.

4. The movable, hinged,

reflective panel can be adjusted to the optimum angle of the sun's elevation, regardless of the season and geographical location.

5. The moving of the hinged reflective panel does not require complex tracking assemblies.

6. This type of system can easily be retrofitted into the attic structure of a house of conventional design and construction.

### 7.4b Architectural Component Considerations/ Storage Systems

Other than requiring sufficient space and access within the structure, a storage system does not usually pose a major architectural problem. The most common location for storage has been the basement space. The storage facility should be located within the space that is to be heated and/or cooled to avoid unnecessary heat exchanges without outside walls or unheated, uncooled spaces. Storage facilities could be incorporated in the structure

of the building, thereby providing a dual function as a wall or floor.

### 7.5 General Systems Sizing

The equations discussed below are sufficient for design calculations and are not intended for actual size determinants. The equations are included to establish the interrelationships that exist between available solar radiation, thermal performance of collector, collector size, and heat storage capacity. The following equations are adapted from *Solar Energy and the Natural House* by Edward Hoskins.

Thermal performance of a flat-plate solar collector can be found by the following equation:

(1) $q_u = 0.64[q_a - U_L(t_{ef} - t_a)]$

where:

$q_u$ = net amount of useful heat collected, BTU/sq. ft. of collector/day

$q_a$ = amount of solar energy absorbed inside the collector, BTU/sq.ft. of collector/day

(2) $q_a = f(I)$

where:

$I$ = total amount of radiation falling on the surface of the collector, BTU/sq.ft. Appendix A-1

$f$ = fraction of incident total solar radiation that is usefully absorbed in the collector (values of $f$ found in Appendix A-2)

$U_L$ = total heat loss coefficient (values of $U_L$ found Appendix A-2)

$t_{ef}$ = daily average temperature of the entering

heat removal fluid; for design purposes, $t_{ef}$ is assumed to be $20°F$ below the collector's surface temperature, therefore it can be found from Appendix A-2

$t_a$=daily average outdoor air temperature (during operating hours) found from Appendix A-3

0.64=approximate design value for collector flow factor and overall collector efficiency

*The total area of collector required can be computed from:*

(3) $A_{coll} = \dfrac{Q_{coll}}{q_u}$

$q_u$=net amount of useful heat collected; obtained from equation (1)

$Q_{coll}$=total daily heat output of the solar collector

(4) $Q_{coll} = Q_d + Q_{rchg}$

where:

$Q_d$=daily building heat loss (from section 3.7)

$Q_{rchg}$=amount of heat required per day to recharge storage unit in BTU's

(5) $Q_{rchg} = Q_{stor}(\dfrac{1}{Z})$

(6) $Q_{stor}=n(Q_d)-n(Q_{dLs})$

where:

$Q_{stor}$=amt. of useful heat in storage unit in BTU's

n=number of days which storage is required (3 days equals economical optimum

$Q_d$=design value for daily building heat loss (see section 3.7)

$Q_{dLs}$=daily, unutilized heat loss from the storage unit

Z=number of sequential clear days that are likely to occur throughout the winter (found from U.S. Weather Bureau records)

*Heat Storage Sizing*

(7) Volume of storage material required; computed from:

$V_{storage}=\dfrac{Q_{stor}}{q_{stor}}$

where:

$V_{storage}$=volume of storage material, cu.ft.

$Q_{stor}$=amount of useful heat in storage unit (see equation 6)

$q_{stor}$=amount of heat in storage, BTU/cu.ft.

*Storage Capacity Required*

(8) $q_{stor}=C(t_h-t_l)$

where:

$q_{stor}$=amount of heat in storage, BTU/cu.ft.

C=unit heat capacity of the storage material, BTU/cu.ft./°F (found in Table 7.11)

$t_h$=maximum storage temperature (°F); Appendix A-2

$t_l$=lowest useful storage temperature, (°F); depends upon requirements of heat retrieval system

155

## 7.6 Low Technology Solar Design

*This crisis is not one of sustaining an unnecessarily, undesirably and dangerously high energy habit but a simpler one of getting any energy at all and of getting it without becoming enslaved by debt. This energy is not needed to drive elaborate heating and ventilating equipment and other electro-mechanical gear of dubious necessity. It is needed for more direct applications.*
Colin Moorcraft AD 10/73 p. 634.

It seems appropriate at this time to distinguish between low technology and high technology. The fundamental approach to low (impact) technology design is to generate simple solutions to simple problems. To elaborate further, the following principles and concerns are most likely to be evident where a low technology approach is pursued:

- common, regional materials of low cost are used rather than industrially sophisticated materials of generally high cost
- impact on the environment is of utmost concern, from the materials chosen (including their method of manufacturing) to their ease of installation
- mechanical energy is held to a minimum due to necessary periodic part replacement and the often necessary expertise required for installation and repair
- conversions of energy are held to a minimum and manipulations of energy are avoided such as from thermal to electrical and back to thermal.

Probably one of the simplest uses of solar energy for heating is the solar window. Basically, this is a large expanse of glass which permits solar radiation to penetrate on winter days to augment the standard furnace system. In some cases fuel bills have been between 18% and 30% lower when the window and house were designed properly. The greenhouse effect (discussed earlier) is largely responsible for this, because glass easily transmits shortwave light radiation but not longwave thermal radiation. The light energy changes to thermal energy when it strikes an interior surface. Unfortunately, at least three factors were overlooked in many of the designs: (1) transmission losses through the glass at night, (2) the thermal heat capacity of the interior surfaces, being struck by the solar radiation was not high enough to store the heat, and (3) the time lag was not calculated to assure the release of the heat at a cooler period of time, such as at night. Where the windows were not insulated or covered at night whatever heat gain occurred during the day was lost. Adequate insulation is necessary in the wall structure as well as the glazed surface. An insulating shutter system on the interior could also aid in inhibiting heat transmission. The "bead wall" (discussed in Chapter 3) is also an excellent method. When the wall material's thermal capacities were not accounted for, the spaces often required venting during the day. As the result of this venting, the heating bill was higher due to the lack of stored energy and the large glass

area.

It is well-known that due to several reasons, the quantity of solar radiation penetrating a glazed surface in winter is greater than that filtering in during the summer. There are a number of reasons for this. Some of these are:

1. There are more hours of daylight during the summer than winter but due to the high angle of the sun, less energy strikes the south facing surface. When the sun rises it is (say at 35° N latitude) often north of east and may set north of west. This obviously will vary with each latitude, especially if shading prohibits any direct summer sun from penetrating the surface.
2. Since the sun is closer to the horizon during the winter than the summer, the rays strike the windows at angles closer to 90°, reducing reflective losses.
3. Winter sky radiation (due to atmospheric scattering is twice the amount of summer sky radiation.

What is commonly referred to as the solar wall abides by the same principles as solar windows, but more often is assumed to supply a higher percentage of the heat load. To do this, each designer has found it necessary to view the indoor thermal environment as a complete, integrated man/structure/lighting/ventilating system. Such is the case with the St. George's School in Wallasey, Cheshire (more than 53° north latitude) designed and built by Emslie Morgan in 1961. Figure 7.25 illustrates a section through the building. Basically, the building has a large double glazed solar wall facing south to supply thermal heat during the winter. This thermal energy is used in conjunction with wasted heat from electric lights and the heat given off by the inhabitants. Morgan combines this with a massive structure (9" brick walls, 7" concrete roof) wrapped in five inches of external foamed polystyrene insulation. The solar wall consists of two panes of glass,

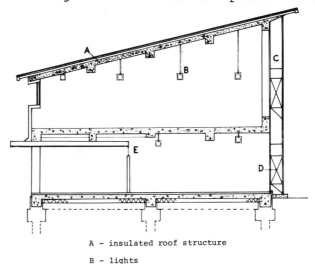

A - insulated roof structure

B - lights

C - double glass wall

D - ventilation windows

FIGURE 7.25 SECTION THROUGH ST. GEORGES SCHOOL.

separated by 24". The inner pane is obscured glass and the outer one completely transparent. This shines a diffused light on the interior. The building has been criticized because of its visual environment and at times inadequate ventilation, but overall the building is a great success. The auxiliary hot water heating system was even removed. Surfaces of the gymnasium and assembly hall had black painted masonry walls where the amount of thermal energy was regulated by white wooden shutters.

Very successful "sun-tempered" dwellings have been built utilizing a black or grey interior plaster wall which absorbs the solar radiation and emits the heat to the space behind it at night. A grey concrete slab can also be used as an effective radiator of stored energy at night. This requires careful insulation to keep the heat from being lost to the ground or an adjacent crawl space under the floor. This also includes heavy edge insulation (figure

3.11.)

Another version of the solar wall is when the collector and storage are integrated in the wall. A successful and well-publicized solar wall of this type was designed by Professor Trombe (director of the Solar Energy Laboratory of the C.N.R.S. in the French Pyrenees) and Jacques Michel. As shown in figure 7.26 the system is very simple. It operates upon the following principles: (1) the use of vertical south facing walls as collectors, (2) the use of the

greenhouse effect, (3) natural convection of heated air, and (4) storing heat in the high thermal capacity of concrete (enough to take care of about two days and two nights). Vents are located at the top and bottom to allow for ventilating the heat, should it not be desired.

A greenhouse may also act as an effective collector of solar energy. This has been successfully done in the arid southwest where humidity from the plants presents no problems to human comfort. The greenhouse

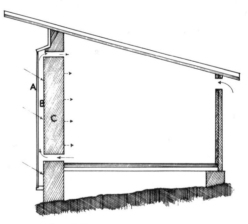

A - 2 layers of glass

B - black roughcast surface

C - concrete wall, structural and heat storage

FIGURE 7.26 THE TROMBE-MICHEL SOLAR WALL. *Source: Architectural Design, October 1973.*

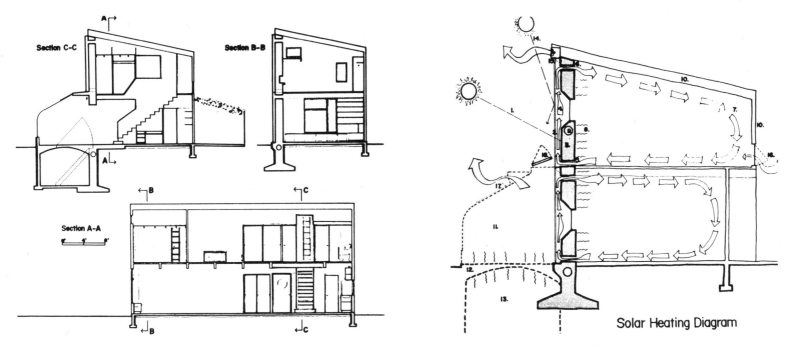

Section C-C

Section B-B

Section A-A

Solar Heating Diagram

FIGURE 7.27   THE PRINCETON HOUSE.   *Reprinted with permission from Dough Kelbaugh.*

is oriented south with a black-coated opposite wall adjacent to the living spaces.  The black wall absorbs the radiation and stores it with its massive thickness.  Rock storage can also be placed underneath the living spaces.  This can be used to store excess heat build-up in the greenhouse.  If an additional collector is integrated into the design, it may supply heat either to the space directly or to the storage.

In Princeton, N.J., archi-tect Doub Kelbaugh and his wife designed and built their home which is heated by a Trombe-Michel solar wall.  The residence is 1900 square feet distributed over two levels. (See figure 7.27)  Solar energy passes through two layers of glazing and a 6" air space to strike a vertical 15" thick concrete wall with a slightly selective coating.  Every room, except the bathrooms, has contact with the solar

wall which functions similarly to the Trombe wall.  The residence also incorporates a double-glazed greenhouse with a thick concrete floor for thermal storage.  The sun provides approximately two-thirds of the heating needs.  In the summer the wall ventilates at the eave allowing for passage of the warmed air.[15]

Steve Baer of Zomeworks Corporation in Albuquerque, New Mexico, has designed and built a house utilizing

a drum-wall. The house is one-story and made up of about 10 rooms. Each room has about 10 faces and is referred to as a zome(or zomohedron). The important features include a reflective operable wall which is opened during the day to allow solar radiation to strike blackened, 55 gallon drums filled with water. Four of the zomes have south facing walls of 25 drums (5 X 5 stack), in a metal framework behind one layer of glass. The insulating reflective wall is composed of a styrofoam core covered with aluminum skin weighing about 1.5 pounds per square foot and could cost about $2.00 a foot.[16] When the wall is down, the drums can pick up 1200 BTU's per square foot of collector. The glass acts to inhibit the outward flow of energy. At night the walls are retracted so that the heat has no where to go but inside. Some cooling effect is noted during the summer when the operable insulating walls are closed during the day and opened at night to allow for irradiation of absorbed heat to the sky. This is also the basic principle behind Harold

Hay's solararchitecture Skytherm house in California.

The Skytherm house is located halfway between Los Angeles and San Francisco at about 35°27' north latitude. The house is similar in many ways to his Phoenix house discussed in Chapter 4. Again, the roof is the collector with four large plastic water bags which lie between five extruded aliminum tracks on a ribbed steel roof with 12' spans. The average depth of water is 10" and the total quantity of water is about 7000 gallons.

There are nine large rectangular polyurethane foam panels laid on the horizontal which move along the tracks. For heating during the day, the panels are stacked above the carport. The solar radiation is absorbed by the water bags and the black plastic sheet under the bags. The four 8' X 38' bags are of tedlar film. At night the panels ride on the trackways by either manual means or by a 1/4 hp motor with sprockets and chains to cover the water bags and force the heat by conduction and radiation to the interior space. In the

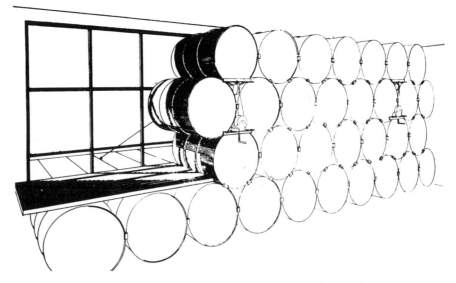

FIGURE **7.28** THE BAER DRUMWALL. *Reprinted with permission from Zomeworks.*

summer, for cooling, the panels cover the bags during the day, insulating them from the radiation. At night the panels are stacked over the carport to allow for any absorbed heat to be irradiated to the atmosphere. The load-bearing walls of the structure are of concrete blocks. Some wall cavities are filled with sand to aid in heat storage.

A regional, labor intensive source of energy has the potential to rally community involvement in the environment and promote more regionally adapted building forms. Low energy applications that are derived from naturally available materials, simple techniques and reaching relatively high efficiencies (in contrast to those elaborate machines which theoretically only promise 18 percent efficiency) promise to contribute more to our energy needs with least negative impact on the environment than considerably higher technology involvements.

Similar to the Skytherm system, in that water is used as both collector and storage, is the "Thermic Diode" solar panel. The "Thermic Diode" solar panel was developed at M.I.T. by Professor Shawn Buckley. The panels are intended to replace the building skin (not the structure). Their approximate size is 4' X 8' X 6" thick. They act as collector, storage and control units for the metabolic requirements of the internal space. The panels are passive devices using no moving parts.

Each panel has a control box. This modulates the flow of heat between the outside and inside of the panel. The box contains two short tubes, one connected to the sensor layer (inlet riser) and the other connected to the storage layer (outlet). On top of the water in the control box is a floating thin layer of oil.

The sensor layer is exposed to the sun where the water becomes heated and rises. As it rises it passes through the inlet riser into the storage layer. A return port at the base of the panel permits cooler water from the storage layer to flow into the sensor layer completing the convective loop. At night when the sensor layer cools down, oil is sucked into the inlet riser. This prevents convective flow and keeps the warmed water in the storage layer to radiate warmth to the interior.

The summer operation requires that the inlet riser in the control box be switched to the storage area. During a summer day the oil floating on top of the diode is sucked into the inlet riser preventing a convective flow. At night as the sensor layer of water is cooled by longwave radiation to the sky it gradually replaces the warmer water in the storage layer by convection through the return port.[17]

FOOTNOTES:

1. Winston, R. "Solar Concentrators of a Novel Design," Paper presented at ISES Conference, Ft. Collins, Colorado, 1974, p. 22.

2. Hoskins, Edward. "Solar Energy and the Natural House," Paper presented

at ISES Conference, Ft. Collins, Colorado, 1974, p. A.1(d).

3. Westinghouse Electric Corporation. *Solar Heating and Cooling of Buildings*, National Science Foundation, 1974, vol. 2, pp. M-10-M-11. (NSF-RA-N-74-023D)

4. TRW. *Solar Heating and Cooling of Buildings*, National Science Foundation, 1974, vol. 2, p. 3.7-37. (NSF-RA-N-74-022B)

5. *Op.cit.* Westinghouse Electric Corp., p. M-14.

6. Yellott, John. "Solar Energy Utilization for Heating and Cooling," *ASHRAE 1974 Applications Handbook*, p. 59.13.

7. *Op.cit.* Westinghouse Electric Corp., p. M-16.

8. *Ibid.*, pp. M-17-M-19.

9. Tybout, R.A. and G. Lof. "Solar House Heating," *Natural Resource Journal*, vol. 10, April 1970, p. 4.

10. *Op.cit.* Westinghouse Electric Corp., p. M-35.

11. *Op.cit.* TRW, p. 3.8-30-3.8-31.

12. Lindsley, E.F. "Air Conditioning Cold from Any Source of Heat," *Popular Science*, August 1974, p. 60.

13. Falbel, Gerald. "Solar House Heating Using Reflective Pyramid Optical Condensing System," Paper presented at ISES Conf., Ft. Collins, Colorado, 1974, p. 3

14. *Op.cit.* Westinghouse Electric Corp., p. M-12.

15. Kelbaugh, D. "Princeton Solar House," Paper delivered to Passive Energy Systems Conference, Albuquerque, N.M., May 1976.

16. *Alternative Sources of Energy*, Book One, p. 39.

17. Buckley, S. "Thermic Diode Solar Panels," Paper presented at the A.S.M.E. Winter Meeting, November, 1974.

REFERENCES:

Anderson, Bruce. *Solar Energy and Shelter Design*, Master's thesis, College of Architecture, Massachusetts Institute of Technology, 1973.

Bennett, Iven. "Monthly Maps of Mean Daily Insolation for the U.S.," *Solar Energy*, vol. 9, no. 3, July-September 1965.

Bhardwaj, R.K.; B.K. Gupta, and R. Prakash. "Performance of a Flat-Plate Solar Collector," *Solar Energy*, vol. 11, July-December 1967.

Boer, K. "A Combined Solar Thermal Elecrrical House," (Paper no. E-H-108, ISES Congress), Paris, 1973.

Burda, E.J., ed. *Applied Solar Energy Research*, Stanford Research Institute, Stanford, California, 1955.

Daniels, Farrington, *Direct Use of the Sun's Energy*, Ballantine Books, New York, 1974.

Daniels, Farrington and John Duffie. *Solar Energy Research*, University of Wisconsin Press, Madison Wisconsin, 1961.

Danz, Ernest. *Architecture and the Sun*, Thames and Hudson, London, 1967.

Davis, C.P. and R.L. Lippen. "Sun Energy Assistance for Air-Type Heat Pumps," *ASHRAE Transactions*, vol. 64, 1958, p. 97.

*A Design Approach for Application of a Solar Energy Heating System to a Geodesic Structure*, Dept. of Design, Southern Illinois University, 1971.

Farber, E.A. "Solar Energy Conversion and Utilization," *Building Systems Design*, June 1972.

Farber, E.A. "Design and Performance of a Compact Solar Refrigeration System," *Engineering Progress at U. of Florida*, Gainesville, vol. 24, no. 2, 1970, p. 70.

General Electric. "Solar Heating and Cooling of Buildings," National Science Foundation, May 1974 (NFS-RA-N-74-021 B).

Green, W.P. *Utilization of Solar Energy for Air Conditioning and Refrigeration in Florida*, Master's thesis, University of Florida, 1936.

Hamilton, Richard, ed. *Space Heating with Solar Energy*, Cabot Solar Energy Research, MIT Press, 1954.

*Handbook of Fundamentals*, (Heating, Refrigerating, Ventilating, and Air Conditioning), published by the American Society of Heating, Refrigeration, and Air Conditioning, New York, 1974.

Halacy, Daniel S. *The Coming Age of Solar Energy*, Harper and Row, New York, 1964.

Hay, H.R. and J.I. Yellott. "Natural Air Conditioning with Roof Ponds and Movable Insulation," *ASHRAE Transactions*, vol. 75, pt. 1, 1969, p. 165.

"Heat from the Sun," *Architectural Forum*, January 1956, vol. 104, no. 1, p. 148.

Hottel, H.C. and B.B. Woertz. "The Performance of Flat-Plate Solar-Heat Collectors," *ASHRAE Transactions*, February 1942, pp. 71-104.

Hottel, H.; Lawrence, A.; and A. Whillier. *Solar Heating Design Problems*.

Solar Energy Research, University of Wisconsin Press, Madison, 1961.

Hoskins, Edward. "Solar Energy and the Natural House," Research Report No. 74-7, Cogswell/Hausler Associates, Chapel Hill, North Carolina, 1974.

Lof, G.O.G. and J.A. Duffie. "Optimization of Focusing Solar Collector Design," *Journal of Engineering for Power*, July 1963, pp. 221-228.

"Low Temperature Engineering Applications of Solar Energy," ASHRAE Technical Committee on Solar Energy Utilization, New York, 1967.

MacKillip, Andrew. "Living Off the Sun," *Ecologist*, Wadebridge, Cornwall, England, vol. 3, no. 7, July 1973, pp. 260-265.

Moorcraft, Collin. "Solar Energy in Housing," *Archi-*

*tectural Design,* October 1973, p. 634 (3-part series).

*The Mother Earth News Handbook of Homemade Power,* Bantam Books, New York, 1974.

Olgyay, Aladar. "Solar Heating for Houses," *Progressive Architecture,* March 1959, pp. 195-203.

"Solar Effects on Building Design," Building Research Institute, Publication No. 1007, 1962.

Swartman, R.K.; Vinh Ha; and A.J. Newton. "Review of Solar Powered Refrigeration," Paper No. 73-WA/Sol-6, ASME, 1974.

Teagan, W.P. and S.L. Sargent. "A Solar-Powered Combined Heating and Cooling System," Paper No. EH-94, ISES Congress, Paris, 1973.

Telkes, Maria. "Space Heating with Solar Energy," *The Scientific Monthly,* vol. 49, no. 6, December 1949.

Telkes, Maria. "Storing Solar Heat in Chemicals," *Heating and Ventilating,* November 1949, p. 80.

Telkes, Maria. "Solar Heat Storage," Paper No. 64-WA/SOL-9, ASME, New York, 1964.

TRW. "Solar Heating and Cooling of Buildings," National Science Foundation, NSF/RA/N-44-023 B, 1974. 3 volumes

Whillier, Austin. "Principles of Solar House Design," *Progressive Architecture,* May 1955, pp. 122-126.

Whillier, Austin. *Solar Energy Collection and Its Utilizationfor House Heating,* Master's thesis, M.I.T., 1953.

Zarem, A.M. and Duane D. Erway. *Introduction to the Utilization of Solar Energy,* McGraw Hill, New York, 1963.

# 8. Organic Fuels

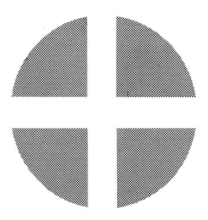

The disposal of both organic and inorganic waste is a serious question to all concerned about our environment. Lately, there has been increasing concern over the pollution of rivers and lakes due to the raw sewage which is being dumped by municipal systems. Table 8.1 gives the approximate amount of available organic wastes generated in 1971. The problems associated with the disposing of this waste is, in many cases, the problem of designers, especially those associated with community development. There exist situations where adding to the municipal sewage system would further perpetuate environmental pollution, or, if a septic tank is used, the residue may endanger the purity of the water table. This chapter deals with specific alternatives to those problems and many others. Sections 8.2 - 8.6 explain how a system may be developed which extracts usable energy from waste decomposition.

## 8.1  Alternative Waste Disposal Systems

The "average" North American family uses 88,000 gallons of water, and 40% of this is used for toilet flushing.[1] McGill University's School of Architecture, in coordination with the Brace Research Institute,[2] conducted a survey of alternatives to the flush toilet. This survey is the primary source of information in this section. The alternatives to the wasteful consumption of water not only apply to people in those areas of the world where water is scarce, but in any place where there is a concern about water pollution and/or an interest in storing waste for anaerobic digestion and methane generation on either the individual or community scale.

Winblad[3] classifies waste disposal systems by their various processes: first, *infiltration*, the absorption and dispersion of human excreta in the soil and ground water; second, *removal*, referring to the transportation of excreta by vehicle or pipe to sewage oxidation ponds, bodies of water, or further processing; third, *destruc-tion*, wherein the waste is reduced by combustion; and *decomposition*, where microbiological action occurs.

Infiltration is the oldest, and probably the most widespread, method of disposal. This process can occur with or without water and is not affected by temperature variations. It is dependent only upon the absorption capacity of the soil (percolation) and whether a sufficient area is allowed for dispersion. The pit latrine uses no water and operates on the basic principle of infiltration and decomposi-

| Source: | | 1971 | 1980 |
|---|---|---|---|
| Manure..........million tons/year | | 200 | 266 |
| Urban refure...........do......... | | 129 | 222 |
| Logging and wood manufacturing residues...............do........ | | 55 | 59 |
| Agriculture crops and food wastes[1] ...................,.....do......... | | 390 | 390 |
| Industrial wastes[2].....do....... | | 44 | 50 |
| Municipal sewage solids.........do | | 12 | 14 |
| Miscellaneous organic wastes....do | | 50 | 60 |
| Total......,.....do.......... | | 880 | 1,061 |
| Net oil potential[3]........:million barrels................... | | 1,098 | 1,330 |
| Net gas for fuel potential[4]....... trillion cubic feet.....،........ | | 8.8 | 10.6 |

[1] Assuming 70 percent dry organic solids in major agricultural crop waste solids (6).

[2] Based on 110 million tons of industrial wastes per year in 1971 (5-6).

[3] Quantities of oil are based on conversion of wastes to oil by reacting carbon monoxide and water. Net oil produced based on 1.25 barrels per ton of dry organic waste.

[4] Gas estimate is based on 5.0 cubic feet of methane produced from each pound or organic material (7).

**TABLE** 8.1   ESTIMATES OF ORGANIC WASTE GENERATED IN 1971 and 1980. *Source: Energy Potential from Organic Wastes: A Review of the Quantities and Sources, by L.L. Anderson, U.S. Government Printing Office, 1972.*

tion. It consists of a hole dug in the ground, a squatting plate, fly screen and a waterproof shelter. The liquid waste infiltrates into the ground and the solid waste decomposes. When the pit is filled, the shelter can be moved to another area. This method does not adapt to heavy usage, such as in urban areas, due to its slow processes.

The aqua privy system utilizes only about one quart of water per usage but is dependent upon a high capacity of absorption by the

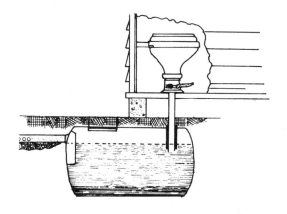

FIGURE 8.1 AQUA PRIVY.
*Source: Stop the Five Gallon Flush! School of Architecture, McGill University.*

soil and can be utilized only where no ground water pollution can occur. The system consists of a tank made of steel or concrete, sometimes divided into two or three compartments, and maintains a constant water level. A vertical pipe extends down from the toilet seat to below the liquid level. (See figure 8.1) The one quart of water added after each use displaces the effluent to outlet pipes when only one compartment tank is used. If two or more are used then the waste is displaced from the first anaerobic decomposition compartment to an aerobic decomposition compartment. All gases in this case are vented to the outside. The wastes then go to leaching pits or direct absorption by the soil. By the nature of the system, the solids build up and must be removed at infrequent intervals.

The septic tank is probably the next most common type of infiltration system. It operates in a similar manner to an aqua privy, but the holding tank is not directly under the toilet. This system still uses about five gallons of water to wash the

waste to the tank and requires infrequent removal of solids, usually by a vacuum tank.

Within the removal classification there are two categories: manual and mechanical. There are many forms of manual removal, the simplest being the bucket type. Waste is deposited in the bucket and then the bucket is removed and cleaned. This process uses no water and requires little investment. It is potentially dangerous to health however, and disposal of the waste can produce some problems. The chemical manual removal type is basically a bucket with chemicals added to reduce the rate of decomposition and odors. The bucket is sometimes vented to the outside. The toilet itself is inexpensive but the chemicals used are not, and they must be handled carefully, as they usually contain lye. Another form of chemical toilet is one that operates an electric pump and recycles the chemicals for flushing. This is a relatively expensive type,

and entails the same problems of disposal. These are of the type used on passenger planes.

The freeze toilet, developed in Sweden, consists of a plastic bag into which the waste is deposited. The bag is then frozen. This eliminates the health hazard, and the waste can be composited. No water is used, but either gas or electricity is required. It entails a high initial cost, but the operating expenses are low.

The packing toilet, also developed in Sweden, uses plastic bags which are sealed, then dropped into a larger bag. This requires no water, electricity or potentially dangerous chemicals, but the larger bag must be dumped at intervals.

The water-borne system is the most frequently found type of Mechanical Removal System. This is the system by which flush toilets are used and the waste is transferred by water to a point of discharge, sometimes a sewage treatment plant but all too often, *directly into a river or lake*. These **toilets** use between two and seven gallons of water with each flushing. Most toilets use five. The water-borne system works ideally for urban density areas. Alternatives should be sought, not for the toilet, but for our waste disposal system as a whole, to prevent sewage from going directly into rivers and lakes with little or no treatment.

The vacuum truck, or privy vault, is another form of mechanical removal. A ventilated steel tank or concrete vault is located directly below the toilet, and the waste falls directly into the tank. Accessibility of the vacuum truck must be maintained as the tank requires emptying at frequent intervals. A disadvantage is that odors are released at the time the tank is being emptied, but there is no need for water or chemicals.

In Sweden, a vacuum network system of interconnected toilets was developed in 1957. Waste is sucked into a holding tank by a vacuum having a pressure of -0.5 atmospheres. Each use requires one quart of water. The waste can be transported 640 feet horizontally and 16 feet vertically at the above in-network pressure.

Similar to the vacuum truck system is the chemical toilet whose tank is accessible from the exterior of the building. A 150 gallon tank may contain about 25 lbs. of lye and about 12 gallons of water. The chemicals kill bacteria, inhibit decomposition and liquify much of the solid material, but again, this tank must be emptied and its contents disposed of cautiously.

Under development in the United States is a recirculating fluid toilet which uses a water-tight tank inside or outside the house where a fluid is substituted for water. This liquid is not miscible with the waste. At the tank the waste and fluid are separated and the fluid is recycled for flushing. Several fixtures can use one tank. No water or dangerous chemicals are used, but the tank must periodically be emptied.

Within the destruction classification is the incinerating toilet. This

toilet consists of a bowl and a combustion chamber below it. It requires electricity, oil, or propane gas and destructs the waste thoroughly, leaving only ashes. The ashes must be removed periodically and can be used as a fertilizer. Some systems use a liner which absorbs the liquid waste and is combusted also. Fumes are vented to the outside. They are used primarily in cold regions such as Scandinavia, Canada or the Arctic.

Decomposition of wastes can be done by composting or continuous aeration. Composting offers the potential to decompose animal and human waste for fertilizer. Compost privys range from the simple to the mechanically complex. In Sweden, a small scale privy that uses human and kitchen waste is manufactured by Clivus A B. This system has a garbage chute, toilet, exhaust duct and a decomposition chamber as one single fiberglas unit. The unit is quite large and demands several design considerations. At the lowest point in the tank, an access door is needed to remove the fertilized humus, which is about 10% of the original matter. Some of these systems use electric coils or hot air to heat the chamber. Figure 8.2 illustrates the unit.

The continuous aeration system combines aerobic decomposition with the flush toilet. This system requires one or two tanks into which waste is discharged. Each tank must be continuously aerated by a pump. The aerated liquid is recycled for flushing. Aeration can be achieved by circulating the water continuously in the system. The water must be changed at least once a year. This system is not without problems; over-use creates odors, but if it is not used frequently enough, the bacteria die. This causes the flush water to smell for the first few days of use. McGill University built a small unit that operates off a 12 volt windmill-operated aquarium pump.

The Bio-Pure Company of Tulatatin, Oregon markets a home aerobic sewage unit. This system uses an electrically-driven air compressor mounted externally atop the unit to bring sewage, water and oxygen-using (aerobic) bacteria together in an atmosphere promoting bacterial decomposition at efficiencies up to 99%. The system has a high initial cost. It was designed for areas where sewage systems are outlawed or where a central sewage facility is out of the question. This system is better than septic tank

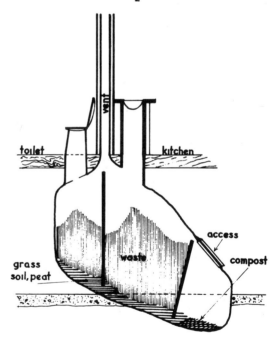

FIGURE 8.2 THE CLIVUS WASTE DISPOSAL UNIT. *Source: Malcolm Wells, Architect, Cherry Hill, New Jersey.*

systems because there is no chance of ground water pollution.

Graham Caine has experimented in London with an algae digester for decomposition. It is a closed loop system of handling waste disposal which produces gas and fertilizer. It combines a solar heated algae tank, a digester and a compost privy. The ultra-violet rays break down pathogens. The algae and the solids are then composted for methane gas ($CH_4$). This system will be discussed further in Chapter 9.

These alternatives were presented for the purpose of making available several means for disposing of human waste. There are many cases where the disposing of waste can be used to benefit other life functions (ex. $CH_4$, fertilizer, etc.) in areas where either a waterborne system cannot operate or is not feasible, or where environmental problems exist.

## 8.2 Anaerobic Digestion for the Production of Methane Gas

Methane is a by-product of aerobic decomposition of organic waste. The fuel gas has a BTU factor of between 400 and 900 and is the main constituent of natural gas. The natural gas used in North America has a BTU factor of between 1000 to 1200. Methane has the potential to substitute for contemporary uses of natural gas, which is facing depletion.

The architectural concerns of methane gas focus primarily on the community - village scale. The rural homestead is, at present, probably the optimum existing condition, but by the nature of the scale there is little or no contact with the building industry and designers. As both high-cost and low-cost communities begin to replace the sprawling, suburban, single-layer approach to solving the housing crisis, waste disposal and fuel requirements are critical questions. The integration of these concerns offers potentials for a community to operate on total

natural energy systems. The integration of wind generators, solar energy and waste disposal for methane gas is discussed with examples in the next chapter. Here the focus will be on the processes, hardware and potential for community and rural homestead systems of waste disposal.

The phenomena of photosynthesis supports all levels of life from the crudest to the most advanced. It is the process by which plants convert light, primarily from the blue and red bands of the visible spectrum, into chemical energy. During the process plants take in carbon dioxide, water and solar radiation to form long molecules known as carbohydrates. Figure 8.3 illustrates the process. The entire photosynthetic process requires only one-tenth of one percent of the total solar radiation reaching the earth's surface to sustain life.[4] These carbohydrates and many other chemicals are found in all life forms that consume plants and their waste. When the plants and animals die and decompose in the earth or in a body of water, several

different reactions may occur depending upon the active environmental influences. When decomposition occurs in the absence of oxygen, that is, in an aerobic medium such as lake bottoms, marshes, swamps, or within the earth's crust, methane is given off. When decomposition occurs under pressure in the earth, fossil fuels are the result. Assisting in the decomposition that occurs under lake and swamp bottoms and in specifically-designed digesters, are anaerobic bacteria. These bacteria live within certain temperature ranges and break down carbon (in the form of carbohydrates) and nitrogen (as proteins, nitrates, ammonia, etc.). The bacteria usually consume about 30 times as much carbon as nitrogen. The ratio of carbon to nitrogen is very important in the production of methane.

The digestion of organic waste can be carried out in similar conditions to those mentioned above in the controlled atmosphere of a digester. If methane is to be trapped and used as a fuel, then a considerable amount of organic waste (vegetable or manure) must be present. The homesteader is in a good position to generate enough gas to sustain his needs from farm animal waste and be able to utilize the fertilizer resulting from the decomposition. The community gains by having its organic waste disposal problem solved and by obtaining a fuel suitable to answer a proportion of its needs.

The designer(s) involved in community planning must take responsibility for the consequences of organic waste disposal. To ignore the potential resources from this waste may in the future prove to be suicidal. Much energy and resources are involved in current forms of waste disposal, and they still prove to be polluting. Water-borne sewage pouring into the oceans, rivers and lakes accelerate the loss of phosphorus (33 million tons a year)[5] from the biosphere, and, combined with nitrates, endanger present forms of aquatic life. When the same bodies of water are the source for drinking water, extensive chemical and energy-intensive processes

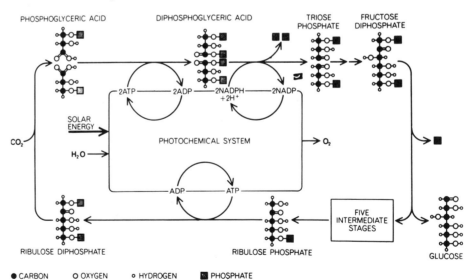

FIGURE 8.3 From "The Biosphere" by G. Evelyn Hutchinson. Copyright © 1970 by Scientific American, Inc. All rights reserved.

171

are required for purifying.

Combined anaerobic and aerobic decomposition of waste on both the community and rural home scale offers a far more ecological response. Figure 8.4 illustrates a typical unit. Assuming a typical family generates 51 pounds of waste a day, it is possible to generate 15-20 cubic feet of gas per day, which is enough to meet cooking requirements.[6] Table 8.2 gives the data of the available organic waste in the United States and what the total fuel value of methane is at present.

Figure 8.5 illustrates a waste cycle for a small community. The scale could be enlarged or reduced to adapt to larger villages or the homestead. It should be noted that flush toilets, as commonly used in America, could not be used due to the excess amount of water required.

The uses of the bio-gas (term used by Ram Bux Singh)[7] can be extended to any usage where natural gas is presently employed. This can include internal combustion engines (cars, gasoline-powered generators, farm equipment, etc.), cooking, lighting and heating. Depending upon the amount of calculated gas received, the operations usually focus on refrigeration and cooking with some storage for small engines. As discussed earlier in Chapters 6 and 7, heating could better be supplied by solar energy and electrical demands by wind or water energy.

Table 8.3 gives the approximate cubic feet of gas required for particular

needs. To compress methane gas into methane liquid is only about 25% efficient.[8] According to studies done by the New Alchemy Institute, at 25% compressor efficiency it would take .52 hp/hr or 1320 BTU to compress 25,300 BTU of Biogas to provide 6350 BTU worth of work, 75% of the available energy is lost in heat. The laws of thermodynamics state that each quantity of energy has a quality called *entropy*. Entropy is the measurement of disorder associated with the energy. The Second law states that any

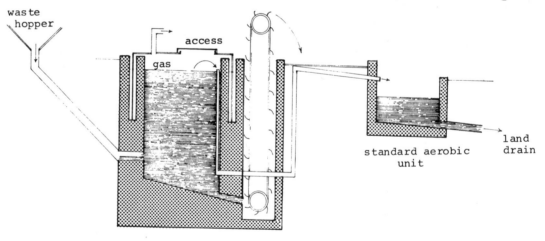

Domestic Sewage Unit Utilizing
Anaerobic & Aerobic Processes

FIGURE 8.4  DIAGRAM OF A DOMESTIC SEWAGE PLANT. *Source: Andrew MacKillop, Low Impact Technology.*

transformation of energy, either mechanical or thermal, increases in entropy. The more often a source of energy is transformed, the less the efficiency.

It is far more efficient to use the gas directly.

With two billion tons of manure produced annually by livestock alone in the United States, and city organic matter, the questions of sanitary collection and disposal are staggering. Ram Bux Singh has outlined a projected cost for installing a bio-gas plant in the United States.  Table 8.4 gives approximate costs. It would be pointless to relate cost factors anymore, since every aspect is subject to fluctuation.

*8.3  The Process and Requirements*

The production of methane is done within a *digester*. There are two forms of digesters; the *batch-load* and the *continuous feed*.  The batch-load digesters are filled once, sealed, and emptied after the gas has been produced.  The

I.  Fuel Value of U.S. Methane Resources
  A.  Organic wastes in U.S./year.........2 billion tons (wet weight), 800 million tons (dry weight)
  B.  Dry organic waste readily collectable.......136.3 million tons
  C.  Methane available from "B"........1.36 trillion $ft^3$/year (@ 10,000 $ft^3$/ton)*
  D.  Fuel value of methane from "C"......1,360 trillion BTU/yr (1000 BTU/$ft^3$)

II.  Fuel Consumption of U.S. Farm Equipment
  A.  Total gasoline consumed (1965).......7 billion gallons/year
  B.  Total energy consumed by "A".......945 trillion BTU/year (1 gallon gasoline = 135,000 BTU)

III.  Total U.S. Natural Gas Consumption (1970)....19,000 trillion BTU

IV.  Total U.S. Energy Consumption (1970)......64,000 trillion BTU

*Urban refuse; higher figure for manure and agricultural wastes.

TABLE 8.2  AVAILABLE ORGANIC WASTE AND THEIR FUEL VALUE. *Source:  New Alchemy Institute Newsletter No. 3.*

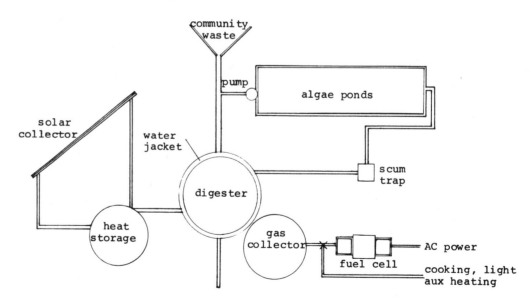

FIGURE 8.5  COMMUNITY ORGANIC WASTE SYSTEM.

| Use | Ft$^3$ |
|---|---|
| Lighting | 2.5 mantle/hr |
| Cooking | 8-16/hr/2-4"burner |
| | 12-15/person/day |
| Incubator | .5-.7 ft$^3$/hr/ft$^3$ incubat |
| Gas Refrigerator | 1.2/ft$^3$/hr/ft$^3$ refrig. |
| Gasoline Engine* | |
|   CH$_4$ | 11/brake Hp/hr |
|   Bio-Gas | 16/brake Hp/hr |
| For Gasoline | |
|   CH$_4$ | 135-160/gallon |
|   Bio-Gas | 180-250/gallon |
| For Diesel Oil | |
|   CH$_4$ | 150-188/gallon |
|   Bio-Gas | 200-278/gallon |

*25% efficiency

TABLE 8.3   USES FOR METHANE. *Source:   New Alchemy Institute Newsletter No. 3.   To obtain write New Alchemy Institute-West, P. O. Box 376, Pescadero, California 94060.   $3.00*

continuous feed digester is fed a certain amount regularly so that fertilizer and gas are continuously being produced. In this type a "slurry," which is a mixture of water and waste, is fed daily. The slurry flows into one end and displaces the previously fed load, which has already begun to decompose. Each load distributes itself down the digester to a point where the bacteria are active and gas is being produced. As the digestion slows down towards the outlet, the contents stratify into layers. Figure 8.6 illustrates this stratification. The inorganic matter, such as sand, is at the base. The sludge is the manure and other waste reduced to about 40% of its original volume. This is an excellent fertilizer for crops or algae cultures. The supernatant is actually the spent liquids of the original slurry compound. The scum is a course, fibrous material which can, in small amounts, act as an insulator but in large amounts inhibit the continual action of the digester. Before this occurs, it must be removed.

As mentioned before, the

COST OF THE PLANT. At present level of prices the installation cost of different sizes of Bio-Gas plant is estimated as below:

| No. Size of the Plant | | Approximate Cost of the Installation in India | Approximate Cost of the Installation in U.S.A. | Remarks |
|---|---|---|---|---|
| 1 | 2 | 3 | 4 | 5 |
| 1. 100 cu.ft. gas production/day | | $ 140 | $ 400 | Family Size |
| 2. 250 cu.ft. gas production/day | | $ 350 | $ 900 | Joint Family Size |
| 3. 500 cu.ft. gas production/day | | $ 600 | $1800 | Farm Size |
| 4. 1250 cu.ft. gas production/day | | $1500 | $4000 | Industrial Size |
| 5. 2000 cu.ft. gas production/day | | $2250 | $5500 | Industrial Size |

TABLE 8.4   COST OF A BIO-GAS PLANT. *Source:   Ram Bux Singh, Bio-Gas Plant.*

anaerobic digestion process involves a complex series of reactions stimulated by a mixed culture of bacteria. The decomposition can be broken down into two phases: a liquefaction stage and a gasification stage, where the products of the first phase are used in the second. The bacteria occur naturally in excrement and, as the process continues, will propagate. Sometimes it is useful to put into the mixture some of the remains of the previous mixture to aid in bacteria growth of subsequent batches. The liquefaction stage occurs when enzymes catalyze the hydrolysis of complex carbohydrates into sugars and alchohols; proteins to peptides and amino acids and fats to fatty acids.[9] These then continue to break down.

The gasification stage reduces the products of the liquefaction phase into final products of carbon dioxide, methane and an inert organic residue or digested sludge. The two phases are dependent upon the environmental conditions surrounding the process and the composition of whatever material is being decomposed. Since two forms of bacteria are present at different times, the two factors mentioned will dictate which is in control and when.

When methane gas is the primary concern, it is important to maintain a balance between the bacteria that produce organic acids during the liquefaction phase and the bacteria that produce methane gas during the gasification phase. Close attention must be paid to the environment of these bacteria, most especially to pH (a (acidity or basisity), liquid content and the composition of the waste.

Digestion by bacteria will occur at temperatures ranging between 32°F to 156°F. However, there are two ranges in which optimum gas production occurs. These ranges are characterized by the types of gas-producing bacteria which favor them. The ranges are 85°F to 105°F and 120°F to 140°F. The upper range bacteria or "thermophilic" (heat-loving) are less stable in fluctuating environmental conditions. Within the lower range, gas is produced more rapidly and is optimum at about 95°F. In the next section we discuss the manner by which the digester's contents are maintained in a stable condition. It should be noted that temperature suggestions can only be general, due to the varying compositions of the waste which could support different forms of bacteria.

When the digestion process begins, more carbon dioxide ($CO_2$) is given off than methane ($CH_4$). Further

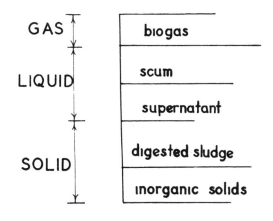

FIGURE 8.6  LAYERING OF PRODUCTS IN A DIGESTER. *Source: New Alchemy Institute Newsletter No. 3.*

175

along, the mixture becomes less acid and methane fermentation begins. The successful pH range is 6.0-8.0, with the best results achieved when the pH is about 7.0 for sewage digesters. When the pH level is slightly alkaline (above 7.0) the acidic carbon dioxide that is formed will tend to bring it down, but if it becomes too acidic, it will be toxic to the bacteria and digestion may stop. When raw animal and vegetable matter are the primary constituents of the mixture, a slightly more alkaline range (8.0-8.5) is advisable. The pH level may be checked with pH paper dipped into the effluent coming from the outlet.

The potential fermentation of the organic matter is further dependent upon the ratio of liquid to solid. The type of materials usually digested contain at least 18% solids and should be diluted down to 7-9% solid prior to feeding into the digester.

As mentioned earlier the carbon to nitrogen (C/N) ratio is a critical factor

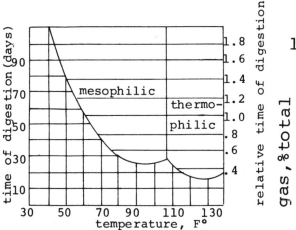 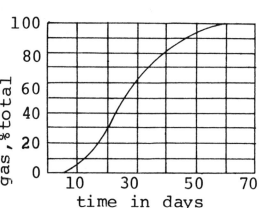

GRAPHS OF DIGESTION TIME, TEMPERATURE AND GAS PRODUCTION
*Source: Alternatives, Autumn 1973*

to the continued action of the bacteria. The basic idea of anaerobic fermentation is to convert the available carbon to methane and carbon dioxide, which as little loss of available nitrogen as possible so the fertility of the fertilizer is not decreased.[10] The basic C/N ratio is 30:1, where the carbon is consumed thirty times faster than nitrogen. It is best to have a sample of the types of waste to be used analyzed in a laboratory prior to digestion to help establish the ratio.

There are other nutritional substances which aid digestion which usually occur in the mixture. These substances include calcium, magnesium, potassium, zinc and iron. The primary nutrients, of course, are carbon, nitrogen, phosphorus and sulphur.

There are some elements which are basically toxic. These are: heavy dosages of metals such as chromium (Cr), copper (Cu), nickel (Ni), zinc (Zn) and mercury (Hg), ammonia gas ($NH_3$) and synthetic detergents. In house-

hold use, these must be spared any form of input.

## 8.4 Digester Design and Types

Digester design is by no means new. Anaerobic decomposition is a standard procedure in sewage treatment. Rarely though, do treatment plants ever recover the methane generated. When they do, it is recycled to heat the plant and its operations, and the remaining gas is discharged into the atmosphere. As mentioned before, the production methods are easily adapted to the community scale, even where a sewage treatment plant exists. The capital invested to adapt the techniques could be recovered in the production of gas.

The two types of digesters currently used, the batch-feed and the continuous-feed, have individual advantages and disadvantages. The batch-feed type is characterized by its sporadic input and production of gas, little daily attention required, and suitability to inputs containing large lumps of solid matter. Batch digesters generally require more labor in loading and emptying than continuous-feed systems. Because of the inconsistancy in gas production and cycle lengths, it is advisable to operate several digesters simultaneously, and out of phase with each other, so that a continuous supply of gas is assured.

The continuous-load digesters utilize a small quantity of raw material every day. This involves little labor, but if difficulties occur, shutdown of the whole plant may result. Continuously feeding diges-

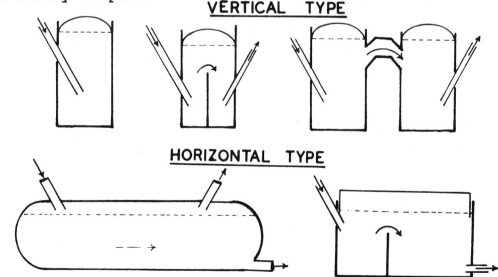

**VERTICAL TYPE**

**HORIZONTAL TYPE**

FIGURE 8.7 TYPES OF CONTINUOUS FEEDING DIGESTERS. *Source:  New Alchemy Institute Newsletter No. 3.*

ters can be of two designs: the vertical mixing and the displacement. Figure 8.7 illustrates these basic designs. In the vertical mixing digester, there are two vertical chambers into which the raw material is put. Raw sewage is loaded into one chamber, and the sludge is drawn off in the other. With the second chamber, further decomposition and production of methane can occur.

The displacement digesters are linear in shape and operate on principles similar to the intestines of an animal. The waste is put in at one end, passes an area of "maximum fermentation," where the bacteria are most active and then is passed through an output. These digesters are easy to operate because the material may be recirculated by reversing its flow within the cylinder, if any form of "souring" or other complications arise. Scum is less likely to form on its greater surface area. When cleaning is necessary due to periodical accumulation of scum and undigestable solids, the displace-

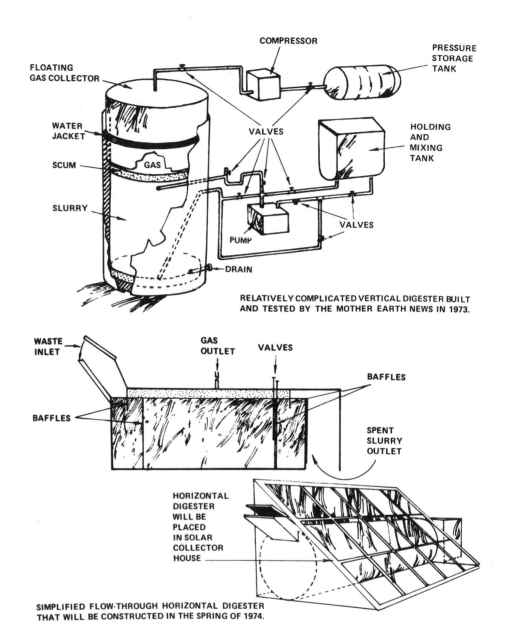

RELATIVELY COMPLICATED VERTICAL DIGESTER BUILT AND TESTED BY THE MOTHER EARTH NEWS IN 1973.

SIMPLIFIED FLOW-THROUGH HORIZONTAL DIGESTER THAT WILL BE CONSTRUCTED IN THE SPRING OF 1974.

MOTHER'S METHANE MAKERS. *Reprinted with permission from Mother Earth News.*

ment digester is easier to maintain than a vertical design.

The size of the digester required for particular functions is dependent upon: (1) the type of digester used; (2) availability of raw materials; (3) length of digester time, which is related to cubic feet of gas required; (4) daily feed volume and (5) the amount of space needed for sludge and effluent. The amount of gas required should be adjusted to the gas production potential of the raw materials available. Table 8.5 gives the expected amount of methane from various sources.

Loading rate for daily feed volume is defined as the amount of raw material (often in pounds of volatile solids) fed to the digester in cubic feet of digester space. Volatile solids (VS) is the amount of solids actually converted to methane by the bacteria. It is actually a measurement of organic solids burned off at about 1000°F. This is basically the carbon-containing material which can be converted to methane. It comes to close to 80%

of most dry materials. What remains after ignition is technically inert material of fixed solids (FS). Table 8.6 gives the data for available VS, FS and total solids (TS). The materials suitable for digestion can be animal or human manure, garbage (vegetable, leftovers, spoiled food), grass clippings, weeds, leaves or any material acceptable for a normal compost pile.

Detention time of the waste material is dependent on the temperature and consistency of the input material and volume of the digester. If manure is used, then it must be diluted from about 18% solids to 7-9%. The slurry might be about the consistancy of cream.[11] As you dilute the raw material the detention time is reduced, but if too much water is used, good fermentation will not occur.

As mentioned before, the optimum temperature is about 95°, but keeping a digester at an operating temperature that high may involve more energy than is worth the time it may save. Figure 8.8 gives the relative gas production according to

Methane Expectations -
(energy efficiency = 80% burning)
1 cow ---- 30 ft.$^3$ biogas per day
            25 pounds shit per day
1 pound corn straw ---- 13 ft.$^3$ biogas
1 pound dry leaves ---- 7.2 ft.$^3$ biogas
1 pound dry straw ---- 15 ft.$^3$ biogas
1 pound "volatile solids" destroyed ---- 18 ft.$^3$ biogas
                                          1.25 lb. biogas
                                          12,000 BTU
1 pound cowshit ---- 0.18 lb. dry solid
  (fresh)            0.14 lb. volatile
                     1 ft.$^3$ biogas at 60°F
                     1.5 ft.$^3$ biogas at 95°F
1 pound dry matter ---- 80% volatile solids
1 kg. dry matter ---- 450 L. gas at 50°F
                      610 L. gas at 68°F
                      760 L. gas at 86°F
1 foot$^3$ biogas ---- 600-700 BTU
1 foot$^3$ natural gas ---- 1,000 BTU
1 foot$^3$ methane ---- 963 BTU
1 foot$^3$ biogas ---- 0.0555 hp-hr.
1 gallon gasoline (US) ---- 200-250 feet biogas
1 gallon gasoline (US) ---- 170 ft.$^3$ washed biogas
1 person ---- 1.2 feet$^2$ gas per day

Useful conversions -
1 hp-hour ---- 2,545 BTU
1 BTU ---- 778 ft.-lb.
1 hp ---- 550 feet lb./second
1 hp ---- 42.4 BTU/minute
1 kw ---- 0.745 kw
1 kw ---- 1.34 hp
1 kw-hr ---- 3413 BTU
1 kw-hr ---- 0.24 lb. carbon burned

TABLE 8.5  DESIGN DATA.
*Source: Methane Digestor Design, Alternatives, Autumn 1973, Vol. 3, No. 1.*

| Average Adult Animal | lbs/day/animal Urine | Feces | Total Solids/Day 20% of Feces | Volatile Solids/Day 80% of TS- 85% for Swine | Livestock Units |
|---|---|---|---|---|---|
| BOVINE (1000 lbs.) | 20 | 52 | 10 | 8.0 | |
| Bulls | | | | | 130-150 |
| Dairy cow | | | | | 120 |
| Under 2 yrs | | | | | 50 |
| Calves | | | | | 10 |
| SWINE (160 lbs.) | 4.0 | 7.5 | 1.5 | | |
| Boar, sow | | | | | 25 |
| Pig 160 lbs. | | | | | 20 |
| Pig 160 lbs. | | | | | 10 |
| Weaners | | | | | 2 |

| | Portion | Amount | %TS | TS/Day | %VS | VS/Day | |
|---|---|---|---|---|---|---|---|
| HUMANS (150 lbs.) | Urine | 2 pints, 2.2 lbs. | 6% | .13 | 75% | .10 | 5 |
| | Feces | 0.5 lbs. | 27% | .14 | 92% | .13 | |
| | Both | 2.7 lbs. | 11% | .30 | 84% | .25 | |
| FOWL | Geese, Turkey (15 lb) | 0.5 | | | | | 2 |
| | Ducks (6 lb) | | | | | | 1.5 |
| | Layer Chicken (3-1/2 lb) | 0.3 | 35% | .10 | 65% | .06 | 1 |
| | Broiler Chicken | 0.1 | | | | | |

TABLE 8.6 Quantity of MANURE GENERATED BY ANIMALS.
*Source: New Alchemy Institute, Newsletter No. 3.*

various temperatures. Depending on the thermal conditions of the area, the methods of heating and/or insulating will vary. In India or other hot areas, the digesters can be above ground and painted black for solar heat absorption. In temperate areas the digesters should be at least partially underground, encased in insulation and heated. The methods of heating are varied. One of the better ways is to run hot water pipes into the digester where either spent bath water, solar-heated water or waste heat from engines near by goes through a heat exchanger. Another method is a water-jacket which surrounds the digester. This method is adequate for a vertical digester with more of the content surface area exposed to the container walls, but in large displacement digesters it may be inadequate. Gas-heated water boilers are one alternative but they do use some of the gas. Insulating materials that are very porous could trap gas mixtures, making the entire plant very dangerous.

Styrofoam sheets are recommended over spun-glass types.

Agitation is required to keep the sludge moving upward in vertical digesters, control scum build-up, and keep large particles from collecting on the bottom. Gas valves, meters, and thermometers should be used to regulate temperature, high pressure in the digester and low pressure in the gas accumulator. Flame arresters are advisable.

The compression of methane should be done with extreme

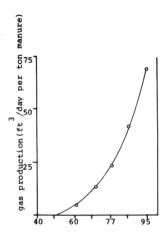

FIGURE 8.8 GRAPH OF RELATIVE GAS PRODUCTION.
*Source: New Alchemy Institute Newsletter No. 3.*

caution. The very first batch of gas that is enough to fill the pipes, scum accumulator and storage tanks should be discharged into the atmosphere. Generally this first gas has too high a proportion of air to gas which makes it highly inflammable to the point of volatility. All transfer lines for transportation and/or compression should be purged of air. This can be done by maintaining a slight positive pressure of gas in the pipelines and storage. Certain appliances require the gas to be stored at specific pressures.

For the gas to be used in conventional natural gas appliances, it must first be scrubbed. This will separate the methane from carbon dioxide and other elements. Carbon dioxide, $CO_2$, and ammonia, $NH_3$, can be removed by bubbling it through lime water (calcium hydroxide, $CaOH_2$). Hydrogen sulfide, $H_2S$, can be scrubbed out by passing it through iron filings. Water vapor may also exist which can be removed through absorptive chemicals if it should be considered a problem. Scrubbed methane is odorless.

Conclusions by the New Alchemy Institute[12] conclude that anaerobic digestion is about 60 to 70 percent efficient in converting organic waste to methane. This does not include the energy required to maintain its processes. If this is included, then the above figure could be called a "conversion rate." Efficiency of digestion can also be determined by a quantifying analysis of the amount of carbon entering the system and the amount of carbon leaving.

It is well known that the remaining sludge is an excellent fertilizer. The content of the fertilizer is dependent upon the amount of nitrogen (N), phosphorus (P), potassium (K) and metallic salts remaining after fermentation. The nitrogen contained in the sludge is in the form of ammonium $(NH_4)$. Many plants, both land and water (algae), prefer the nitrogen in this form rather than in the oxidized form of nitrites following aerobic organic decomposition.[13]

If the sludge is not de-sired as a fertilizer, it may be processed through the ground in a conventional septic tank system or used as a food source for certain strains of algae which when processed may in turn produce more methane gas. Algae (chlorella spp. and scenedesmus spp.) are the optimization of photosynthesis because each cell is a photosynthetic converter.[14] Several experiments by the Sanitary Engineering Research Laboratory (SERL) at Richmond, California and also by Arthur D. Little, Inc. have demonstrated that algae grown on a mixture of nutrients including $CO_2$, harvested and deposited in a methane digester are a viable source of methane gas, however, at this time the problems outweigh the benefits. One main area of concern is the quantity of land required if the algae are grown in ponds. It is estimated that 15 kwh is all that could be generated from a one acre pond under excellent conditions. The other serious problem is that algae production requires a good deal of energy input even if the sun can maintain the temperatures needed. It does have the advantage of a high

turnover rate of organic matter and, if decomposed quickly, it can be integrated into a closed nutritional system which leaves a high nitrogen sludge after decomposition which, in turn, can be used for fertilizer.  In Chpater 9, page 199, Graham Caine's Eco House, which uses an algal regenerative system, is discussed.

*8.5  Fuel Cells*

Fuel cells have their greatest applicability when more than one natural energy source is to be used.  The fuel cell operates around three basic elements:  the *reformer*, which converts hydrocarbon fuels (such as methane) to processed fuel; the *fuel cell*, which produces direct current electricity; and the *inverter*, which converts direct current to alternating current.

The reformer takes hydrocarbon fuels like methane, hydrogen, natural gas or oil through a chemical transformation that disassociates the carbon and hydrogen elements of the fuel.  The

carbon is then combined with oxygen and with the hydrogen is fed as a fuel to the fuel cell.  When using wind energy, the power can operate an electrolysis process to produce hydrogen.  The fuel cell then generates D.C. power that is taken to a static inverter to become A.C. power for conventional use.

Existing means of converting fuel to electricity burn the carbon or hydrocarbon fuels to produce heat, and then from the heat, mechanical energy. The maximum practical cycle

efficiency of these engines is between 40 to 43 percent. The fuel cell, however, eliminates the heat phase and mechanical cycles and converts the chemical energy of fuel directly into electrical energy at twice the efficiency of the best engines.[15]

The basic characteristics of demonstrated fuel cells prove them to be clean, quiet, vibrationless, capable of continual unattended operation, and requiring only minimal maintenance.  They are flexible and adapt to modular installations.

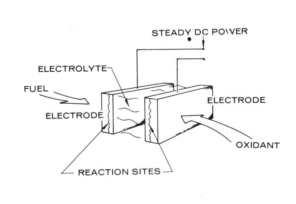
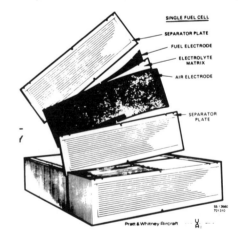

FIGURE 8.9   FUEL CELL ASSEMBLY. *Reprinted with permission of Pratt and Whitney Aircraft.*

## 8.6 Wood Utilization

Wood and other proposed bio-mass fuels offer some outstanding advantages compared to other sources of energy. First and foremost are their renewability. As long as the sun shines and the biosphere remains in balance wood can be available forever if it is harvested on a sustained yield basis. Secondly, nature has provided trees and plants with collectors (the leaves with their chlorophyl) and their own energy accumulators (plant material) which, as long as the plant is still alive, are protected from drastic energy loss through plant deterioration by the plant's natural protective mechanisms. Thirdly, the air pollution aspect of wood combustion is virtually superior to all fossil fuels. Wood contains very little sulfur dioxide ($SO_2$). It generally contains less than 0.1 percent to .05 percent. Fossil fuels such as oil and coal contain 1 to 3 percent sulfur. Sulfur dioxide is the compound which has been linked to various lung diseases and has been found to inhibit the growth rate of plants. Because emissions from fossil fuels contain high percentages of this compound it necessitates its costly removal. Fourthly, the use of wood as a fuel will not interfere with the carbon dioxide balance of the earth. Unlike fossil fuels the forest consumes as much carbon dioxide as it will ultimately release when it is burned. The carbon dioxide that is released when wood is burned will have been collected during the relatively recent past whereas the combustion of fossil fuels will release $CO_2$ that was withdrawn from circulation millions of years ago resulting in a $CO_2$ increase. Carbon dioxide was not normally considered a pollutant at all. It has been recently theorized that if the atmosphere changes significantly the climates of the earth may change. This is a result of carbon dioxide increasing the earth's "greenhouse effect," thus increasing the earth's temperature. Some of the consequences of a temperature rise might include: a shift in global circulation patterns altering the temperatures of land masses which in turn would alter precipitation patterns and possibly flood land masses due to rising sea levels from the melting of polar regions.

No one should draw the conclusion that by-products of wood combustion are completely harmless. Studies and research are now being done by the U.S.D.A. to determine the full environmental impact of burning wood. There is one advantage in that there is a great similarity between these intermediate products of combustion and those liberated in the forest by decay.

We have yet to completely understand the delicate relationships that exist in ecological processes. It is for this reason that the full environmental impact of wood as a fuel source is yet to be determined. Before widespread implementation is to be considered detailed analyses will have to be done to determine the interrelationships that do exist and to determine the load limits that exist for the natural processors that eliminate pollutants from wood combustion.

With the potential increase in the use of wood as a fuel source, it becomes obvious that woodburning devices must be so designed as to attain as complete combustion as possible. The net result of complete combustion is twofold-- one, the heating potential from a given amount of wood is greater, thus reducing the quantity of wood needed and in turn lessening the environmental strain on the wood source. Secondly, the more complete combustion is, the closer we can come to just producing carbon dioxide and water vapor, eliminating harmful pollutants that would normally be released.

## 8.6a   Availability

Larry Gay, in his book *The Complete Book of Heating with Wood*, states that "there is presently an abundance of wood available in the United States, despite many stories in our press to the contrary. It is a fact, however, that there is a serious shortage of certain species, particularly the big trees of high quality. This is of little consequence to woodburning devices since any type of wood can be used.

With the potential of increased usage of forest areas comes the problem of environmental effects. Soil erosion and nutrient loss are both potential problems, especially if whole trees are harvested since then the nutrient-rich small branches, twigs and leaves would not be left in the forest. The question then becomes one of not how much potential wood is available from a forest, but rather what fraction of the volume we can take without upsetting the forest ecosystem.

Forest productivity can actually be increased by thinning and cutting less productive individual trees and using these as a fuel source. There is also a tremendous resource in wood waste such as hogged wood, sawdust, bark, planer shavings and sander dust that has largely remained untapped as a fuel source.

Only through efficient wood-burning devices that utilize wood waste or low grade wood can we guarantee their fuel availability as well as providing a minimum amount of environmental impact.

## 8.6b   Combustion Process

Wood burns in three distinct phases. First, the moisture within the wood is driven off. In the second phase wood breaks down into charcoal where volatile gases and liquids are produced. Finally, the charcoal itself burns.

The volatile gases that are produced in the second phase contain 60 percent of the heat potential in a given quantity of wood. In a fireplace these volatile gases escape combustion and are carried up the chimney. This is one contributing factor to the large inefficiency of fireplaces. In order to utilize the potential of these gases the wood needs to be combusted in a controlled environment. This is where we can see a distinct advantage of enclosed combustion chambers as in a wood stove. Here we have control over the amount of air reaching the flame as well as the path of the volatile gases. With this in mind we can outline the criteria for complete combustion to occur. There must be:

1. adequate air intake,
2. intimate mixture of combustible gases and air,
3. ignition of gas-air mixture, and
4. adequate space for the gases to burn completely.

To better understand this process the following example is given:

In a fireplace the main air supply for combustion is introduced under and around the wood fuel. The charcoal consumes the incoming oxygen in proportion to its thickness, therefore a two-inch bed will consume all the oxygen that it comes in contact with. A thicker bed will burn incompletely, producing carbon monoxide. What results is incomplete combustion with insufficient oxygen to combine with the volatile gases. So the unburned gases escape up the chimney to condense on the flue walls producing creosote.

In a properly designed wood stove secondary air can be induced above the coals to combine with the volatiles so that they can be burned. The more complete combustion is the closer we come to producing only carbon dioxide and water vapor.

## 8.6c Development of a Woodburning Device for Combination with Thermal Storage

The development of a woodburning device or wood furnace system that integrates with a heat storage system eliminates the need to constantly fuel and regulate the output of the wood stove. Instead, the heat given off by the device rather than being circulated all at once into the building is then stored until called for to heat the building.

Conventional wood stoves control excess heat output by reducing the amount of air the fire receives and thereby reducing the heat output by cutting off the air supply to the wood. However, this greatly reduces the efficiency of combustion and therefore the heat output from the furnace per pound of fuel. A reduction in efficiency also means that air pollution is increased because incompletely combusted material escapes as stack gases.

If a woodburning device is combined with some form of thermal storage, there is no need to use inefficient regulation methods, rather, the furnace can be allowed to burn rapidly at high temperatures to insure complete combustion with a minimum of air pollution. One such device which uses the high temperature concept is a wood furnace developed by Richard C. Hill, University of Maine. The furnace is to be installed as an auxiliary heating source to a solar system in the Maine Audubon headquarters. (See figures 8.10 and 8.11).

The wood furnace is the secondary heat source with the 2,000 square foot flat-plate air collector expected to provide 60 to 70 percent of the overall heating needs for the building. The 25 to 40 percent deficit will be provided by the wood furnace. This is equivalent to approximately three cords of hardwood a year. At $50 a cord, the cost per year for supplemental fuel amounts to $150.

**185**

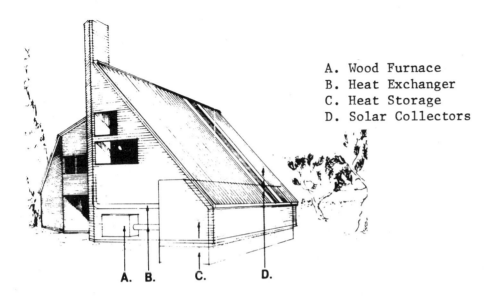

A. Wood Furnace
B. Heat Exchanger
C. Heat Storage
D. Solar Collectors

FIGURE 8.10  MAINE AUDUBON HEADQUARTERS.

friction and the energy needed to circulate the air.

The heat storage capacity of the rock bed will carry the building over two sunless days while the outside air temperature is 25°F. Depending on the monitored rock-bed temperature and predicted weather a decision will be made by the building manager whether or not to start the auxiliary furnace.

The design of the furnace necessitates that it be heavily insulated so that the heat generated by

Heated air from the solar collectors and the wood furnace goes to a common heat storage system composed of 105 tons of crushed granite of an average diameter of one inch. The stones rest on a galvanized steel grate 70 feet in length by 10 feet in width. The stones are stacked to a height of 3 feet along this grate. The incoming heated air is circulated by fans along the vertical axis of the stone bed rather than through the much longer horizontal axis to reduce

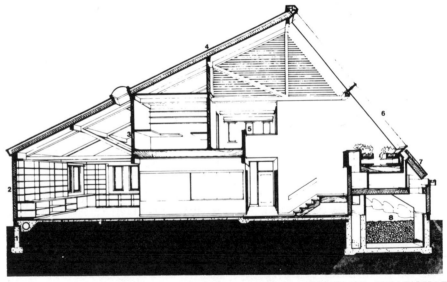

FIGURE 8.11  CROSS SECTION - MAINE AUDUBON HEADQUARTERS.
*Reprinted with permission from the architect, G. Terrien.*

**186**

combustion is carried out of the furnace in the flue gas to the storage bed with a minimum amount of heat transfer out of the sides of the furnace. Therefore, the material must be capable of insulating plus be able to withstand temperatures in excess of 1000°F. The material used in the construction of the furnace are: insulating firebrick for wall surfaces with castable refractory material forming the interior sections and an added layer of perlite providing insulation between a double wall construction.

As previously stated the Maine Audubon furnace does not need to control heat output because excess heat is stored in the gravel until needed by the building. This allows the furnace to burn rapidly at high temperatures by injecting excess air into the furnace. This insures complete combustion and a minimum of air pollution.

The furnace operation is as follows (figs. 8.12, 8.13): A 50 cfm blower injects air into the combustion chamber via a plenum chamber and venturi section. As the air

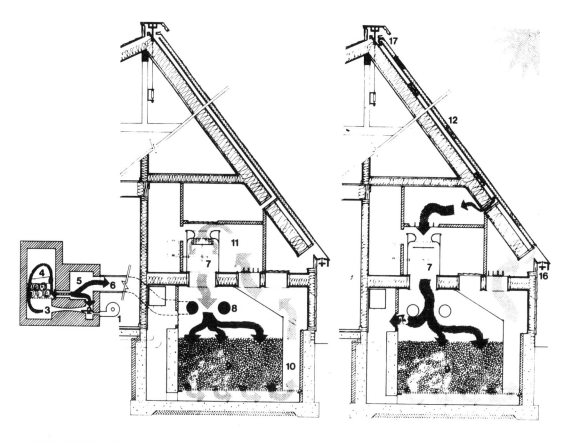

**WOOD BURNING FURNACE & HEAT COLLECTED FROM FURNACE**

HIGH VELOCITY BLOWER ① FORCES HIGH PRESSURE AIR UNDER STEEL PLATE ② AND THROUGH VENTURI ③. PULLING HOT COMBUSTION GASES FROM EXHAUST CHAMBER ⑤ THROUGH VENTURI ALSO. AFTER PASSING THROUGH GRATE AND FIRE ④. COMBUSTION GASES ENTER EXHAUST CHAMBER ⑤ FOR RECYCLING TO HIGHER TEMPERATURES AND FOR EXIT THROUGH EXHAUST FLUE ⑥. FAN ⑦ CYCLES AIR PAST EXHAUST FLUE LOOP ⑧ TO HEAT THE ROCK STORAGE BED ⑨. UP BYPASS DUCTS ⑩. AND BACK INTO FAN CHAMBER ⑪.

**HEAT COLLECTED FROM SUNSHINE**

FAN ⑦ CYCLES HOT AIR FROM COLLECTOR ⑫ TO HEAT THE ROCK STORAGE BED ⑨ AND BACK THROUGH THE COLLECTOR BYPASS DOOR ⑬ SHUNTS AIR HEATED BY COLLECTORS OR BY FURNACE PAST STORAGE. OPERABLE VENTS AT EAVE ⑯ AND RIDGE ⑰ PERMIT SUMMER VENTILATION OF COLLECTOR. VENTS ARE SHOWN OPEN FOR CLARITY BUT WOULD BE SHUT IN WINTER DURING COLLECTOR OPERATION

FIGURE 8.12   COMBINED WOOD AND SOLAR HEATING SYSTEM, MAINE AUDUBON HEADQUARTERS.   *Reprinted with permission from the architect, G. Terrien.*

is injected into the venturi section it is accelerated to a high velocity flow which has a tendency to create a partial vacuum on the edge of its path. This vacuum pulls uncombusted gases from the combustion chamber back into the fire to be completely burned. Essentially, the fire burns upside down on the grate as the recirculated gases are burned. The flow continues on its path into the exhaust chamber where it starts over again by heating the steel plate and mixing with new incoming air in the plenum chamber. Not only does this arrangement provide for an intimate mixture of combustible gases and air but it also provides for the preheating of the incoming air. Only those gases which are at a sufficiently high temperature escape through the exhaust flue to the storage bed.

Heat exchange from the exhaust gases to the storage bed is accomplished by ducting them over the length of the gravel storage bed. Since the heat exchange surface is not in intimate contact with the gravel surface a fan is used to transfer the

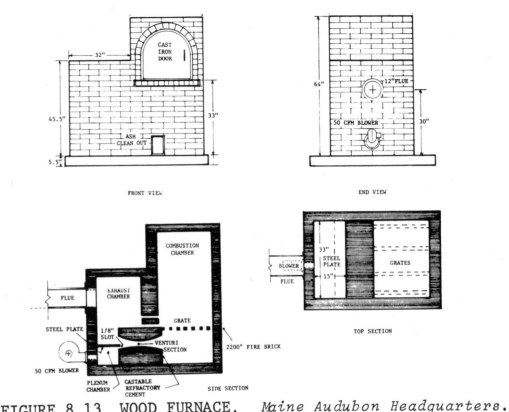

FIGURE 8.13 WOOD FURNACE. *Maine Audubon Headquarters.*

heat by blowing air across the pipes and then on through the gravel.

The heat exchanger, which is the flue pipe, consists of standard 8" ribbed and galvanized steel culvert pipe. As the flue gases travel the 140' pipe suspended over the rock storage, their temperature drops from as high as 1000°F to 150°F. Because of

this extreme temperature drop the flue gases no longer have enough buoyancy to keep rising. Therefore, a stack draft-inducing fan is necessary to exhaust the gas.

The heat exchanging flue pipe gives the storage system an added opportunity to recover the sensible heat of the water vapor in the exhaust gases. Moisture is

always a by-product of combustion even in the case of oven-dry wood. Wood contains hydrogen, which during combustion is converted largely into water vapor. Water vapor is said to contain "latent" heat (as opposed to "sensible"). If the water vapor condenses to liquid water, it releases its stored latent heat as sensible heat-- roughly 1040 BTU per pound of water-- the same amount of energy it takes to evaporate a pound of water.

But when wood is burned in a stove or fireplace, the water vapor in the flue gases rarely condenses where the heat can be used. This heat loss can be quite significant.

To summarize, the combination of a solar system and wood auxiliary is particularly attractive for the following reasons:

- they are lower in cost than conventional systems

- the wood fuel source can be obtained at lower costs than conventional fuels

- because of wood's wide range of availability it can be classified as a decentralist fuel, therefore, it cannot be controlled by large interests. This provides a fuel source that has a stable price base and low escalation rate.

- the wood fuel draws from a renewable resource base thus putting a minimum strain on finite fossil fuel resources

- the environmental impact from burning wood is much lower than other fuels

- because of the inherent simplicity of woodburning devices, they are extremely reliable and easy to maintain

- woodburning devices can operate at different levels of energy demand therefore providing a tremendous amount of flexibility in the sizing of solar components (i.e., the overall collector area can be reduced by the amount of dependency on the woodburning device and user participation.

FOOTNOTES:

1. "Stop the Five Gallon Flush!" School of Architecture, McGill University, 1973.

2. *Ibid*.

3. Winblad, Uno. *Evaluation of Waste Disposal Systems for Urban Low Income Communities in Africa*, Scan Plan Report No. 3, Copenhagen, 1972.

4. Moorcraft, Colin. "Plant Power," *Architectural Design*, Jan. 1974, vol. 44, no. 1, p. 19.

5. Deevey, E. "Mineral Cycles," *Scientific American*, Sept. 1970, vol. 223, no. 3.

6. MacKillop, Andrew. "Low Energy Housing," *The Ecologist*, Dec. 1972, vol. 2, p. 8.

7. Ram Bux Singh. *Bio-Gas Plant*, Gobar Gas Research Station, Ajitmal, Etawah (u.p.), India.

8. *Methane Digesters*, New Alchemy Institute, Newsletter No. 3, Spring, 1973.

9. Bell, Boulter and Keiller Dunlop. *Methane, Fuel of the Future,* published by Andrew Singer, Bottisham Park Mill, Bottisham, Cambridgeshire, England.

10. *Op.cit.* Ram Bux Singh, p. 26.

11. *Op.cit.* New Alchemy Institute, p. 21.

12. *Ibid.,* p. 24.

13. Ministry of Agriculture, Fisheries & Food, 1964, Nitrogen and Soil Matter, National Agricultural Advisory Service, Her Majesty's Stationery Office, London.

14. Daniels, Farrington. *Direct Use of the Sun's Energy,* Ballantine Books, Inc., 1964, p. 225.

15. *Powercells in Ground Applications,* Pratt & Whitney Aircraft, East Hartford, Connecticut.

16. Meier, R. L. "Biological Cycles in the Transformation of Solar Energy into Useful Fuels," *Solar Energy Research,* ed., F. Daniels & J. A. Duffy, p. 180.

17. *Alternative Sources of Energy,* Book One, ed. Sandy Eccli, et.al., 1974 by A.S.E., p. 112.

REFERENCES:

*Alternative Sources of Energy,* "Special Eco Section," No. 11, July 1973, pp. 12-24.

Anderson, L.L. "Energy Potential from Organic Wastes: A Review of the Quantities and Sources," U.S. Gov't Printing Office, 1972.

Appell, H.R., et.al. "Converting Organic Wastes to Oil," Bureau of Mines, Report of Inv. 7560, 1971.

"The Biosphere," *Scientific American,* No. 3, vol. 223, September 1970, p. 10.

Bloodgood, D. and F. A. Sanders. "The Effect of Nitrogen to Carbon Ratio on Anaerobic Decomposition," *Journal of Water Pollution Conf. Fed.,* no. 37, 1965, p. 1741.

Bohn, Heinrich L. "A Clean New Gas," *Environment,* vol. 13, no. 10, pp. 4-9.

Boyle, G. and P. Harper, ed. *Radical Technology,* Pantheon Books, New York, 1976.

Cook, J., ed. *Wood Burning Quarterly,* (quarterly publication available from Wood Burning Quarterly, 8009-34th Avenue, S. Minneapolis, Minnesota, 55420.)

Daniels, F. and J.A. Duffie, ed. *Solar Energy Research,* University of Wisconsin Press, Madison, Wisc, 1961.

Davis, E.G., Feld, I.L. and J.H. Brown. "Combustion Disposal of Manure Wastes and Utilization of the Residue."

Dugan, G.L., et.al. "Recycling System for Poultry Wastes," *Journal W.P.C.F.,* vol. 44, no. 3, March 1972, pp. 432-439.

Feldman, H.F., et.al. "Cattle Manure to Pipeline Gas: a process study," *Mech. Engr.,* October 1973, pp. 36-40.

Feldman, H.F. "Pipeline

Gas from Solid Wastes," *Chem. Engr. Progress*, vol. 67, no. 12, December 1971, pp. 51-52.

Fisher, A.W., Jr. "Economic Aspects of Algae as a Potential Fuel," *Solar Energy Research*, F. Daniels and J.A. Duffie, ed.

"Fuel from Wastes: a Minor Energy Source," *Science*, vol. 178, November 1972, pp. 599-602.

Gay, Larry. *The Complete Book of Heating with Wood*, Garden Way Publishing, Charlotte, VT, 1974.

Golueke, C.G. and W.J. Oswald. "An Algal Regenerative System for Single-Family Farms and Villages," *Compost Science - Journal of Waste Recycling*, May-June, 1973, vol. 14, no. 3.

Golueke, C.G. and W.J. Oswald. "Biological Conversion of Light Energy to the Chemical Energy of Methane," *Applied Microbiology*, vol. 7, 1959, pp. 219-227.

Golueke, C.G., et.al.

"Anaerobic Digestion of Algae," *S.E.R.L.*, Dept. of Engineering, Univ. of Calif., Berkeley, vol. 5, 1957, pp. 47-55.

Gotaas, H.B. and W.J. Oswald. "Utilization of Solar Energy for Waste Reclamation," *Trans. of the Conference on the Use of Solar Energy*, vol. 4, Tucson, Arizona, October 31 - November 1, 1955.

*Handbook of Homemade Power*, Mother Earth News, Bantam Books, N.Y., May 1974.

Havens, David. *The Woodburners Handbook*, Media House Publications, Portland, Maine, 1973.

Hughes, F.P. "The Eco House," *Mother Earth News*, no. 20, March 1973, pp. 62-65.

Hydrocarbon Powercells for U.S. Air Force Missions, Pratt & Whitney Aircraft.

Kern, K. *The Owner-Built Home*, Owner-Builder Publ., Oakhurst, Calif., 1974.

Kern, K. *The Owner-Built Homestead*, Owner-Building Publ., Oakhurst, Calif.,

1974.

Kotze, J.P., et.al. "Anaerobic Digestion II," *Water Research*, vol. 3, no. 7, July 1969.

Leicke, J., et.al. *Other Homes and Garbage*, Sierra Club Books, San Francisco, Calif., 1975.

Maine Audubon Society, *Maine Audubon Headquarters Energy Systems*. (Blueprints and system description, $8.00. Available from Maine Audubon Society, 53 Baxter Blvd., Portland, Maine, 04101)

Merrill, R., et.al. *Energy Primer*, Portola Institute, Menlo Park, Calif., 1974.

"Methane Power," *Architecture Design*, February 1972, vol. 42, no. 2, p. 131.

Oswald, W.J. and C.G. Golueke. "Solar Power via a Botanical Process," *Mech. Engr.*, February 1964, pp. 40-43.

"Plowboy Interview with Ram Bux Singh," *Mother Earth News*, No. 18, pp. 7-13.

Shelton, J. *The Woodburners Encyclopedia*, Vermont

Crossroads Press, Vermont, 1976.

Singh, Ram Bux. *Bio-Gas Plant Designs with Specifications*, Gobar Gas Research Station, Hjitmal, Etawah (v.p.), India.

Swift, Wesley R. "Methane Digester Design," *Alternatives*, Autumn 1973, vol. 3, no. 1.

Weichett, Stephen. "An Organic Answer to the Fuel Shortage," *Environment Action Bulletin*, December 15, 1973.

Winkleman, Hans. *Wood Burning*, Occasional Paper No. 1, Food and Agriculture Organization of the United Nations, Rome, Italy, December 1958.

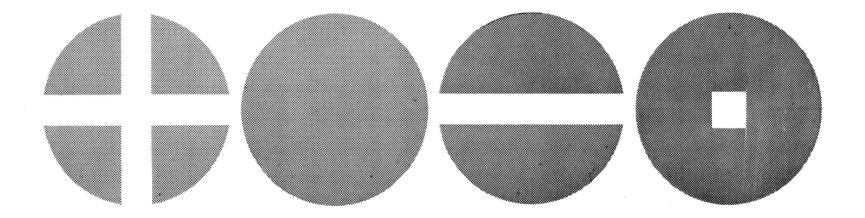

Integration allows waste
heat, water and ambient
energy sources, such as sun
and wind, to be brought
together in a single unit.
An integrated system
interfaces these diverse
forms of energy into a
central matrix for the
retention and distribution
of energy for domestic
needs.

Past attempts to meet total
energy needs by natural
means have generally been
based upon the utilization
of only one intermittent
energy source. These
attempts have largely been
inadequate because certain
parameters, such as physical
size and cost, have been
excessive.

If one energy source were
allowed to work in harmony
with another, the overall
system reliability would
increase, simply because
each energy source would
provide a backup for the
other. In an integrated

**193**

system, the devices used for the extraction of ambient energy sources can be of smaller capacity than would be necessary in a nonintegrated system. When separate systems are integrated, each performs multi-function jobs that can reduce overall systems requirements.

The integration of subsystems is largely dependent upon the type of storage system compatable with the form of energy input. Some existing types of storage are: *Chemical Storage*, batteries, hydrogen production/storage; *Mechanical Storage*, flywheels; *Biological Storage*, algae production/ energy extraction with methane digester; *Thermal Storage*, specific heat storage (water, rocks), heat of fusion (eutectic salts). Possible combinations and different levels of interaction will suggest themselves upon analyzation.

Following are some considerations basic to choosing appropriate conversion and interaction designs:

A. Environmental Impact

B. Conversion Efficiencies

C. Ease of Integration or Compatibility with Other Systems

D. Adaptability to a Common Storage System

E. Ability to Recycle, to Maximize Efficiencies within the System

F. Economic Restraints

A wide range of representative designs of integrated systems have been chosen for further investigation. Upon analyzation, it is possible to obtain an insight into alternative energy sources: how they integrate with themselves, the environment, the shelter that surrounds them; and, most important, how they interface with the individual that lives within. The following designs are included not to suggest a particular life style (even though the functioning of some subsystems is dependent upon such) or a particular building type or architectural statement, but to suggest different ways in which a multiplicity of factors (energy sources, food production, waste treatment, shelter design, the individual, etc.) can come together into a harmonious matrix.

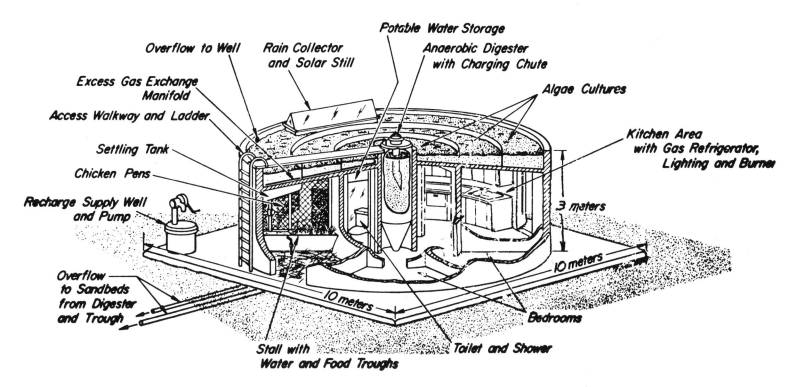

The figure contains the following labels:

Overflow to Well
Rain Collector and Solar Still
Potable Water Storage
Anaerobic Digester with Charging Chute
Excess Gas Exchange Manifold
Algae Cultures
Access Walkway and Ladder
Settling Tank
Kitchen Area with Gas Refrigerator, Lighting and Burner
Chicken Pens
Recharge Supply Well and Pump
3 meters
10 meters
Overflow to Sandbeds from Digester and Trough
10 meters
Bedrooms
Stall with Water and Food Troughs
Toilet and Shower

FIGURE 9.1   SINGLE FAMILY DWELLING UNIT WHICH INCORPORATES A MICROBIOLOGICAL RECYCLING SYSTEM.   *Reprinted with permission from Compost Science.*

*A Recycling System for Single-Family Farms, and Villages*

C.G. Golueke and W.J. Oswald from the University of California, Berkeley, have designed a microbiological recycling system that recycles organic wastes and utilizes solar energy. Their objective was to develop a unit that placed a minimum burden on the environment and available resources. This was accomplished through the integration of human habitation with the environment. The integration involved the development of localized systems in which residues were directly recycled into the living unit from which they emanated. This design is the closest approximation of a natural cycle to date. Energy is produced by a complete cycle of the interaction of plant and animal life as it occurs in nature.

It is felt that the minimum practical scale at which this design could be operable would provide waste disposal and nutrient recycling for four persons, one cow, and 50 chickens.

**195**

The basic components of this system are:

A. An anaerobic digester

B. A series of algal growth chambers

C. A sedimentation chamber

D. Gravel bed

E. Solar still

F. Gas exchanger

All of the above is provided for livestock and humans in a living space 33' in diameter and 10' high.

*System Operation and Systems Components*

All organic wastes (manure, urine, wasted food, night-soil, and clean-up water) are fed at least once a day to a 55-cu-ft anaerobic digester. Methane gas produced by the bacterial decomposition is collected in the top part of the digester (an inverted dome-type cover). The gas will accumulate under the dome at a pressure sufficiently

above atmosphere to force the gas from the collector to the living space where it is used for household purposes. Organic wastes are fed to the digester through a charging chute which introduces the wastes below the digester's cul-

ture surface. The digester is located in the center of the living space and situated such that the insulation of the structure and the metabolic heat given off by the occupants, keep the digester at

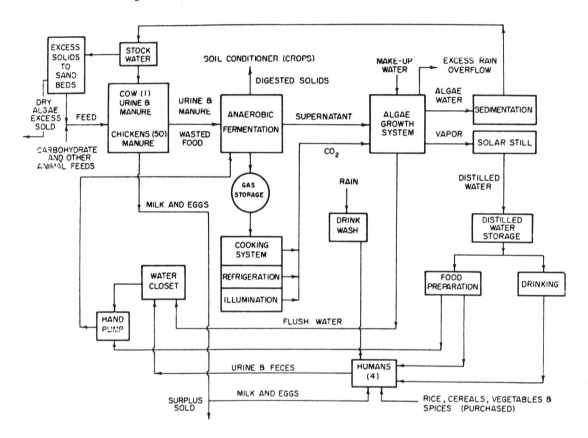

FIGURE 9.2  SCHEMATIC DIAGRAM OF SINGLE FAMILY ORGANIC WASTE RECYCLING SYSTEM. *Reprinted with permission from Compost Science.*

optimum operating temperatures.

When organic material is added to the digester, the material displaces a soluable substance which moves into the algae culture tank located on the roof. This soluable substance acts as a substrate for algal growth. The roof pond consists of three concentric ponds. The outer pond or the final treatment stage is equipped with a collection hopper to serve as a sump in which settled algae are collected. These algae, along with water, can be fed to the cow, thereby forcing it to consume algal protein in the wet form. The algae slurry can also be discharged on to sand beds for drying and then used as chicken feed. The roof pond area could be increased in size to provide additional algae to supplement organic material for the digester. Carbon dioxide formed by the combustion of the methane, is vented by convection to the algal culture where part of it is used as a carbon source by the growing algae.

A potable water supply is provided by a solar still. The solar distilling apparatus extracts water from the algae culture producing sufficient water to meet the drinking and cooking needs of four humans. The solar still can also be used as a catchment for rainwater. A supplement of water is needed for bathing and general cleansing purposes; this can be provided by ground or surface water.

The system can be expected to provide an ample and hygienic environment for a family and its essential livestock. The unit can be constructed of local materials at a relatively low cost. Because the system operation is dependent on algae growth, the area of operation is dependent upon the climatic range in which certain algae can survive. In extreme climatic areas, covering the roof pond with a transparent dome might extend the feasibility range of operation.

*The Ecol Operation*

The Ecol House, developed by the Minimum Cost Housing Group at McGill University, Montreal, Canada, shows that a home built at minimum cost to ecological principles can be a practical and attractive reality.

Two of the objectives of the Brace Research Team were to develop a low-cost construction technique and to reduce the high level of current water usage in present water and sewage systems.

*Sulfur Block Construction*

Sulfur is one of the world's most plentiful, but least utilized, raw materials. Some of the advantages of using sulfur as a building material are as follows:

A. Availability

B. High bond strength

C. Water resistance

D. Good insulation when mixed with other aggregates (sand, gravel and earth)

E. Compressive strength comparable to that of concrete

F. Low energy requirement for liquification (114°C - 119°C)

G. Easily remelted and recycled

H. Termite resistant

The biggest advantage of the sulfur material is that it liquifies at a low temperature range (114-119°C) which is easily obtained by primitive heating methods. At McGill University the concrete is made in a conventional cement mixer, modified to accept fiberglas insulation and a butane heater source. Sand and other aggregates are added to the molten sulfur which is then preheated in an electric melting pot. It was found that the highest strength block is obtained with the use of 40% sulfur mixed with 60% sand.

The heated sulfur is poured into a mortarless interlocking block form where it sets in a few minutes. The interlocking block form is

an ideal shape for use by unskilled laborers. The first course, and the most critical to the final shape of interlocking sulfur blocks, is laid over a poured concrete footing. After the first course is made level and true, the interlocking block is self-aligning.

The roof of the living unit is made from asbestos-cement sewer pipe. Each pipe is cut into four lengthwise sections. These sections are formed into interlocking channels and bolted down to a precut and notched cedar log building system (Canadian Pan-Abode).

*Bathroom Unit*

The bathroom unit is separated from the main living space. The walls are 1/2" asbestos-cement panels. Formed integral to the roof is a combined rain collector and solar still. Collected rainwater is stored in an overhead tank to be used for showering and washing. All spent water is stored in a 45 gallon oil drum (holding drum) located under the bathroom floor. From this

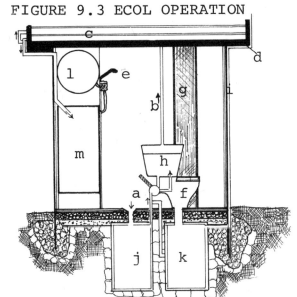

FIGURE 9.3 ECOL OPERATION

a-hand pump   b-to the still
c-solar still   d-insulation
e-shower        f-toilet
g-window        h-toilet basin
i-vent
j-shower waste water storage
k-toilet waste water
l-rain water storage
m-drinking water storage

point, the water can be pumped to the roof where solar distillation makes it potable or it can be pumped to the toilet cistern for flushing purposes. After two consecutive uses, this water is then transferred to a second tank or the waste treatment tank located beneath the toilet.

**198**

The treatment tank receives a constant flow of bubbled air provided by a 12-volt aquarium pump so that the aerobic decomposition process is accelerated. An overflow pipe for the treatment tank leads to a conventional stone-filled sump. It is estimated that solid residues will accumulate at a rate of 2 to 3 inches per year, a rate which suggests that pumping out will only be required at 5-year intervals.

Another water-saving feature is that the wash basin and toilet pedestal are formed into one unit. The basin is mounted over the toilet cistern so that dirty basin water can be used for flushing purposes.

## Electrical Installation

A German-designed 12-pole wind generator (Lubing Maschinenfabrik) provides 12-volt direct current for use in cooking, lighting, and water heating. Storage facilities for the wind generator plant are provided through 12-volt storage batteries. Elec-tricity from the storage batteries also operates the aquarium pump for the waste treatment system.

The McGill University Ecol Operation not only shows that intermediate technologies and ecological principles can be readily adapted to housing, but also that these principles can be supplied at a low cost. Total cost for the house construction excluding land and labor was just under $2,000; the sanitation system cost about $450 including washroom construction; and the electrical installation cost about $1,000 bringing the total cost to $3,450.

## Grahame Caine Ecohouse

This ecological house is a self-sufficient, domestic unit attempting to rely on the solar infra-structure to generate a life-sustaining biological cycle and to assist in creating comfort conditions. The designer of the ecological house is a 5th-year student at the Architectural Association of London.

The major component of the ecological house is a two-compartment anaerobic digester. One of the compartments is loaded with liquid organic waste, while the other is loaded with solid organic material. After the organic material in both phases undergoes partial decomposition, it is transferred to a **second** tank that is conducive to algal growth. The algae helps breakdown and digest the sewage further. Any dangerous microorganisms or pathogens in the human excreta portion of the sewage should be destroyed in this second tank by oxygen and the ultraviolet radiation of the sun. Although algae require a light intensity of only

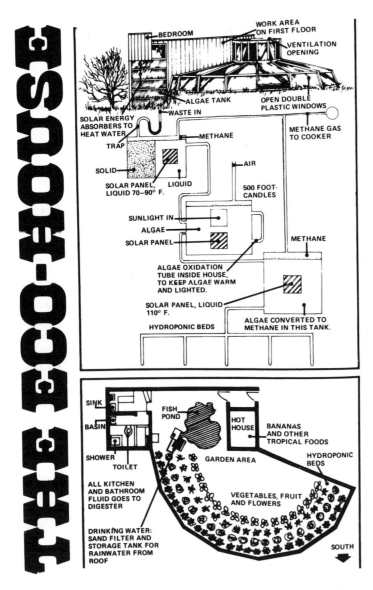

FIGURE 9.4 GRAHAME CAINE ECO-HOUSE.
*Reprinted with permisson from the
Mother Earth News.*

500-foot-candles, the natural illumination levels during winter, in some areas, may be inadequate for continous photosynthesis. Supplemental lighting is used in Caine's design: the indoor section of the algae pool is illuminated by a 40-watt fluorescent tube.

When the algae has finished decomposing the organic material, liquid is passed on to a final tank, a second digester, where it is transformed to methane gas. Methane gas and gas from the first digester are piped to the kitchen stove.

Both digester tanks are kept at optimum operating temperatures (70-95°F) with a warm water jacket heated by a flat-plate collector. The collector provides a temperature of 70° throughout winter to assure algae production.

The final material that is left in the second digester (digested algae, human and vegetable organic material) is used as a hydroponic plant culture

medium. Growing beds are located in a 500 square foot greenhouse, incorporated into the living space. Caine expects 250 square feet of cultivated space in the greenhouse to provide him with 8 pounds of vegetables per square foot. This should be enough to provide all the needed vegetables all year around.

A potable water supply is obtained from collected rainfall. Rainwater, falling on the 600 square foot roof area, is collected and filtered through sand filters. This filtering process removes any particulate matter, washed out of the atmosphere. The water then goes to another storage tank from which it is then transferred to an activated charcoal filter bed before use. It is important to note that if rainwater is collected from urban skies, more sophisticated filtering techniques will have to be used to remove high lead contents.

The solar collection system for the hot water supply consists of an array of black-painted hot water radiators on the south wall of the dwelling. Hot water is stored in a 30-gallon tank and a backup source of heat is provided by an immersion heater connected to a conventional power source.

Caine plans to incorporate a wind generator power system in the near future to bring the ecohouse closer to full autonomy.

*Project Ouroboros*

Ouroboros was a mythological dragon who survived by consuming its own tail. It is a fitting representation of our own existence on this planet. Project Ouroboros is a two-story residence built by students in the University of Minnesota School of Architecture. Constructed in 1973, it represents an approach to residential scale design through the study and application of the many different "rhythms and flows of energy through our environment and to design interactive systems to use those energies compatibly." The trapezoidal building shape is to minimize heat loss surface and maximize the south orientation. The solar collector is 576 square feet for a floor area of 1,500 square feet. The greenhouse with a southern exposure collects further heat. The earth beams protect the surface area from extreme weather and minimize fluctuating surface temperatures. The sod roof further assists in summer cooling. Low energy furniture, a downdraft wood burner, aerobic sewage composting, water reduction devices, and a 4 kw wind generator all combine with basic energy conservation principles to bring about an integrated low energy dwelling. The designers state that the house is 100 percent solar heated and have plans for investigating water recycling processes and methane generation.

Project Ouroboros brings up the issue of sod roofs. Its quite obvious that sod roofs are not very common in the United States, but in northern Europe they were and still are quite common. Sod roofs are frequently considered more expensive due

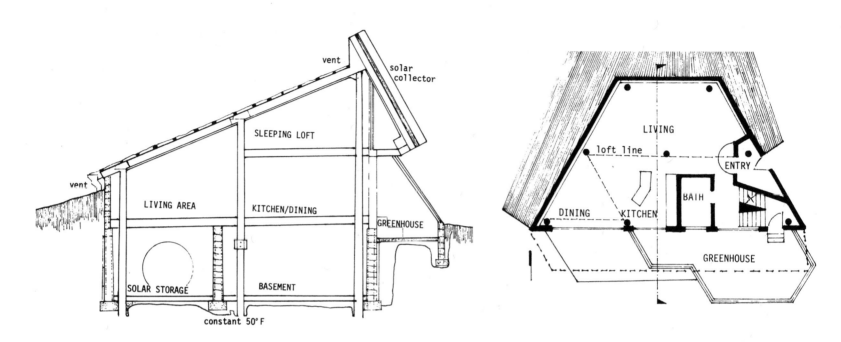

FIGURE 9.5  PROJECT OUROBOROS.  *College of Architecture, University of Minnesota.*

to increased structural requirements. The actual cost depends on whether it is owner applied and whether it is native or commercial sod as well as to what the cost is being compared with. Asphalt shingle roof may cost as much as $35 per square and last between 15 and 25 years.

A sod roof generally lasts about 60 years.

A typical roof construction could include a layer of roll roofing, a coating of selvage cement and a layer of 6 mil black polyethelene, with another layer of cement. The sod may then be placed on top. It

is estimated that 6" of sod would equal about 3" of fiberglass insulation. As well as its insulative quality, sod slows down water runoff and assists in summer cooling. It is important to base a decision as to using a sod roof or not on more than economics alone.

*Integrated Life Support Systems*

About one hour outside of Albuquerque is the research and working laboratory of Robert Reines called *Integrated Life Support Systems*. Along with colleagues he has constructed two domes. The first dome, the residence, is 31'6" in diameter and has a usable area of 655 square feet on the ground level and 200 square feet in loft space. The construction of the dome is pressed steel segmented sections with three inches of flame-resistant polyurethane insulation concealed within the steel. For heating the first dome, three banks of double-glazed solar collectors were constructed up the hill. The second dome has collectors integral to the dome. Storage is contained in a remote 3,000 gallon water-glycol solution and heat distribution to the space is accomplished with water run through radiators. For electrical needs, three wind generators, a bank of storage batteries and solid-state power conditioning equipment supply all the needs of the residence, darkroom, drafting room and workshop.

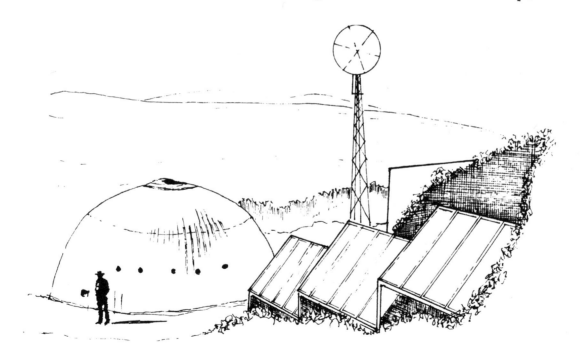

FIGURE 9.6 INTEGRATED LIFE SUPPORT SYSTEMS.

## Integrated Core Unit

The issue of integration does not only need to be applied to experimental applications but may also be facilitated in conventional cooking and heating systems. Components and equipment within a house are normally uncoordinated in that they function separately from one another, creating inefficiencies in the conversion and use of energy. As a result, a large percentage of energy used by appliances and mechanical equipment is transformed into waste heat.

Integrating the mechanical system into a central core or unit would reduce the inefficiencies that exist by allowing waste heat and water to be recycled. The collection of waste heat, the prevention of its dissipation, and the transfer of it back into the energy core maximize the overall system's efficiency.

The major component of the system and the component upon which its effectiveness depends is the *Thermal Storage Unit*. Collectable heat may be stored in the form of sensible heat in a solid or liquid medium or in the form of heat of fusion. The transportation of waste heat from the domestic unit to the thermal storage tank can be accomplished through the use of heat pipes and heat exchangers. Heat pipes can be used to transport waste heat from stack gases in open flameburning devices, from stoves, and from most heat-producing appliances. Heat exchangers can be used to transfer thermal waste from hot water to the thermal heat sink.

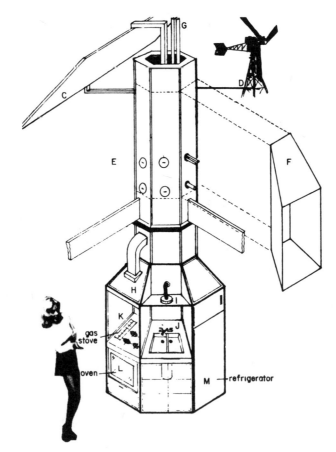

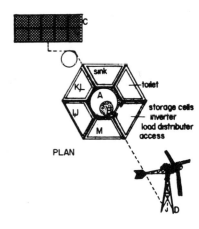

PLAN

A. THERMAL HEAT SINK

B. METHANE DIGESTER

C. SOLAR COLLECTOR

D. WIND GENERATOR

E. STRUCTURAL & MECHANICAL CORE

F. POTENTIAL 2nd FLOOR UNITS

G. VENTS

H. FAN & HEAT EXCHANGER

I. LIGHT

J. KITCHEN SINK

FIGURE 9.7 INTEGRATED CORE UNIT.

*Everett Barber Residence*

The Everett Barber residence was designed by the owner (President of Sunworks) in collaboration with the architectural firm of Charles W. Moore Associates. The 1,300 square foot, three bedroom residence incorporates a wide range of energy conservation features and alternative energy sources.

The roof of the Barber residence, inclined at a 57° angle and oriented south, contains 450 square feet of collector area. Energy storage is provided by specific heat (water) contained in a vertical storage tank, 5' in diameter and 12' high. Solar energy is expected to supply 60 percent of the annual heating requirements. Auxiliary heat is provided to the storage with an oversized hot water heater.

A large stone fireplace will also be used to supply supplemental heat to the storage tank. Water-circulating tubes will be incorporated above the smoke shelf of the fireplace to extract heat which would normally escape up the chimney. The heated water is circulated by gravity flow to the solar heat storage tank. Proper combustion within the fireplace is augmented by preheating incoming air. Preheating is accomplished by having the air-intake duct parallel to the fireplace flue with heat exchange occurring between the two. Heat loss through the chimney flue is prevented by a thermostatically controlled damper which closes when the fire is extinguished.

The chimney also provides natural ventilation during hot weather. A belvedere on top of the chimney vents warm air from within the living space. This helps induce natural air circulation which occurs when the air inside the house is warmer than the air outside. Warm air leaving through the louvers allows cool air to enter the house through windows on the ground floor. The circulation of unwanted heat from the solar collectors through several finned coils located in the throat of the belvedere facilitates natural circulation by providing a greater temperature differential between incoming and outgoing air.

The roof section includes overhangs designed to utilize winter sun angles and to block summer sun. Overhangs are also provided above east- and south-facing windows. Sliding shutters are provided on the west-facing sliding doors to prevent heat buildup from summer sun in the afternoons. All glass areas are largely concentrated on the south side of the house to facilitate winter solar heating and the use of natural light. The north wall has few windows, and what windows are provided incorporate insulating shutters on the inside to prevent heat loss on cold nights.

The structure is largely constructed of concrete block and a 3", sprayed-on layer of polyurethane foam. It has been shown that use of insulation on the exterior of the masonry construction is more effective than use of the same insulation on the interior. The insulation

serves as a buffer between the comparatively large thermal mass of the masonry unit and the outside temperature extremes.

Domestic hot water heating represents a large portion of a house's total energy requirements. The Barber residence incorporates three methods by which the incoming water temperature can be boosted before the water is supplied to the hot water heater. The hotter the incoming water source, the less the energy expenditure of the hot water heater. With the first method, a heat exchanger is utilized to extract heat from waste hot water to preheat water going to the domestic hot water heater. With the second method, excess heat produced by the condenser on the refrigerator is utilized as a preheat source. This also increases the refrigerator's operating efficiency by allowing the condenser to operate at lower temperatures. With the third method, the solar heat storage tank is utilized as a preheat source.

Reducing energy by providing

a preheat source need not be limited to hot water applications. The energy consumed by heating elements in both electric dryers and dishwashers can be reduced by preheating the air entering both units. Air entering both the clothes dryer and dishwasher could pass through a heat exchanger containing solar heated

water.

Plans are being made to incorporate a recycling system so that waste water can be reclaimed to furnish water for flushing purposes.

Two 10'- diameter windmills are being used without storage to augment local utility company power.

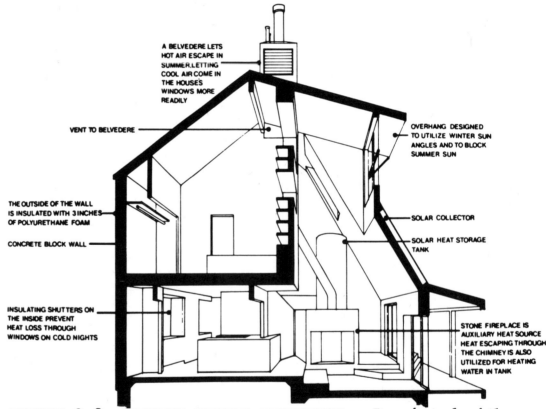

A BELVEDERE LETS HOT AIR ESCAPE IN SUMMER,LETTING COOL AIR COME IN THE HOUSE'S WINDOWS MORE READILY

VENT TO BELVEDERE

OVERHANG DESIGNED TO UTILIZE WINTER SUN ANGLES AND TO BLOCK SUMMER SUN

THE OUTSIDE OF THE WALL IS INSULATED WITH 3 INCHES OF POLYURETHANE FOAM

CONCRETE BLOCK WALL

SOLAR COLLECTOR

SOLAR HEAT STORAGE TANK

INSULATING SHUTTERS ON THE INSIDE PREVENT HEAT LOSS THROUGH WINDOWS ON COLD NIGHTS

STONE FIREPLACE IS AUXILIARY HEAT SOURCE HEAT ESCAPING THROUGH THE CHIMNEY IS ALSO UTILIZED FOR HEATING WATER IN TANK

FIGURE 9.8 EVERETT BARBER RESIDENCE. *Reprinted with permission from Sunworks.*

*New Alchemy Institute Ark for Prince Edward Island*

The New Alchemy Institute was established in 1969 as an organization dedicated to a science of the future. Integrating scientific practicality and philosophy, N.A.I. has been foremost in the United States if not the world in fusing ecological principles, internal food cycles and renewable energy sources. One way chosen to do this is with the "backyard fish farm-greenhouses." From this research came the mini-ark, a solar heated and wind powered food growing complex.

With further research came the Cape Cod ark. The concept behind it was to determine whether a well designed bioshelter could produce enough food to pay itself and provide an income for its owners.

The latest effort of N.A.I. is the ark for Prince Edward Island, a small Canadian province north of Nova Scotia. The ark is unique in that it integrates components previously unconnected. The greenhouse, solar ponds and solar collectors all interface with a 25 kw wind generator to be a self-sufficient organism. The concept behind the P.E.I. ark is to develop a structure which generates its own power, uses its own wastes and provides food without placing a drain on its environment.

Prince Edward **Island** has since decided against a nuclear future and now will focus on a coal/wind/solar energy future.

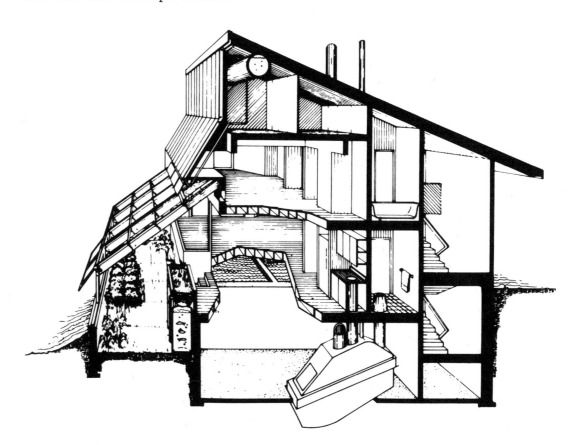

FIGURE 9.9  PRINCE EDWARD ISLAND ARK.  *Reprinted with permission from the New Alchemy Institute.*

*The Biosphere*

The biosphere is an integration of a house, a greenhouse, a solar heater, and a solar still. Several of the functions required of a living area-- food, heat, fresh water, and waste treatment-- are superimposed on a modified greenhouse.

The greenhouse shares a common wall with the living space and is oriented along a north-south axis. The growing area of the greenhouse is one-half to two-thirds of the floor area of the living space. The transparent section of the greenhouse is provided with removable, 3", foil-covered, foam plastic. The insulating panels are hinged so they can be removed or repositioned depending upon the greenhouse's thermal needs.

Thermal storage can be provided in either of two ways-- heat can be trapped in wet earth in the greenhouse or excess heat can be stored in the massive common wall between the living space and the collector.

Located at the base of the heat storage wall and the collector surface are troughs to catch condensed water running off of their surfaces. Inasmuch as this is distilled water, it is fit for human consumption. To minimize water losses, a waterproof sheet is buried a foot or two beneath the soil in the greenhouse, making it a sealed unit.

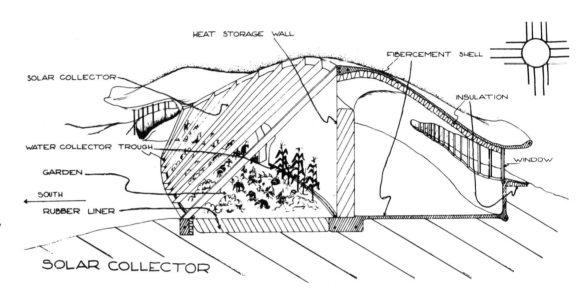

FIGURE 9.10   THE BIOSPHERE HOUSE.  *Reprinted with permission from Biotechnic Press.*

## Organic Living Experiment

The organic living experiment was created in the summer of 1971 by John Shore. The geodesic structure houses an indoor growing area with thermal heat provided by solar water heaters and with electrical energy provided by savonious wind generators.

## Systems Description

Rainwater is fed into a sand filter made from a 15-cm-diameter pipe, 50 cm long. The lower end of the pipe is capped and a valve is fitted to regulate the filtration speed. The action of the water filter is physical, rather than biological. During heavy storms, water can overflow the filter and fall into a large storage tank. From there, the water can be drawn, either by hand or wind pump, to the roof-mounted storage tank. This tank feeds the drinking water filter, solar heaters, and irrigation system for the growing bin. For a potable water supply, this rainwater undergoes a second filtration, a cascade system using

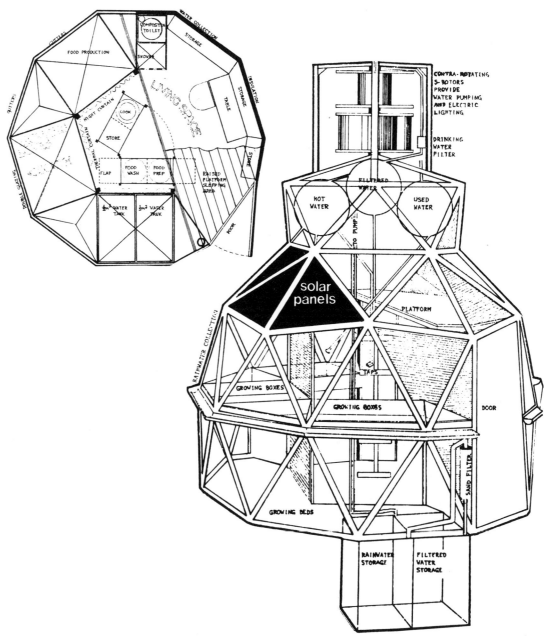

FIGURE 9.11  ORGANIC LIVING EXPERIMENT NO. 1.  *Reprinted with permission from John Shore.*

two sand filters.

An aerobic composter digests the human excreta and the dead plant tissue and turns it into a rich growing medium. The composter is an insulated container with internal gratings which support the decomposing material. An air inlet and an exhaust vent pipe provide air circulation throughout the compost mass. Here, aerobic biological decomposition will destroy pathogenic bacteria of a thermal sensitivity lower than the compost temperature.

The area cultivated within the dome cannot supply one person's food, but can extend the growing seasons for the cultivation of selected crops. Water heated by a parabolic focusing concentrator provides temperatures sufficient for the slow cooking of chopped foods in vacuum flasks. Flat-plate collectors are used for water heating.

Wind energy is extracted by two contra-rotating savonious rotors.

FIGURE 9.12  SOLAR DWELLING NO. 1.  *Reprinted with permission from John Shore.*

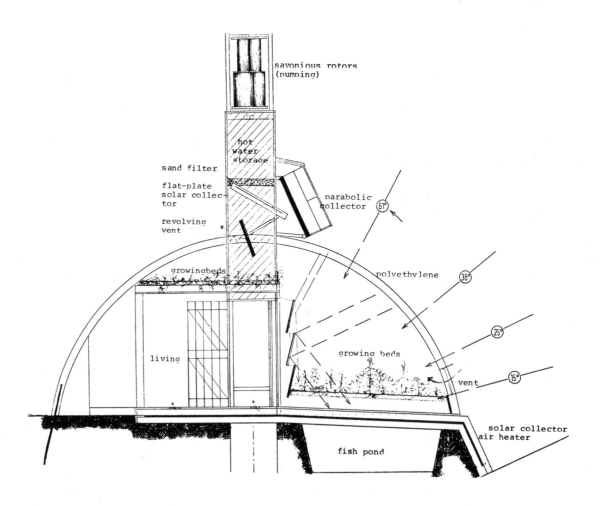

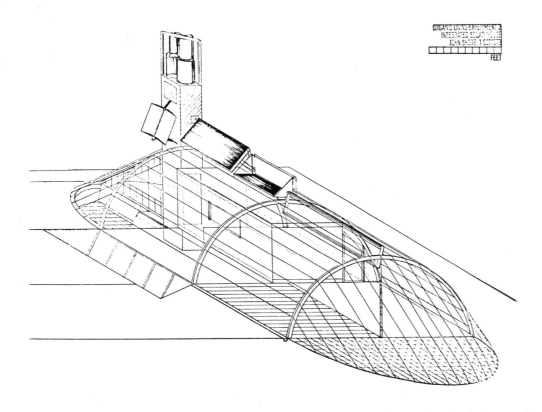

FIGURE 9.13 SOLAR DWELLING NO. 1. *Reprinted with permission from John Shore.*

Savonious rotors were selected because of their simplicity and ease of construction. The savonious rotors are supported at either end and in the middle by Sturmey-Archer-Dynohub alternators. Inasmuch as the rotors and alternators are connected directly, complex gearing mechanisms are eliminated. The

alternator, located between the two contra-rotating rotors, is connected by its magnet to the top rotor and by its armature to the bottom one. Because both parts of this alternator are allowed to rotate past each other, it achieves almost twice the speed and output as the alternators located on the ends. A slip-ring

assembly transfers the current from the center alternator armature into the living space. In place of the alternator, water pumps could be used as support bearings for the rotor.

The organic living experiment was built in May 1971 and ran until December 1973. Since then, John Shore has developed two more integrated solar dwellings. The first integrated solar house design, developed in October 1973, was rejected because large areas of plastic would have been required. A second design was developed with the intention of making the unit more easily constructable. Both designs are described together inasmuch as the systems' operations are basically the same; only the structures differ.

The living area of the integrated solar dwelling unit is highly insulated and surrounded by lean-to walls of natural timber and a vapor barrier, supporting 2' of earth with a grass-clover surface.

The wall between the living area and the growing area

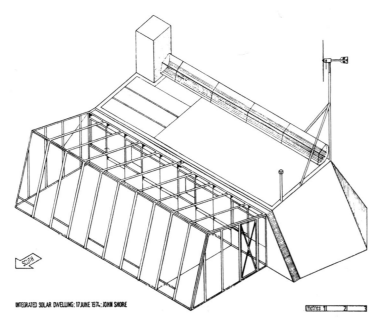

INTEGRATED SOLAR DWELLING: 17 JUNE 1974.: JOHN SHORE

metres 1 2 3

is a heat storage wall which absorbs thermal heat and redistributes it to the living space. By using various forms of construction, materials, and color, the thermal lag or the rate at which thermal heat is exchanged with the living space can be controlled.

The indoor growing area is used to extend the growing season. The growing space has an extension which expands the living and

FIGURE 9.14   SOLAR DWELLING NO. 2.   *Reprinted with permission from John Shore.*

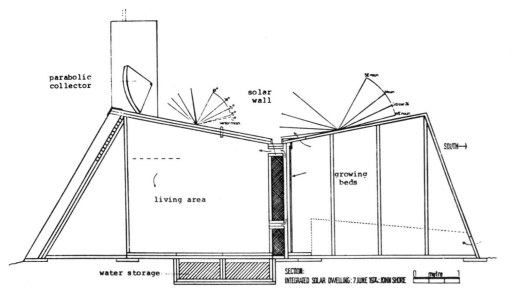

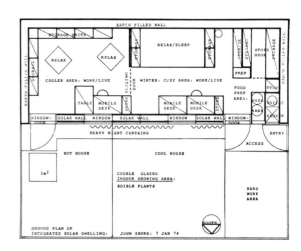

working area. The growing area is divided into two sections, 1) a hot house for growing vegetables, 2) a cool area for growing fruit. The addition of a pond provides aqua culture for growing fish or other aquatic foods.

Under the living space, there are water tanks for rain and hot water storage. The tower on the roof contains insulated hot water tanks for the solar water heater.

Solar air heaters are used to provide supplemental heat to the living space. The solar collector located at ground level circulates heated air through ducts created with concrete blocks. The ducts exchange heat with the sand or soil covering the unit.

*Grassy Brook Village*

Grassy Brook Village will be a development of 20 residential living units designed to make a minimum impact on the natural environment and provide life-support systems that derive their energy from natural and nonpolluting sources.

Grassy Brook Village, presently under construction, is located on a 43-acre tract of woodland in the town of Brookline, Vermont. The architect of Grassy Brook is Robert F. Shannon of People/Space Company of Boston; the design engineer for the integrated system is Fred S. Dubin, of Dubin-Mindell-Bloome Associates, New York; and the project developer is Richard Blazej of Brookline, Vermont. Phase One, the construction of the first cluster, is slated for completion in 1974. After the evaluation of Phase One, Phase Two, the second cluster of 10 houses, will be built.

Each cluster consists of approximately 10 10,000-sq-ft, 3-bedroom houses.

These houses will utilize one common central solar heating system and one common waste handling system.

The solar heating system will utilize 4,500 sq. ft. of collector surface which will be inclined at 57° and will be located on a south-facing slope, west of the cluster of houses. The use of a separate, common solar collector frees the house designs from the constraints of accommodating south-oriented collectors on the roofs. The separation of the solar collector from the houses may result in some efficiency losses, but the planners feel that these will be more than offset by the gains resulting from having a single central system as opposed to 10 individual solar heating systems.

Each house is equipped with fan coil units that can receive thermally conditioned water from the heat pump. These units are located in the perimeter walls of each room. There are two units per room, each of which will be

FIGURE 9.15  GRASSY BROOK VILLAGE. *Reprinted with permission from Grassy Brook Village, Inc.*

by an oil-fired boiler.

The living units are so designed that the heating demand per unit is approximately 7,500 BTU/degree day. This reduction in energy needs has been accomplished as a result of the incorporation of the following conservation features:

A. Common walls permitted by the clustering of the units (provide minimum exposed surface area)

B. Heavy insulation in ceilings and floors (fiberglass)

thermostatically controlled. The centrally-located heat pump will provide hot water for heating, or chilled water for cooling. The heat source for the heat pump will be warm water either from the storage tank or from the solar collector when warm water is available at a minimum temperature of 50°F. Well water may also be used as a low-grade source of heat when the collector cannot provide adequate temperatures.

When the temperature supplied by the flat-plate collector is greater than

110°F during the winter heating period, the heat pump will be bypassed, and hot water from the collector will flow directly to the fan coil units, located in the living space.

The thermal storage tank, located under the housing units, has a capacity of 20,000 gallons. The storage tank is sectioned off to permit storage of water at different thermal gradients. When extended periods of cloudiness or extreme cold weather are encountered, supplemental heat is provided to the storage tank

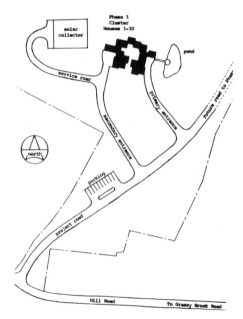

FIGURE 9.16   SITE PLAN.

FIGURE 9.17 PROPOSED GRASSY BROOK LIFE SUPPORT SYSTEM. *Reprinted with permisson from the Mother News.*

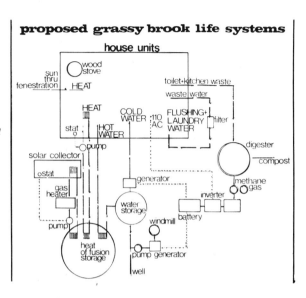

**proposed grassy brook life systems**

house units

C. Foam urethane insulation on exterior walls

D. Double glazing of case-ment and fixed windows

E. Triple glazing of skylights

F. Urethane-insulated doors

G. Insulated panels to close over large windows at night.

The houses have flat roofs with gardens which provide additional insulation. The stabilization of tempera-ture and moisture condi-tions at the roof line as a result of the heavy layer of garden soil and plant life and the heavy insulation in the struc-ture itself, will elimi-nate the usual leakage problems.

A small wood-burning stove is also included in each house to provide addition-al heat should it be needed.

A conventional sewage system must be installed (to meet Vermont state regulations). It will serve as backup to the various experimental units under construction such as the anaerobic digester, aerobic composter, and aerator. These experi-mental units are designed as plug-in units, so they may be removed if they do not work.

Some of the systems to be incorporated into the later phases of work include:

A. Use of wind-generated electricity to power electrolysis units in which water would be separated into its two components, hydrogen and oxygen. Hydrogen would then be fed to a fuel cell to produce direct current. The direct current would be convert-ed to usable house current through an inverter.

B. A vacuum pump transferral system in which human excreta would be carried by a vacuum to the anaerobic digester. This feature would save water and prevent over-loading of the digester

due to excess water.

C. Recycling systems in which bath, sink, and laundry water would be piped off to a dry well where the water would be filtered and pumped for flushing purposes.

The above systems are under investigation and may prove to be unworkable because of their inherent cost and limited capability in a project on the scale of Grassy Brooks.

Not only is Grassy Brooks an experiment in the integration of alternative energy sources, but it is also an experiment in sociological interaction. The success of Grassy Brooks is dependent upon the cooperation and willingness of the inhabitants to live within the constraints imposed by natural energy sources. Each person has a share of the responsibility, and depends on the exercise of that responsibility by all the others in the group on an equal basis. In such a housing arrangement-small-scale life-support systems whose power is derived from natural,

nonpolluting, renewable resources rather than from remote, complicated systems requiring the use of non-renewable fuels that degrade the environment--the individual may be expected to develop a changing feeling about his relationship to nature and his fellow man.

REFERENCES:

*Recycling System for Single-Family Farms and Villages*

Clarence G. Golueke and W. J. Oswald
University of California, Berkeley
Sanitary Research Lab
1301 S. 46th Street
Richmond, CA 94804

Golueke, C. G. and W. J. Oswald. "An Algal Regenerative System for Single-Family Farms and Villages," *Compost Science*, vol. 14, no. 3, May-June 1973.

*Ecol Operation*

Minimum Cost Housing Group
Brace Research Institute
McGill University
Montreal, Canada

Ferrabee, Linda. "Waste Watcher's Sulfur House," *Design*, no. 296, August 1973, pp. 72-75.

Ecol Operation, *Architectural Design*, no. 243, April 1973, p. 242.

*Graham Caine Eco-House*

Grahame Caine

c/o Architectural Assoc.
of London
London, England

Hughes, F. P. "The Eco-House," *The Mother Earth News*, no. 20, March 1973, p. 62.

Caine, Grahame. "The Ecological House," *Architectural Design*, no. 141, March 1973, p. 140.

*Project Ouroboros*

Boyle, G. and P. Harper *Radical Technology*, Pantheon Books, New York, 1976.

Marcovich, S. "Autonomous Living," *Popular Science*, December 1975, p. 80.

*Integrated Core Unit*

Clinton G. Bush, Jr.
President
Concepts & Directions, Inc.
Oyster Bay, New York

Bush, Clinton G. "Super-core," *Catalyst*, vol. 3, no. 2, 1973, p. 22.

*Everett Barber Residence*

Everett Barber
Sunworks, Inc.
669 Boston Post Road
Cuilford, Conn. 06437

Watson, Donald and Everett Barber, Jr. "Energy Conservation in Architecture," *Connecticut Architect*, March/April 1974.

*Prince Edward Island Ark*

Todd, John. "The New Alchemist," *Coevolution Quarterly*, Spring 1976, pp. 54-65.

*The Biosphere*

Day Chahroudi
Massachusetts Institute of Technology
77 Massachusetts Avenue
Cambridge, Mass. 02139

*Organic Living Experiment*

John Shore
36 Bedford Square
London, WCIB 3ES
England

Shore, John. "Organic Living Experiment #1," *Undercurrents*, no. 6, January 1973.

*Grassy Brook Village*

Grassy Brook Village, Inc.
R.F.D. 1, Box 39
Newfane, Vermont 05345

"Grassy Brook Village... An Ecologically Sound Community in the Works," *Lifestyle*, no. 2, December 1972, p. 76.

Blazej, Richard D. and Philip M. Moriarty. "Living within Our Means," *Grassy Brook Village*, 1974.

Eccli, Sandy, *et.al.*, eds. *Alternative Sources of Energy: Book One*, A.S.E., 1974, p. 19.

**219 NOTES**

APPENDIX A: *Daily Values of "Direct Beam" Solar Radiation Computed for Selected Slopes, Aspects and Days at Varying Latitudes*[1]

Hourly solar radiation was computed for: slopes in 15° increments ranging from level to a vertical wall; 16 aspects, in 22-1/2° increments; latitudes in 10° increments, from 0 to 60° north; and atmospheric transmission coefficient of 0.9. The 0.9 is representative of atmospheric conditions on a clear day. Other values will be needed for areas where atmospheric pollution is severe. The Smithsonian Institute (1958) presents seasonal totals of direct solar radiation with different atmospheric coefficients at many latitudes.

The values given in the tables were derived by the following method: (see figure A-1)

A sample surface is directly overhead at point $p$ on meridian $lg$ with a declina-

tion 8. The sample surface is located at latitude $\emptyset$, point $r$, on meridian $mg$ which has an hour angle h from the meridian $lg$. The surface $cfgi$ has a slope $\alpha$ from the horizontal $jo$, a deviation of $\theta$ from the vertical $cd$, and an aspect $\beta$ from the north $no$.

The sun's rays are striking the surface at $r$ with an altitude angle $Sok$, called $A$, from the horizontal. The altitude $A$ is given by:

Sin $A$ = sin $\phi$ sin $\delta$ + cos cos $\delta$ cos $h$
*and* azimuth $AZ$ from the north, where $AZ = Z + 90°$, is given by:
$$\sin AZ = -\cos \delta \sin \lambda / \cos A.$$
The solar intensity $I$ on the surface $cfgi$ is:
$$I = I_o p^{(l/sin\ A)} \sin \theta$$
where:
$$\sin = \sin A \cos \alpha - \cos A \sin \alpha \sin(Z - B).$$

$I_o$ is the radiation at the top of the atmosphere ($I_o$ or the solar constant is 2.00 cal/cm$^2$ - min$^4$ or 442 BTU/hr-ft$^2$) on a surface normal to the sun's rays and p is the atmospheric transmisson coefficient.
Diagram F.1 is a geometric represntation of the relationships discussed above.

NOTE: The values given in Appendix A are given in Langleys per day, which can be converted to BTU/sq.ft./day by multiplying by the factor of 3.687.

Latitude 20° North, Jan. 21

| Slope (°) | N | NNE NNW | NE NW | ENE WNW | E W | ESE WSW | SE SW | SSE SSW | S |
|---|---|---|---|---|---|---|---|---|---|
| | | | | | ASPECT | | | | |
| 0 | 533 | 533 | 533 | 533 | 533 | 533 | 533 | 533 | 533 |
| 15 | 374 | 385 | 417 | 464 | 516 | 569 | 614 | 645 | 656 |
| 30 | 194 | 226 | 298 | 387 | 481 | 575 | 654 | 713 | 734 |
| 45 | 29 | 85 | 190 | 312 | 433 | 550 | 653 | 732 | 761 |
| 60 | 0 | 8 | 115 | 244 | 376 | 499 | 611 | 702 | 737 |
| 75 | 0 | 0 | 65 | 185 | 311 | 429 | 531 | 623 | 663 |
| 90 | 0 | 0 | 37 | 134 | 243 | 342 | 422 | 502 | 544 |

Latitude 30° North, Jan. 21

| Slope (°) | N | NNE NNW | NE NW | ENE WNW | E W | ESE WSW | SE SW | SSE SSW | S |
|---|---|---|---|---|---|---|---|---|---|
| | | | | | ASPECT | | | | |
| 0 | 410 | 410 | 410 | 410 | 410 | 410 | 410 | 410 | 410 |
| 15 | 244 | 259 | 295 | 345 | 402 | 456 | 504 | 537 | 549 |
| 30 | 76 | 111 | 187 | 279 | 381 | 479 | 565 | 628 | 650 |
| 45 | 0 | 13 | 107 | 225 | 352 | 478 | 590 | 675 | 707 |
| 60 | 0 | 0 | 63 | 180 | 313 | 448 | 576 | 677 | 716 |
| 75 | 0 | 0 | 39 | 140 | 269 | 401 | 524 | 632 | 675 |
| 90 | 0 | 0 | 25 | 107 | 218 | 333 | 442 | 544 | 589 |

Latitude 20° North, Mar. 21

| Slope (°) | N | NNE NNW | NE NW | ENE WNW | E W | ESE WSW | SE SW | SSE SSW | S |
|---|---|---|---|---|---|---|---|---|---|
| | | | | | ASPECTS | | | | |
| 0 | 716 | 716 | 716 | 716 | 716 | 716 | 716 | 716 | 716 |
| 15 | 623 | 628 | 647 | 672 | 699 | 724 | 743 | 756 | 761 |
| 30 | 487 | 502 | 545 | 600 | 653 | 697 | 726 | 747 | 754 |
| 45 | 317 | 350 | 429 | 514 | 588 | 640 | 672 | 688 | 695 |
| 60 | 127 | 200 | 315 | 423 | 508 | 558 | 581 | 585 | 589 |
| 75 | 0 | 95 | 224 | 334 | 419 | 459 | 466 | 449 | 443 |
| 90 | 0 | 47 | 151 | 250 | 325 | 353 | 340 | 294 | 267 |

Latitude 30° North, Mar. 21

| Slope (°) | N | NNE NNW | NE NW | ENE WNW | E W | ESE WSW | SE SW | SSE SSW | S |
|---|---|---|---|---|---|---|---|---|---|
| | | | | | ASPECT | | | | |
| 0 | 651 | 651 | 651 | 651 | 651 | 651 | 651 | 651 | 651 |
| 15 | 530 | 538 | 563 | 598 | 636 | 673 | 702 | 721 | 728 |
| 30 | 373 | 393 | 452 | 524 | 598 | 663 | 710 | 744 | 756 |
| 45 | 190 | 238 | 338 | 446 | 545 | 624 | 681 | 718 | 731 |
| 60 | 0 | 115 | 245 | 370 | 478 | 558 | 612 | 642 | 657 |
| 75 | 0 | 56 | 174 | 297 | 402 | 473 | 513 | 530 | 538 |
| 90 | 0 | 31 | 123 | 228 | 318 | 375 | 394 | 385 | 383 |

Latitude 20° North, Jun. 22

| Slope (°) | N | NNE NNW | NE NW | ENE WNW | E W | ESE WSW | SE SW | SSE SSW | S |
|---|---|---|---|---|---|---|---|---|---|
| | | | | | ASPECTS | | | | |
| 0 | 800 | 800 | 800 | 800 | 800 | 800 | 800 | 800 | 800 |
| 15 | 821 | 818 | 807 | 792 | 774 | 756 | 739 | 729 | 725 |
| 30 | 786 | 779 | 759 | 740 | 714 | 682 | 645 | 616 | 601 |
| 45 | 698 | 688 | 668 | 656 | 631 | 586 | 527 | 472 | 444 |
| 60 | 562 | 549 | 544 | 551 | 532 | 478 | 397 | 313 | 264 |
| 75 | 387 | 373 | 413 | 440 | 426 | 366 | 271 | 157 | 90 |
| 90 | 186 | 209 | 291 | 330 | 319 | 259 | 159 | 37 | 0 |

Latitude 30° North, Jun. 22

| Slope (°) | N | NNE NNW | NE NW | ENE WNW | E W | ESE WSW | SE SW | SSE SSW | S |
|---|---|---|---|---|---|---|---|---|---|
| | | | | | ASPECT | | | | |
| 0 | 833 | 833 | 833 | 833 | 833 | 833 | 833 | 833 | 833 |
| 15 | 825 | 823 | 819 | 816 | 810 | 804 | 796 | 790 | 786 |
| 30 | 760 | 757 | 753 | 755 | 751 | 739 | 722 | 700 | 692 |
| 45 | 644 | 640 | 643 | 664 | 671 | 652 | 617 | 573 | 551 |
| 60 | 483 | 478 | 513 | 560 | 574 | 547 | 492 | 422 | 387 |
| 75 | 290 | 292 | 389 | 452 | 468 | 432 | 357 | 258 | 206 |
| 90 | 119 | 179 | 280 | 345 | 358 | 316 | 226 | 108 | 42 |

Latitude 40° North, Jan. 21

| Slope (°) | N | NNE NNW | NE NW | ENE WNW | E W | ESE WSW | SE SW | SSE SSW | S |
|---|---|---|---|---|---|---|---|---|---|
| 0 | 278 | 278 | 278 | 278 | 278 | 278 | 278 | 278 | 278 |
| 15 | 123 | 136 | 171 | 218 | 272 | 327 | 373 | 405 | 416 |
| 30 | 0 | 21 | 87 | 170 | 262 | 357 | 444 | 504 | 526 |
| 45 | 0 | 0 | 42 | 135 | 249 | 370 | 485 | 569 | 600 |
| 60 | 0 | 0 | 24 | 110 | 230 | 361 | 492 | 595 | 633 |
| 75 | 0 | 0 | 15 | 89 | 200 | 335 | 468 | 581 | 623 |
| 90 | 0 | 0 | 11 | 58 | 169 | 287 | 414 | 527 | 570 |

Latitude 50° North, Jan. 21

| Slope (°) | N | NNE NNW | NE NW | ENE WNW | E W | ESE WSW | SE SW | SSE SSW | S |
|---|---|---|---|---|---|---|---|---|---|
| 0 | 151 | 151 | 151 | 151 | 151 | 151 | 151 | 151 | 151 |
| 15 | 24 | 36 | 65 | 103 | 149 | 195 | 236 | 263 | 273 |
| 30 | 0 | 0 | 19 | 77 | 150 | 230 | 304 | 358 | 377 |
| 45 | 0 | 0 | 8 | 63 | 149 | 251 | 353 | 428 | 455 |
| 60 | 0 | 0 | 4 | 53 | 144 | 259 | 377 | 469 | 502 |
| 75 | 0 | 0 | 3 | 46 | 132 | 250 | 377 | 478 | 515 |
| 90 | 0 | 0 | 2 | 36 | 117 | 224 | 351 | 455 | 492 |

Latitude 40° North, Mar. 21

| Slope (°) | N | NNE NNW | NE NW | ENE WNW | E W | ESE WSW | SE SW | SSE SSW | S |
|---|---|---|---|---|---|---|---|---|---|
| 0 | 564 | 564 | 564 | 564 | 564 | 564 | 564 | 564 | 564 |
| 15 | 420 | 431 | 461 | 503 | 551 | 598 | 636 | 659 | 669 |
| 30 | 248 | 276 | 346 | 435 | 523 | 606 | 668 | 713 | 729 |
| 45 | 59 | 134 | 248 | 372 | 485 | 587 | 666 | 719 | 738 |
| 60 | 0 | 60 | 181 | 313 | 436 | 541 | 621 | 675 | 698 |
| 75 | 0 | 34 | 134 | 258 | 376 | 474 | 545 | 589 | 610 |
| 90 | 0 | 22 | 99 | 204 | 306 | 388 | 439 | 466 | 480 |

Latitude 50° North, Mar. 21

| Slope (°) | N | NNE NNW | NE NW | ENE WNW | E W | ESE WSW | SE SW | SSE SSW | S |
|---|---|---|---|---|---|---|---|---|---|
| 0 | 456 | 456 | 456 | 456 | 456 | 456 | 456 | 456 | 456 |
| 15 | 298 | 310 | 344 | 393 | 447 | 500 | 545 | 573 | 584 |
| 30 | 119 | 157 | 238 | 336 | 435 | 526 | 600 | 653 | 671 |
| 45 | 0 | 60 | 167 | 290 | 415 | 529 | 623 | 688 | 713 |
| 60 | 0 | 32 | 128 | 253 | 384 | 505 | 604 | 677 | 706 |
| 75 | 0 | 21 | 101 | 214 | 341 | 459 | 555 | 620 | 651 |
| 90 | 0 | 15 | 77 | 178 | 288 | 389 | 467 | 526 | 552 |

Latitude 40° North, Jun. 22

| Slope (°) | N | NNE NNW | NE NW | ENE WNW | E W | ESE WSW | SE SW | SSE SSW | S |
|---|---|---|---|---|---|---|---|---|---|
| 0 | 843 | 843 | 843 | 843 | 843 | 843 | 843 | 843 | 843 |
| 15 | 802 | 803 | 805 | 811 | 819 | 825 | 828 | 828 | 827 |
| 30 | 705 | 707 | 715 | 739 | 762 | 774 | 775 | 765 | 761 |
| 45 | 561 | 564 | 589 | 645 | 685 | 697 | 688 | 664 | 650 |
| 60 | 378 | 382 | 462 | 546 | 594 | 599 | 573 | 526 | 498 |
| 75 | 175 | 231 | 353 | 444 | 491 | 484 | 439 | 365 | 326 |
| 90 | 98 | 154 | 264 | 343 | 382 | 362 | 299 | 199 | 147 |

Latitude 50° North, Jun. 22

| Slope (°) | N | NNE NNW | NE NW | ENE WNW | E W | ESE WSW | SE SW | SSE SSW | S |
|---|---|---|---|---|---|---|---|---|---|
| 0 | 830 | 830 | 830 | 830 | 830 | 830 | 830 | 830 | 830 |
| 15 | 762 | 765 | 773 | 788 | 807 | 824 | 835 | 842 | 845 |
| 30 | 642 | 648 | 666 | 712 | 758 | 792 | 807 | 809 | 807 |
| 45 | 478 | 487 | 536 | 626 | 695 | 733 | 742 | 733 | 726 |
| 60 | 282 | 304 | 427 | 539 | 617 | 649 | 643 | 614 | 599 |
| 75 | 156 | 214 | 341 | 453 | 524 | 544 | 518 | 468 | 441 |
| 90 | 109 | 160 | 268 | 364 | 419 | 422 | 376 | 301 | 262 |

## Latitude 60° North, Jan. 21

| Slope (°) | N | NNE NNW | NE NW | ENE WNW | E W | ESE WSW | SE SW | SSE SSW | S |
|---|---|---|---|---|---|---|---|---|---|
| 0 | 41 | 41 | 41 | 41 | 41 | 41 | 41 | 41 | 41 |
| 15 | 0 | 0 | 2 | 19 | 42 | 68 | 92 | 107 | 113 |
| 30 | 0 | 0 | 0 | 12 | 46 | 91 | 135 | 166 | 177 |
| 45 | 0 | 0 | 0 | 10 | 49 | 108 | 170 | 213 | 228 |
| 60 | 0 | 0 | 0 | 9 | 50 | 118 | 193 | 246 | 264 |
| 75 | 0 | 0 | 0 | 7 | 49 | 120 | 203 | 262 | 282 |
| 90 | 0 | 0 | 0 | 6 | 45 | 114 | 199 | 260 | 281 |

## Latitude 60° North, Mar. 21

| Slope (°) | N | NNE NNW | NE NW | ENE WNW | E W | ESE WSW | SE SW | SSE SSW | S |
|---|---|---|---|---|---|---|---|---|---|
| 0 | 333 | 333 | 333 | 333 | 333 | 333 | 333 | 333 | 333 |
| 15 | 169 | 183 | 221 | 273 | 330 | 384 | 431 | 462 | 473 |
| 30 | 0 | 58 | 139 | 233 | 331 | 424 | 505 | 561 | 581 |
| 45 | 0 | 23 | 102 | 210 | 331 | 448 | 549 | 622 | 650 |
| 60 | 0 | 15 | 84 | 193 | 320 | 447 | 557 | 640 | 674 |
| 75 | 0 | 12 | 71 | 173 | 294 | 422 | 534 | 615 | 653 |
| 90 | 0 | 9 | 59 | 147 | 259 | 372 | 474 | 551 | 586 |

## Latitude 60° North, Jun. 22

| Slope (°) | N | NNE NNW | NE NW | ENE WNW | E W | ESE WSW | SE SW | SSE SSW | S |
|---|---|---|---|---|---|---|---|---|---|
| 0 | 802 | 802 | 802 | 802 | 802 | 802 | 802 | 802 | 802 |
| 15 | 716 | 721 | 733 | 753 | 781 | 806 | 825 | 835 | 837 |
| 30 | 582 | 591 | 615 | 677 | 743 | 793 | 818 | 830 | 832 |
| 45 | 408 | 421 | 493 | 609 | 701 | 757 | 778 | 779 | 776 |
| 60 | 248 | 295 | 418 | 548 | 642 | 693 | 703 | 688 | 681 |
| 75 | 193 | 238 | 358 | 479 | 564 | 602 | 593 | 560 | 541 |
| 90 | 156 | 195 | 297 | 400 | 467 | 486 | 455 | 401 | 380 |

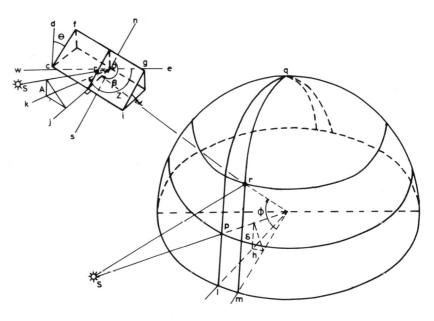

DIAGRAM F.1 Illustration of the angles necessary for the theoretical calculations of solar radiation on a particular surface in the Northern Hemisphere.

APPENDIX A-1 *Day-long direct solar irradiation in BTU/ft² for the 21st day of each month at lattitudes from 24 to 64° north, on a surface normal to the sun's rays; total irradiation on horizontal surfaces and south facing surfaces tilted at the following angles above the horizontal: L - 10°, L + 10° L + 20°, 90°. These tables are reproduced with the permisson of ASHRAE.*

APPENDIX A-2 *Table for use in general system sizing, Section 7.5. Source: Solar Energy and the Natural House.*

| Number of cover plates | | Collector Temp. (above ambient air temperature, °F) | Typical Applications | f = fraction of incident total radiation absorbed in collector | | | | $U_L$ |
|---|---|---|---|---|---|---|---|---|
| Black-painted absorber e=0.9 or 0.95 | Selective absorber e=0.2 | | | Black-painted absorber | | Selective absorber | | |
| | | | | good window glass | poor window glass | good window glass | poor window glass | |
| 0 | 0 | -10 to +10 | heat source for heat pump / air heating for drying | | | | | |
| 1 | 1 | 10 to 60 | summer water heating / solar distillation / spacing heating in non-freezing climates | 0.73 | 0.69 | 0.69 | 0.65 | 1.5 |
| 2 | 1 | 60 to 100 | winter water heating / winter space heating | 0.67 | 0.62 | 0.63 | 0.57 | .84 |
| 3 | 2 | 100 to 150 | summer air conditioning / steam production in summer / refrigeration | 0.62 | 0.56 | 0.58 | 0.51 | .57 |
| 4 | | | | 0.57 | 0.51 | 0.54 | 0.47 | .42 |

[f-values are approximately 15% more for plastic]

| Date | Deg. Lat. | $I_{DN}$ | Total Solar Irradiation, $I_{tH} + I_d$ | | | | | |
|---|---|---|---|---|---|---|---|---|
| | | | Horiz. | L − 10 | L | L + 10 | L + 20 | Vertical |
| Jan. 21 δ = − 20 deg | 24 | 2766 | 1622 | 1984 | 2174 | 2300 | 2360 | 1766 |
| | 32 | 2458 | 1288 | 1839 | 2008 | 2118 | 2166 | 1779 |
| | 40 | 2182 | 948 | 1660 | 1810 | 1906 | 1944 | 1726 |
| | 48 | 1710 | 596 | 1360 | 1478 | 1550 | 1578 | 1478 |
| | 56 | 1126 | 282 | 934 | 1010 | 1058 | 1074 | 1044 |
| | 64 | 306 | 45 | 268 | 290 | 302 | 306 | 304 |
| Feb. 21 δ = − 10.6 deg | 24 | 3036 | 1998 | 2276 | 2396 | 2446 | 2424 | 1476 |
| | 32 | 2872 | 1724 | 2188 | 2300 | 2345 | 2322 | 1644 |
| | 40 | 2640 | 1414 | 2060 | 2162 | 2202 | 2176 | 1730 |
| | 48 | 2330 | 1080 | 1880 | 1972 | 2024 | 1978 | 1720 |
| | 56 | 1986 | 740 | 1640 | 1716 | 1792 | 1716 | 1598 |
| | 64 | 1432 | 400 | 1230 | 1286 | 1302 | 1282 | 1252 |
| Mar. 21 δ = 0.0 deg | 24 | 3078 | 2270 | 2428 | 2456 | 2412 | 2298 | 1022 |
| | 32 | 3012 | 2084 | 2378 | 2403 | 2358 | 2246 | 1276 |
| | 40 | 2916 | 1852 | 2308 | 2330 | 2284 | 2174 | 1484 |
| | 48 | 2780 | 1578 | 2208 | 2228 | 2182 | 2074 | 1632 |
| | 56 | 2586 | 1268 | 2066 | 2084 | 2040 | 1938 | 1700 |
| | 64 | 2296 | 932 | 1856 | 1870 | 1830 | 1736 | 1656 |
| Apr. 21 δ = + 11.9 deg | 24 | 3036 | 2454 | 2458 | 2374 | 2228 | 2016 | 488 |
| | 32 | 3076 | 2390 | 2444 | 2356 | 2206 | 1994 | 764 |
| | 40 | 3092 | 2274 | 2412 | 2320 | 2168 | 1956 | 1022 |
| | 48 | 3076 | 2106 | 2358 | 2266 | 2114 | 1902 | 1262 |
| | 56 | 3024 | 1892 | 2282 | 2186 | 2038 | 1830 | 1450 |
| | 64 | 2982 | 1644 | 2776 | 2082 | 1936 | 1736 | 1594 |
| May 21 δ = + 20.3 deg | 24 | 3032 | 2556 | 2447 | 2286 | 2072 | 1800 | 246 |
| | 32 | 3112 | 2582 | 2454 | 2281 | 2064 | 1788 | 469 |
| | 40 | 3160 | 2552 | 2442 | 2264 | 2040 | 1760 | 724 |
| | 48 | 3254 | 2482 | 2418 | 2234 | 2010 | 1728 | 982 |
| | 56 | 3340 | 2374 | 2374 | 2188 | 1962 | 1682 | 1218 |
| | 64 | 3470 | 2236 | 2312 | 2124 | 1898 | 1624 | 1436 |
| June 21 δ = + 23.45 deg | 24 | 2994 | 2574 | 2422 | 2230 | 1992 | 1700 | 204 |
| | 32 | 3084 | 2634 | 2436 | 2234 | 1990 | 1690 | 370 |
| | 40 | 3180 | 2648 | 2434 | 2224 | 1974 | 1670 | 610 |
| | 48 | 3312 | 2626 | 2420 | 2204 | 1950 | 1644 | 874 |
| | 56 | 3438 | 2562 | 2388 | 2166 | 1910 | 1606 | 1120 |
| | 64 | 3650 | 2488 | 2342 | 2118 | 1862 | 1558 | 1356 |
| July 21 δ = + 20.5 deg | 24 | 2932 | 2526 | 2412 | 2250 | 2036 | 1766 | 246 |
| | 32 | 3012 | 2558 | 2442 | 2250 | 2030 | 1754 | 458 |
| | 40 | 3062 | 2534 | 2409 | 2230 | 2006 | 1728 | 702 |
| | 48 | 3158 | 2474 | 2386 | 2200 | 1974 | 1694 | 956 |
| | 56 | 3240 | 2372 | 2342 | 2152 | 1926 | 1646 | 1186 |
| | 64 | 3372 | 2248 | 2280 | 2090 | 1864 | 1588 | 1400 |
| Aug. 21 δ = + 12.1 deg | 24 | 2864 | 2408 | 2402 | 2316 | 2168 | 1958 | 470 |
| | 32 | 2902 | 2352 | 2388 | 2296 | 2144 | 1934 | 736 |
| | 40 | 2916 | 2244 | 2354 | 2258 | 2104 | 1894 | 978 |
| | 48 | 2898 | 2086 | 2300 | 2200 | 2046 | 1836 | 1208 |
| | 56 | 2850 | 1883 | 2218 | 2118 | 1966 | 1760 | 1392 |
| | 64 | 2808 | 1646 | 2108 | 1008 | 1860 | 1662 | 1522 |
| Sept. 21 δ = 0.0 deg | 24 | 2878 | 2194 | 2432 | 2366 | 2322 | 2212 | 992 |
| | 32 | 2808 | 2014 | 2288 | 2308 | 2264 | 2154 | 1226 |
| | 40 | 2708 | 1788 | 2210 | 2228 | 2182 | 2074 | 1416 |
| | 48 | 2568 | 1522 | 2102 | 2118 | 2070 | 1966 | 1546 |
| | 56 | 2368 | 1220 | 1950 | 1962 | 1918 | 1820 | 1594 |
| | 64 | 2074 | 892 | 1726 | 1736 | 1696 | 1608 | 1532 |
| Oct. 21 δ = − 10.7 deg | 24 | 2868 | 1928 | 2198 | 2314 | 2364 | 2346 | 1442 |
| | 32 | 2696 | 1654 | 2100 | 2208 | 2252 | 2232 | 1588 |
| | 40 | 2454 | 1348 | 1962 | 2060 | 2098 | 2074 | 1654 |
| | 48 | 2154 | 1022 | 1774 | 1860 | 1890 | 1866 | 1626 |
| | 56 | 1804 | 688 | 1516 | 1586 | 1612 | 1588 | 1480 |
| | 64 | 1238 | 358 | 1088 | 1136 | 1152 | 1134 | 1106 |
| Nov. 21 δ = − 19.9 deg | 24 | 2706 | 1610 | 1962 | 2146 | 2268 | 2324 | 1730 |
| | 32 | 2405 | 1280 | 1816 | 1980 | 2084 | 2130 | 1742 |
| | 40 | 2128 | 942 | 1636 | 1778 | 1870 | 1908 | 1686 |
| | 48 | 1668 | 596 | 1336 | 1448 | 1518 | 1544 | 1412 |
| | 56 | 1094 | 284 | 914 | 986 | 1032 | 1046 | 1016 |
| | 64 | 302 | 46 | 266 | 286 | 298 | 302 | 300 |
| Dec. 21 δ = − 23.45 deg | 24 | 2624 | 1474 | 1852 | 2058 | 2204 | 2286 | 1808 |
| | 32 | 2348 | 1136 | 1704 | 1888 | 2016 | 2086 | 1794 |
| | 40 | 1978 | 782 | 1480 | 1634 | 1740 | 1796 | 1616 |
| | 48 | 1444 | 446 | 1136 | 1250 | 1326 | 1364 | 1304 |
| | 56 | 748 | 157 | 620 | 678 | 716 | 734 | 722 |
| | 64 | 24 | 2 | 20 | 22 | 24 | 24 | 24 |

# APPENDIX A-3 *Daily Radiation on Horizontal Surfaces*[3]

## Left column

| Location | | Jan | Feb | Mar | Apr | May | Jun | Jul | Aug | Sep | Oct | Nov | Dec |
|---|---|---|---|---|---|---|---|---|---|---|---|---|---|
| Albuquerque, N.M. Lat. 35°03'N El. 5314 ft | H̄ | 1150.9 | 1453.9 | 1925.4 | 2343.5 | 2560.9 | 2757.5 | 2561.2 | 2387.8 | 2120.3 | 1639.8 | 1274.2 | 1051.6 |
| | K̄t | 0.704 | 0.691 | 0.719 | 0.722 | 0.713 | 0.737 | 0.695 | 0.708 | 0.728 | 0.711 | 0.684 | 0.704 |
| | t₀ | 37.3 | 43.3 | 50.1 | 59.6 | 69.4 | 79.1 | 82.8 | 80.6 | 73.6 | 62.1 | 47.8 | 39.4 |
| Annette Is., Alaska Lat. 55°02'N El. 110 ft | H̄ | 236.2 | 428.4 | 883.4 | 1357.2 | 1634.7 | 1638.7 | 1632.1 | 1269.4 | 962 | 454.6 | 220.3 | 152 |
| | K̄t | 0.427 | 0.415 | 0.492 | 0.507 | 0.484 | 0.441 | 0.454 | 0.427 | 0.440 | 0.347 | 0.304 | 0.361 |
| | t₀ | 35.8 | 37.5 | 39.7 | 44.4 | 51.0 | 56.2 | 58.6 | 59.8 | 54.8 | 48.2 | 41.9 | 37.4 |
| Apalachicola, Florida Lat. 29°45'N El. 35 ft | H̄ | 1107 | 1378.2 | 1654.2 | 2040.9 | 2268.6 | 2195.9 | 1978.6 | 1912.9 | 1703.3 | 1544.6 | 1243.2 | 982.3 |
| | K̄t | 0.577 | 0.584 | 0.576 | 0.612 | 0.630 | 0.594 | 0.542 | 0.558 | 0.559 | 0.574 | 0.543 | 0.573 |
| | t₀ | 57.3 | 59.0 | 62.9 | 69.5 | 76.4 | 81.8 | 83.1 | 83.1 | 80.6 | 73.2 | 63.7 | 58.55 |
| Astoria, Oregon Lat. 46°12'N El. 8 ft | H̄ | 338.4 | 607 | 1008.5 | 1401.5 | 1838.7 | 1753.5 | 2007.7 | 1721 | 1322.5 | 780.4 | 413.6 | 295.2 |
| | K̄t | 0.330 | 0.397 | 0.454 | 0.471 | 0.524 | 0.466 | 0.551 | 0.538 | 0.526 | 0.435 | 0.336 | 0.332 |
| | t₀ | 41.3 | 44.7 | 46.9 | 51.3 | 55.0 | 59.3 | 62.6 | 63.6 | 62.2 | 55.7 | 48.5 | 43.9 |
| Atlanta, Georgia Lat. 33°39'N El. 976 ft | H̄ | 848 | 1080.1 | 1426.9 | 1807 | 2618.1 | 2002.6 | 2002.9 | 1898.1 | 1519.2 | 1290.8 | 997.8 | 751.6 |
| | K̄t | 0.493 | 0.496 | 0.522 | 0.551 | 0.561 | 0.564 | 0.545 | 0.559 | 0.515 | 0.543 | 0.510 | 0.474 |
| | t₀ | 47.2 | 49.6 | 55.9 | 65.0 | 73.2 | 80.9 | 82.4 | 81.6 | 77.4 | 66.5 | 54.8 | 47.7 |
| Barrow, Alaska Lat. 71°20'N El. 22 ft | H̄ | 13.3 | 143.2 | 713.3 | 1491.5 | 1883 | 2055.3 | 1602.2 | 953.5 | 428.4 | 152.4 | 22.9 | - |
| | K̄t | - | 0.776 | 0.773 | 0.726 | 0.553 | 0.533 | 0.448 | 0.377 | 0.315 | 0.35 | - | - |
| | t₀ | -13.2 | -15.9 | -12.7 | 2.1 | 20.5 | 35.4 | 41.6 | 40.0 | 31.7 | 18.6 | 2.6 | -8.6 |
| Bethel, Alaska Lat. 60°47'N El. 125 ft | H̄ | 142.4 | 404.8 | 1052.4 | 1662.3 | 1711.8 | 1698.1 | 1401.8 | 938.7 | 755 | 430.6 | 164.9 | 83 |
| | K̄t | 0.536 | 0.557 | 0.704 | 0.675 | 0.519 | 0.458 | 0.398 | 0.336 | 0.406 | 0.432 | 0.399 | 0.459 |
| | t₀ | 9.2 | 11.6 | 14.2 | 29.4 | 42.7 | 55.5 | 56.9 | 54.9 | 47.4 | 33.7 | 19.0 | 9.4 |
| Bismarck, North Dakota Lat. 46°47'N El. 1660 ft | H̄ | 587.4 | 934.3 | 1328.4 | 1668.2 | 2056.1 | 2173.8 | 2305.5 | 1929.1 | 1441.3 | 1018.1 | 600.4 | 464.2 |
| | K̄t | 0.594 | 0.628 | 0.605 | 0.565 | 0.588 | 0.579 | 0.634 | 0.606 | 0.581 | 0.584 | 0.510 | 0.547 |
| | t₀ | 12.4 | 15.9 | 24.8 | 41.8 | 58.6 | 67.9 | 76.1 | 73.5 | 61.6 | 49.6 | 31.4 | 18.4 |
| Blue Hill, Mass Lat. 42°13'N El. 629 ft | H̄ | 555.3 | 797 | 1143.9 | 1438 | 1776.4 | 1943.9 | 1881.5 | 1622.1 | 1314 | 941 | 592.2 | 482.3 |
| | K̄t | 0.445 | 0.458 | 0.477 | 0.464 | 0.501 | 0.516 | 0.513 | 0.495 | 0.492 | 0.472 | 0.406 | 0.436 |
| | t₀ | 28.3 | 28.3 | 36.9 | 46.9 | 58.5 | 67.2 | 72.3 | 70.6 | 64.2 | 54.1 | 43.3 | 31.5 |
| Boise, Idaho Lat. 43°34'N El. 2844 ft | H̄ | 518.8 | 884.9 | 1280.4 | 1814.4 | 2189.3 | 2376.7 | 2500.3 | 2149.4 | 1717.7 | 1128.4 | 678.6 | 456.8 |
| | K̄t | 0.446 | 0.503 | 0.548 | 0.594 | 0.619 | 0.631 | 0.684 | 0.660 | 0.656 | 0.588 | 0.494 | 0.442 |
| | t₀ | 29.5 | 36.5 | 45.0 | 53.5 | 62.1 | 69.3 | 79.6 | 77.2 | 66.7 | 56.3 | 42.3 | 33.1 |

| Location | | Jan | Feb | Mar | Apr | May | Jun | Jul | Aug | Sep | Oct | Nov | Dec |
|---|---|---|---|---|---|---|---|---|---|---|---|---|---|
| Boston, Mass Lat. 42°22'N El. 29 ft | H̄ | 505.5 | 738 | 1067.1 | 1355 | 1769 | 1864 | 1860.5 | 1570.1 | 1267.5 | 896.7 | 535.8 | 442.8 |
| | K̄t | 0.410 | 0.426 | 0.445 | 0.438 | 0.499 | 0.495 | 0.507 | 0.480 | 0.477 | 0.453 | 0.372 | 0.400 |
| | t₀ | 31.4 | 31.4 | 39.9 | 49.5 | 60.4 | 69.8 | 74.5 | 73.8 | 66.8 | 57.4 | 46.6 | 34.9 |
| Brownsville, Texas Lat. 25°55'N El. 20 ft | H̄ | 1105.9 | 1262.7 | 1505.9 | 1714 | 2092.2 | 2288.5 | 2345 | 2124 | 1774.9 | 1536.5 | 1104.8 | 982.3 |
| | K̄t | 0.517 | 0.500 | 0.505 | 0.509 | 0.584 | 0.627 | 0.650 | 0.617 | 0.566 | 0.468 | | 0.488 |
| | t₀ | 63.3 | 66.7 | 70.7 | 76.2 | 81.4 | 85.1 | 86.5 | 86.9 | 84.1 | 78.9 | 70.7 | 65.2 |
| Caribou, Maine Lat. 46°52'N El. 628 ft | H̄ | 497 | 861.6 | 1360.1 | 1495.9 | 1779.7 | 1779.7 | 1898.1 | 1675.6 | 1254.6 | 793 | 415.5 | 398.9 |
| | K̄t | 0.504 | 0.579 | 0.619 | 0.507 | 0.509 | 0.473 | 0.522 | 0.527 | 0.506 | 0.455 | 0.352 | 0.470 |
| | t₀ | 11.5 | 12.8 | 24.4 | 37.3 | 51.8 | 61.6 | 67.2 | 65.0 | 56.2 | 44.7 | 31.3 | 16.8 |
| Charleston, S.C. Lat. 32°54'N El. 46 ft | H̄ | 946.1 | 1152.8 | 1352.4 | 1918.8 | 2063.4 | 2113.3 | 1649.4 | 1933.6 | 1557.2 | 1332.1 | 1073.8 | 952 |
| | K̄t | 0.541 | 0.521 | 0.491 | 0.584 | 0.574 | 0.567 | 0.454 | 0.569 | 0.525 | 0.554 | 0.539 | 0.586 |
| | t₀ | 53.6 | 55.2 | 60.6 | 67.8 | 74.8 | 80.9 | 82.9 | 82.3 | 79.1 | 69.8 | 59.8 | 54.0 |
| Cleveland, Ohio Lat. 41°24'N El. 805 ft | H̄ | 466.8 | 681.9 | 1207 | 1443.9 | 1928.4 | 2102.6 | 2094.4 | 1840.6 | 1410.3 | 997 | 526.6 | 427.3 |
| | K̄t | 0.361 | 0.383 | 0.497 | 0.464 | 0.543 | 0.559 | 0.571 | 0.559 | 0.524 | 0.491 | 0.351 | 0.371 |
| | t₀ | 30.8 | 30.9 | 39.4 | 50.2 | 62.4 | 72.7 | 77.0 | 75.1 | 68.5 | 57.4 | 44.0 | 32.8 |
| Columbia, Mo Lat. 38°58'N El. 785 ft | H̄ | 651.3 | 941.3 | 1315.8 | 1631.3 | 1999.6 | 2129.1 | 2148.7 | 1953.1 | 1689.6 | 1202.6 | 839.5 | 590.4 |
| | K̄t | 0.458 | 0.492 | 0.520 | 0.514 | 0.559 | 0.586 | 0.585 | 0.588 | 0.606 | 0.562 | 0.510 | 0.457 |
| | t₀ | 32.5 | 36.5 | 45.9 | 57.7 | 66.7 | 75.9 | 81.1 | 79.4 | 71.9 | 61.4 | 46.1 | 35.8 |
| Columbus, Ohio Lat. 40°00'N El. 833 ft | H̄ | 486.3 | 746.5 | 1112.5 | 1480.8 | 1839.1 | (2111) | 2041.3 | 1572.7 | 1189.3 | 919.5 | 479 | 430.2 |
| | K̄t | 0.356 | 0.401 | 0.447 | 0.470 | 0.515 | (0.561) | 0.555 | 0.475 | 0.433 | 0.441 | 0.302 | 0.351 |
| | t₀ | 32.1 | 33.7 | 42.7 | 53.5 | 64.4 | 74.2 | 78 | 75.9 | 70.1 | 58 | 44.5 | 34.0 |
| Davis, Calif. Lat. 38°33'N El. 51 ft | H̄ | 599.2 | 945 | 1504 | 1959 | 2368.6 | 2619.2 | 2565.6 | 2287.8 | 1856.8 | 1288.5 | 795.6 | 550.5 |
| | K̄t | 0.416 | 0.490 | 0.591 | 0.617 | 0.667 | 0.697 | 0.697 | 0.687 | 0.664 | 0.590 | 0.477 | 0.421 |
| | t₀ | 47.6 | 52.1 | 56.8 | 63.1 | 69.6 | 75.7 | 81 | 79.4 | 76.7 | 67.8 | 57 | 48.7 |
| Dodge City, Kan. Lat. 37°46'N El. 2592 ft | H̄ | 953.1 | 1186.3 | 1565.7 | 1975.6 | 2126.5 | 2459.8 | 2400.7 | 2210.7 | 1841.7 | 1421 | 1065.3 | 873.8 |
| | K̄t | 0.639 | 0.598 | 0.606 | 0.612 | 0.594 | 0.655 | 0.652 | 0.663 | 0.654 | 0.650 | 0.625 | 0.652 |
| | t₀ | 33.8 | 38.7 | 46.5 | 57.7 | 66.7 | 77.2 | 83.8 | 82.4 | 73.7 | 61.7 | 46.5 | 36.8 |
| East Lansing, Michigan Lat. 42°44'N El. 856 ft | H̄ | 425.8 | 739.1 | 1086 | 1249.8 | 1732.8 | 1914 | 1884.5 | 1627.7 | 1303.3 | 891.5 | 473.1 | 379.7 |
| | K̄t | 0.35 | 0.431 | 0.456 | 0.406 | 0.489 | 0.508 | 0.514 | 0.498 | 0.493 | 0.456 | 0.333 | 0.349 |
| | t₀ | 26.0 | 26.4 | 35.7 | 48.4 | 59.8 | 70.3 | 74.5 | 72.4 | 65.0 | 53.5 | 40.0 | 29.0 |
| East Wareham, Mass Lat. 41°46'N El. 18 ft | H̄ | 504.4 | 762.4 | 1132.1 | 1392.6 | 1704.8 | 1958.3 | 1873.8 | 1607.4 | 1363.8 | 996.7 | 636.2 | 521 |
| | K̄t | 0.398 | 0.431 | 0.469 | 0.449 | 0.486 | 0.520 | 0.511 | 0.489 | 0.508 | 0.496 | 0.431 | 0.461 |
| | t₀ | 32.2 | 31.6 | 39.0 | 48.3 | 58.9 | 67.5 | 74.1 | 72.8 | 65.9 | 56 | 46 | 34.8 |

| Location | | Jan | Feb | Mar | Apr | May | Jun | Jul | Aug | Sep | Oct | Nov | Dec |
|---|---|---|---|---|---|---|---|---|---|---|---|---|---|
| Edmonton, Alberta Lat. 53°35'N El. 2219 ft | H̄ | 331.7 | 652.4 | 1165.3 | 1541.7 | 1900.4 | 1914.4 | 1964.9 | 1528 | 1113.3 | 704.4 | 413.6 | 245 |
| | K̄t | 0.529 | 0.585 | 0.624 | 0.564 | 0.558 | 0.514 | 0.549 | 0.506 | 0.506 | 0.504 | 0.510 | 0.492 |
| | t₀ | 10.4 | 14 | 26.3 | 42.9 | 55.4 | 61.3 | 66.6 | 63.2 | 54.2 | 44.1 | 26.7 | 14.0 |
| El Paso, Texas Lat. 31°48'N El. 3916 ft | H̄ | 1247.6 | 1612.9 | 2048.7 | 2447.2 | 2673 | 2731 | 2391.1 | 2350.5 | 2077.5 | 1704.8 | 1324.7 | 1051.6 |
| | K̄t | 0.686 | 0.714 | 0.730 | 0.741 | 0.743 | 0.733 | 0.652 | 0.669 | 0.693 | 0.695 | 0.647 | 0.626 |
| | t₀ | 47.1 | 53.1 | 58.7 | 67.3 | 75.7 | 84.2 | 84.9 | 83.4 | 78.5 | 69.0 | 56.0 | 48.5 |
| Ely, Nevada Lat. 39°17'N El. 6262 ft | H̄ | 871.6 | 1255 | 1749.8 | 2103.3 | 2322.1 | 2649 | 2417 | 2307.7 | 1935 | 1473 | 1078.6 | 814.8 |
| | K̄t | 0.618 | 0.660 | 0.692 | 0.664 | 0.649 | 0.704 | 0.656 | 0.695 | 0.696 | 0.691 | 0.658 | 0.64 |
| | t₀ | 27.3 | 32.1 | 39.5 | 48.3 | 57.0 | 65.4 | 74.5 | 72.3 | 63.7 | 52.1 | 39.9 | 31.1 |
| Fairbanks, Alaska Lat. 64°49'N El. 436 ft | H̄ | 66 | 283.4 | 860.5 | 1481.2 | 1806.2 | 1970.8 | 1702.9 | 1247.6 | 699.6 | 323.6 | 104.1 | 20.3 |
| | K̄t | 0.639 | 0.556 | 0.674 | 0.647 | 0.546 | 0.529 | 0.485 | 0.463 | 0.419 | 0.416 | 0.47 | 0.458 |
| | t₀ | -7.0 | 0.3 | 13.0 | 32.2 | 50.5 | 62.4 | 63.8 | 58.3 | 47.1 | 29.6 | 5.5 | -6.6 |
| Fort Worth, Texas Lat. 32°50'N El. 544 ft | H̄ | 936.2 | 1198.5 | 1597.8 | 1829.1 | 2105.1 | 2437.6 | 2293.3 | 2216.6 | 1880.8 | 1476 | 1147.6 | 913.6 |
| | K̄t | 0.530 | 0.541 | 0.577 | 0.556 | 0.585 | 0.624 | 0.624 | 0.653 | 0.634 | 0.612 | 0.576 | 0.563 |
| | t₀ | 48.1 | 52.3 | 59.8 | 68.8 | 75.9 | 84.0 | 87.7 | 88.6 | 81.3 | 71.5 | 58.8 | 50.8 |
| Fresno, Calif. Lat. 36°46'N El. 331 ft | H̄ | 712.9 | 1116.6 | 1652.8 | 2049.4 | 2409.2 | 2641.7 | 2512.2 | 2300.7 | 1897.8 | 1415.5 | 906.6 | 616.6 |
| | K̄t | 0.462 | 0.551 | 0.632 | 0.638 | 0.672 | 0.703 | 0.682 | 0.686 | 0.665 | 0.635 | 0.512 | 0.44 |
| | t₀ | 47.3 | 53.9 | 59.1 | 65.6 | 73.5 | 80.7 | 87.5 | 84.9 | 79.6 | 69.7 | 57.3 | 48.0 |
| Gainesville, Fla. Lat. 29°39'N El. 165 ft | H̄ | 1036.9 | 1324.7 | 1635 | 1956.4 | 1934.7 | 1960.9 | 1895.6 | 1873.8 | 1615.1 | 1312.2 | 1169.7 | 919.5 |
| | K̄t | 0.535 | 0.56 | 0.568 | 0.587 | 0.538 | 0.531 | 0.519 | 0.547 | 0.529 | 0.515 | 0.537 | 0.508 |
| | t₀ | 62.1 | 63.1 | 67.5 | 72.8 | 79.4 | 83.4 | 83.8 | 84.1 | 82 | 75.7 | 67.2 | 62.4 |
| Glasgow, Mont. Lat. 48°13'N El. 2277 ft | H̄ | 572.7 | 965.7 | 1437.6 | 1741.3 | 2127.3 | 2261.6 | 2414.7 | 1984.5 | 1531 | 997 | 574.9 | 428.4 |
| | K̄t | 0.621 | 0.678 | 0.672 | 0.597 | 0.611 | 0.602 | 0.666 | 0.630 | 0.629 | 0.593 | 0.516 | 0.548 |
| | t₀ | 13.3 | 17.3 | 31.1 | 47.9 | 59.3 | 67.3 | 76 | 73.2 | 61.2 | 49.2 | 31.0 | 18.6 |
| Grand Junction, Colo Lat. 39°07'N El. 4849 ft | H̄ | 848 | 1210.7 | 1622.9 | 2002.2 | 2300.3 | 2645.4 | 2517.7 | 2157.2 | 1957.5 | 1394.8 | 960.7 | 793.4 |
| | K̄t | 0.597 | 0.633 | 0.643 | 0.632 | 0.643 | 0.704 | 0.690 | 0.65 | 0.705 | 0.654 | 0.59 | 0.621 |
| | t₀ | 26.9 | 35.0 | 44.6 | 55.8 | 66.3 | 75.7 | 82.5 | 79.6 | 71.4 | 58.3 | 42.0 | 31.4 |
| Grand Lake, Colo. Lat. 40°15'N El. 8389 ft | H̄ | 735 | 1135.4 | 1579.3 | 1876.7 | 1974.9 | 2369.7 | 2103.3 | 1708.5 | 1715.8 | 1212.2 | 775.6 | 660.5 |
| | K̄t | 0.541 | 0.615 | 0.637 | 0.597 | 0.553 | 0.63 | 0.572 | 0.516 | 0.626 | 0.583 | 0.494 | 0.542 |
| | t₀ | 18.5 | 23.1 | 31.0 | 41.5 | 48.7 | 56.6 | 62.8 | 61.5 | 55.5 | 45.2 | 30.3 | 22.6 |
| Great Falls, Mont Lat. 47°29'N El. 3664 ft | H̄ | 524 | 869.4 | 1369.7 | 1621.4 | 1970.8 | 2179.3 | 2383 | 1986.3 | 1536.5 | 984.9 | 575.3 | 420.7 |
| | K̄t | 0.552 | 0.596 | 0.631 | 0.551 | 0.565 | 0.580 | 0.656 | 0.627 | 0.626 | 0.574 | 0.503 | 0.518 |
| | t₀ | 25.4 | 27.6 | 35.6 | 47.7 | 57.5 | 64.3 | 73.8 | 71.3 | 60.6 | 51.4 | 38.0 | 29.1 |

| Location | | Jan | Feb | Mar | Apr | May | Jun | Jul | Aug | Sep | Oct | Nov | Dec |
|---|---|---|---|---|---|---|---|---|---|---|---|---|---|
| Greensboro, N.C. Lat. 36°05'N El. 891 ft | H̄ | 743.9 | 1031.7 | 1323.2 | 1755.3 | 1988.5 | 2111.4 | 2033.9 | 1810.3 | 1517.3 | 1202.6 | 908.1 | 690.8 |
| | K̄t | 0.469 | 0.490 | 0.499 | 0.543 | 0.554 | 0.563 | 0.552 | 0.538 | 0.527 | 0.531 | 0.501 | 0.479 |
| | t₀ | 42.0 | 44.2 | 51.7 | 60.8 | 69.9 | 78.0 | 80.2 | 78.9 | 73.9 | 62.7 | 51.5 | 43.2 |
| Griffin, Georgia Lat. 33°15'N El. 980 ft | H̄ | 889.6 | 1135.8 | 1450.9 | 1923.6 | 2163.1 | 2176 | 2064.9 | 1961.2 | 1605.9 | 1352.4 | 1073.8 | 781.5 |
| | K̄t | 0.513 | 0.517 | 0.528 | 0.586 | 0.601 | 0.583 | 0.562 | 0.578 | 0.543 | 0.565 | 0.545 | 0.487 |
| | t₀ | 48.9 | 51.0 | 59.1 | 66.7 | 74.6 | 81.2 | 83.0 | 82.2 | 78.4 | 68 | 57.3 | 49.4 |
| Hatteras, N.C. Lat. 35°13'N El. 7 ft | H̄ | 891.9 | 1184.1 | 1590.4 | 2128 | 2376.4 | 2438 | 2334.3 | 2085.6 | 1758.3 | 1337.6 | 1053.5 | 798.1 |
| | K̄t | 0.546 | 0.563 | 0.593 | 0.655 | 0.661 | 0.652 | 0.634 | 0.619 | 0.605 | 0.58 | 0.566 | 0.535 |
| | t₀ | 49.9 | 49.5 | 54.7 | 61.5 | 69.9 | 77.2 | 80.0 | 79.8 | 76.7 | 67.9 | 59.1 | 51.3 |
| Indianapolis, Ind Lat. 39°44'N El. 793 ft | H̄ | 526.2 | 797.4 | 1184.1 | 1481.2 | 1828 | 2042 | 2039.5 | 1832.1 | 1513.1 | 1094.4 | 662.4 | 491.1 |
| | K̄t | 0.380 | 0.424 | 0.472 | 0.47 | 0.511 | 0.543 | 0.554 | 0.552 | 0.549 | 0.520 | 0.413 | 0.391 |
| | t₀ | 31.3 | 33.9 | 43.0 | 54.1 | 64.9 | 74.8 | 79.6 | 77.4 | 70.6 | 59.3 | 44.2 | 33.4 |
| Inyokern, Calif Lat. 35°39'N El. ft | H̄ | 1148.7 | 1554.2 | 2136.9 | 2594.8 | 2925.4 | 3108.8 | 2908.8 | 2759.4 | 2409.2 | 1819.2 | 1170.1 | 1094.4 |
| | K̄t | 0.716 | 0.745 | 0.803 | 0.8 | 0.815 | 0.830 | 0.790 | 0.820 | 0.834 | 0.795 | 0.743 | 0.742 |
| | t₀ | 47.3 | 53.9 | 59.1 | 65.8 | 73.5 | 80.7 | 87.5 | 84.9 | 78.6 | 68.7 | 57.3 | 48.9 |
| Ithaca, N.Y. Lat. 42°27'N El. 950 ft | H̄ | 434.3 | 755 | 1074.9 | 1322.9 | 1779.3 | 2025.8 | 2031.3 | 1736.9 | 1320.3 | 918.4 | 466.4 | 370.8 |
| | K̄t | 0.351 | 0.435 | 0.45 | 0.428 | 0.502 | 0.538 | 0.554 | 0.530 | 0.497 | 0.465 | 0.324 | 0.337 |
| | t₀ | 25.2 | 26.5 | 36 | 48.4 | 59.6 | 68.9 | 73.9 | 71.9 | 64.2 | 53.6 | 41.5 | 29.6 |
| Lake Charles, La Lat. 30°13'N El. 12 ft | H̄ | 899.2 | 1145.7 | 1487.4 | 1801.8 | 2080.4 | 2213.3 | 1968.6 | 1910.3 | 1678.2 | 1505.5 | 1122.1 | 875.6 |
| | K̄t | 0.473 | 0.492 | 0.521 | 0.542 | 0.578 | 0.597 | 0.538 | 0.558 | 0.553 | 0.597 | 0.524 | 0.494 |
| | t₀ | 55.3 | 58 | 63.5 | 70.9 | 77.4 | 83.4 | 84.8 | 85.0 | 81.5 | 73.8 | 62.6 | 56.9 |
| Lander, Wyo Lat. 42°48'N El. 5370 ft | H̄ | 786.3 | 1146.1 | 1638 | 1988.5 | 2114 | 2492.2 | 2438.4 | 2120.6 | 1712.9 | 1301.8 | 837.3 | 694.8 |
| | K̄t | 0.65 | 0.672 | 0.691 | 0.647 | 0.597 | 0.662 | 0.665 | 0.649 | 0.647 | 0.666 | 0.589 | 0.643 |
| | t₀ | 20.2 | 26.3 | 34.7 | 45.5 | 56.0 | 65.4 | 74.6 | 72.5 | 61.5 | 48.3 | 33.4 | 23.8 |
| Las Vegas, Nev Lat. 36°05'N El. 2162 ft | H̄ | 1035.8 | 1438 | 1926.5 | 2322.8 | 2629.5 | 2799.2 | 2524 | 2342 | 2062 | 1602.6 | 1190 | 964.2 |
| | K̄t | 0.595 | 0.67 | 0.728 | 0.719 | 0.734 | 0.746 | 0.685 | 0.697 | 0.716 | 0.704 | 0.657 | 0.668 |
| | t₀ | 47.5 | 53.9 | 60.3 | 69.5 | 78.3 | 88.2 | 95.0 | 92.9 | 85.4 | 71.7 | 57.8 | 50.2 |
| Lemont, Illinois Lat. 41°40'N El. 595 ft | H̄ | (590) | 879 | 1255.7 | 1481.5 | 1866 | 2041.7 | 1990.8 | 1836.9 | 1469.4 | 1015.5 | (639) | (531) |
| | K̄t | (0.464) | 0.496 | 0.520 | 0.477 | 0.525 | 0.542 | 0.559 | 0.547 | 0.506 | | (0.433) | (0.467) |
| | t₀ | 28.9 | 30.3 | 39.5 | 49.7 | 59.2 | 70.8 | 75.6 | 74.3 | 67.2 | 57 | | 30.6 |
| Lexington, Ky Lat. 38°02'N El. 979 ft | H̄ | - | - | - | 1834.7 | 2171.2 | - | 2246.5 | 2064.9 | 1775.6 | 1315.6 | - | 681.5 |
| | K̄t | - | - | - | 0.575 | 0.606 | - | 0.610 | 0.619 | 0.631 | 0.604 | - | 0.513 |
| | t₀ | 36.5 | 38.8 | 47.4 | 57.8 | 67.5 | 76.2 | 79.8 | 78.2 | 72.8 | 61.2 | 47.6 | 38.5 |

| Station | | Jan | Feb | Mar | Apr | May | Jun | Jul | Aug | Sep | Oct | Nov | Dec |
|---|---|---|---|---|---|---|---|---|---|---|---|---|---|
| Lincoln, Neb | $\bar{H}$ | 712.5 | 955.7 | 1299.6 | 1587.8 | 1856.1 | 2040.6 | 2011.4 | 1902.6 | 1543.5 | 1215.8 | 773.4 | 643.2 |
| Lat. 40°51'N | $\bar{K}_t$ | 0.542 | 0.528 | 0.532 | 0.507 | 0.522 | 0.542 | 0.547 | 0.577 | 0.568 | 0.596 | 0.508 | 0.545 |
| El. 1189 ft | $t_o$ | 27.8 | 32.1 | 42.4 | 55.8 | 65.8 | 76.0 | 82.6 | 80.2 | 71.5 | 59.9 | 43.2 | 31.8 |
| Little Rock, Ark | $\bar{H}$ | 704.4 | 974.2 | 1335.8 | 1669.4 | 1960.1 | 2091.5 | 2081.2 | 1938.7 | 1640.6 | 1282.6 | 913.6 | 701.1 |
| Lat. 34°44'N | $\bar{K}_t$ | 0.424 | 0.458 | 0.496 | 0.513 | 0.545 | 0.559 | 0.566 | 0.574 | 0.561 | 0.552 | 0.484 | 0.463 |
| El. 265 ft | $t_o$ | 44.6 | 48.5 | 56.0 | 65.8 | 73.1 | 76.7 | 85.1 | 84.6 | 78.3 | 67.9 | 54.7 | 46.7 |
| Los Angeles, Calif. (WBAS) | $\bar{H}$ | 930.6 | 1284.1 | 1729.5 | 1948 | 2196.7 | 2272.3 | 2413.6 | 2155.3 | 1898.1 | 1372.7 | 1082.3 | 901.1 |
| Lat. 33°56'N | $\bar{K}_t$ | 0.547 | 0.596 | 0.635 | 0.595 | 0.610 | 0.608 | 0.657 | 0.635 | 0.641 | 0.574 | 0.551 | 0.566 |
| El. 99 ft | $t_o$ | 56.2 | 56.9 | 59.2 | 61.4 | 64.2 | 66.7 | 69.6 | 70.2 | 69.1 | 66.1 | 62.6 | 58.7 |
| Los Angeles, Calif. (WBO) | $\bar{H}$ | 911.8 | 1223.6 | 1640.9 | 1866.8 | 2061.2 | 2259 | 2428.4 | 2198.9 | 1891.5 | 1362.3 | 1053.1 | 877.8 |
| Lat. 34°03'N | $\bar{K}_t$ | 0.538 | 0.568 | 0.602 | 0.571 | 0.573 | 0.605 | 0.66 | 0.648 | 0.643 | 0.578 | 0.548 | 0.566 |
| El. 99 ft | $t_o$ | 57.9 | 59.2 | 61.8 | 64.3 | 67.6 | 70.7 | 75.8 | 76.1 | 74.2 | 69.6 | 65.4 | 60.2 |
| Madison, Wis | $\bar{H}$ | 564.6 | 812.2 | 1232.1 | 1455.3 | 1745.4 | 2031.7 | 2046.5 | 1740.2 | 1443.9 | 993 | 555.7 | 495.9 |
| Lat. 43°08'N | $\bar{K}_t$ | 0.49 | 0.478 | 0.522 | 0.474 | 0.493 | 0.540 | 0.559 | 0.534 | 0.549 | 0.510 | 0.396 | 0.467 |
| El. 866 ft | $t_o$ | 21.8 | 24.6 | 35.3 | 49.0 | 61.0 | 70.9 | 76.8 | 74.4 | 65.6 | 53.7 | 37.8 | 25.4 |
| Matanuska, Alaska | $\bar{H}$ | 119.2 | 345 | - | 1327.6 | 1628.4 | 1727.6 | 1526.9 | 1169 | 737.3 | 373.8 | 142.8 | 56.4 |
| Lat. 61°30'N | $\bar{K}_t$ | 0.513 | 0.503 | - | 0.545 | 0.494 | 0.466 | 0.434 | 0.419 | 0.401 | 0.390 | 0.372 | 0.364 |
| El. 180 ft | $t_o$ | 13.9 | 21.0 | 27.4 | 38.6 | 50.3 | 57.6 | 60.1 | 58.1 | 50.2 | 37.7 | 22.9 | 13.9 |
| Medford, Oregon H. | $\bar{H}$ | 435.4 | 804.4 | 1259.8 | 1807.4 | 2216.2 | 2440.5 | 2607.4 | 2261.6 | 1672.3 | 1043.5 | 558.7 | 346.5 |
| Lat. 42°23'N | $\bar{K}_t$ | 0.353 | 0.464 | 0.527 | 0.584 | 0.625 | 0.648 | 0.710 | 0.689 | 0.628 | 0.526 | 0.384 | 0.313 |
| El. 1329 ft | $t_o$ | 39.4 | 45.4 | 50.8 | 56.3 | 63.1 | 69.4 | 76.9 | 76.4 | 69.6 | 58.7 | 47.1 | 40.5 |
| Miami, Florida | $\bar{H}$ | 1292.2 | 1554.6 | 1828.8 | 2020.6 | 2068.6 | 1991.5 | 1992.6 | 1890.8 | 1646.8 | 1436.5 | 1321 | 1183.4 |
| Lat. 25°47'N | $\bar{K}_t$ | 0.604 | 0.616 | 0.612 | 0.600 | 0.578 | 0.545 | 0.552 | 0.549 | 0.525 | 0.534 | 0.559 | 0.588 |
| El. 9 ft. | $t_o$ | 71.6 | 72.0 | 73.8 | 77.0 | 79.9 | 82.9 | 84.1 | 84.5 | 83.3 | 80.2 | 75.6 | 72.6 |
| Midland, Texas | $\bar{H}$ | 1066.4 | 1345.7 | 1784.8 | 2036.1 | 2301.1 | 2317.7 | 2301.8 | 2193 | 1921.8 | 1470.8 | 1244.3 | 1023.2 |
| Lat. 31°56'N | $\bar{K}_t$ | 0.587 | 0.596 | 0.638 | 0.617 | 0.639 | 0.622 | 0.628 | 0.643 | 0.642 | 0.600 | 0.609 | 0.611 |
| El. 2854 ft | $t_o$ | 47.9 | 52.8 | 60.0 | 68.8 | 77.2 | 83.9 | 85.7 | 85.0 | 78.9 | 70.3 | 56.6 | 49.1 |
| Nashville, Tenn | $\bar{H}$ | 589.7 | 907 | 1246.8 | 1662.3 | 1997 | 2149.4 | 2079.7 | 1862.7 | 1600.7 | 1223.6 | 823.2 | 614.4 |
| Lat. 36°07'N | $\bar{K}_t$ | 0.373 | 0.440 | 0.472 | 0.514 | 0.556 | 0.573 | 0.565 | 0.554 | 0.556 | 0.540 | 0.454 | 0.426 |
| El. 605 ft | $t_o$ | 42.6 | 45.1 | 52.9 | 63.0 | 71.4 | 80.1 | 83.2 | 81.9 | 76.6 | 65.4 | 52.3 | 44.3 |
| New Port, R.I. | $\bar{H}$ | 565.7 | 856.4 | 1231.7 | 1484.8 | 1849 | 2019.2 | 1942.8 | 1687.1 | 1411.4 | 1035.4 | 656.1 | 527.7 |
| Lat. 41°29'N | $\bar{K}_t$ | 0.438 | 0.482 | 0.507 | 0.477 | 0.520 | 0.536 | 0.529 | 0.513 | 0.524 | 0.512 | 0.44 | 0.460 |
| El. 60 ft | $t_o$ | 29.5 | 32.0 | 39.6 | 48.2 | 58.6 | 67.0 | 73.2 | 72.3 | 66.7 | 56.2 | 46.5 | 34.4 |
| Santa Maria, Calif | $\bar{H}$ | 983.8 | 1296.3 | 1805.9 | 2067.9 | 2375.6 | 2599.6 | 2540.6 | 2293.3 | 1965.7 | 1566.4 | 1169 | 943.9 |
| Lat. 34°54'N | $\bar{K}_t$ | 0.595 | 0.613 | 0.671 | 0.636 | 0.661 | 0.695 | 0.690 | 0.678 | 0.674 | 0.676 | 0.624 | 0.627 |
| El. 238 ft | $t_o$ | 54.1 | 55.3 | 57.6 | 59.5 | 61.2 | 63.5 | 65.3 | 65.7 | 65.9 | 64.1 | 60.8 | 56.1 |
| Sault Ste. Marie, Michigan | $\bar{H}$ | 488.6 | 843.9 | 1336.5 | 1559.4 | 1962.3 | 2064.2 | 2149.4 | 1767.9 | 1207 | 809.2 | 392.2 | 359.8 |
| Lat. 46°28'N | $\bar{K}_t$ | 0.490 | 0.560 | 0.606 | 0.526 | 0.560 | 0.549 | 0.590 | 0.554 | 0.481 | 0.457 | 0.323 | 0.408 |
| El. 724 ft | $t_o$ | 16.3 | 16.2 | 25.6 | 39.5 | 52.1 | 61.6 | 67.3 | 66.0 | 57.9 | 46.8 | 33.4 | 21.9 |
| Sayville, N.Y | $\bar{H}$ | 602.9 | 936.2 | 1259.4 | 1560.5 | 1857.2 | 2123.2 | 2040.9 | 1734.7 | 1446.8 | 1087.4 | 697.8 | 533.9 |
| Lat. 40°30'N | $\bar{K}_t$ | 0.453 | 0.511 | 0.510 | 0.498 | 0.522 | 0.564 | 0.555 | 0.525 | 0.530 | 0.527 | 0.450 | 0.447 |
| El. 20 ft | $t_o$ | 35 | 34.9 | 43.1 | 52.3 | 63.3 | 72.2 | 76.9 | 75.3 | 69.5 | 59.3 | 48.3 | 37.7 |
| Schenectady, N.Y. | $\bar{H}$ | 488.2 | 753.5 | 1026.6 | 1272.3 | 1553.1 | 1687.8 | 1662.3 | 1494.8 | 1124.7 | 820.6 | 436.2 | 356.8 |
| Lat. 42°50'N | $\bar{K}_t$ | 0.406 | 0.441 | 0.433 | 0.413 | 0.438 | 0.448 | 0.454 | 0.458 | 0.426 | 0.420 | 0.309 | 0.331 |
| El. 217 ft | $t_o$ | 24.7 | 24.6 | 34.9 | 48.3 | 61.7 | 70.8 | 76.9 | 73.7 | 64.6 | 53.1 | 40.1 | 28.0 |
| Seattle, Wash | $\bar{H}$ | 282.6 | 520.6 | 992.2 | 1507 | 1881.5 | 1909.9 | 2110.7 | 1688.5 | 1211.8 | 702.2 | 386.3 | 239.5 |
| Lat. 47°27'N | $\bar{K}_t$ | 0.296 | 0.355 | 0.456 | 0.510 | 0.538 | 0.508 | 0.581 | 0.533 | 0.492 | 0.407 | 0.336 | 0.292 |
| El. 386 ft | $t_o$ | 42.1 | 45.0 | 48.9 | 54.1 | 59.8 | 64.4 | 68.4 | 67.9 | 63.3 | 56.3 | 48.4 | 44.4 |
| Seattle, Wash | $\bar{H}$ | 252 | 471.6 | 917.3 | 1375.6 | 1664.9 | 1724 | 1805.1 | 1617 | 1129.1 | 638 | 325.5 | 218.1 |
| Lat. 47°36'N | $\bar{K}_t$ | 0.266 | 0.324 | 0.423 | 0.468 | 0.477 | 0.459 | 0.498 | 0.511 | 0.459 | 0.372 | 0.284 | 0.269 |
| El. 14 ft | $t_o$ | 38.9 | 42.9 | 46.9 | 51.9 | 58.1 | 62.8 | 67.2 | 66.7 | 61.6 | 54.0 | 45.7 | 41.5 |
| Seabrook, N.J | $\bar{H}$ | 591.9 | 854.2 | 1195.6 | 1518.8 | 1800.7 | 1964.6 | 1949.8 | 1715 | 1445.7 | 1071.9 | 721.8 | 522.5 |
| Lat. 39°30'N | $\bar{K}_t$ | 0.426 | 0.453 | 0.476 | 0.481 | 0.504 | 0.522 | 0.530 | 0.517 | 0.524 | 0.508 | 0.449 | 0.416 |
| El. 100 ft | $t_o$ | 39.5 | 37.6 | 43.9 | 54.7 | 64.9 | 74.1 | 79.8 | 77.7 | 69.7 | 61.2 | 48.5 | 39.3 |
| Spokane, Wash. | $\bar{H}$ | 446.1 | 837.6 | 1200 | 1864.6 | 2104.4 | 2226.5 | 2479.7 | 2076 | 1511 | 844.6 | 486.3 | 279 |
| Lat. 47°40'N | $\bar{K}_t$ | 0.478 | 0.579 | 0.556 | 0.602 | 0.603 | 0.593 | 0.684 | 0.656 | 0.616 | 0.494 | 0.428 | 0.345 |
| El. 1968 ft | $t_o$ | 26.5 | 31.7 | 40.5 | 49.2 | 57.9 | 64.6 | 73.4 | 71.7 | 62.7 | 51.5 | 37.4 | 30.5 |
| State College, Pa | $\bar{H}$ | 501.8 | 749.1 | 1106.6 | 1399.2 | 1754.6 | 2027.6 | 1968.2 | 1690 | 1336.1 | 1017 | 580.1 | 443.9 |
| Lat. 40°48'N | $\bar{K}_t$ | 0.381 | 0.413 | 0.451 | 0.448 | 0.493 | 0.539 | 0.536 | 0.512 | 0.492 | 0.496 | 0.379 | 0.376 |
| El. 1175 ft | $t_o$ | 31.3 | 31.4 | 39.8 | 51.3 | 63.4 | 71.8 | 75.8 | 73.4 | 66.1 | 55.6 | 43.2 | 32.6 |
| Stillwater, Okla | $\bar{H}$ | 763.8 | 1081.5 | 1463.8 | 1702.6 | 1879.3 | 2235.8 | 2224.3 | 2039.1 | 1724.3 | 1314 | 991.5 | 783 |
| Lat. 36°09'N | $\bar{K}_t$ | 0.484 | 0.527 | 0.555 | 0.528 | 0.523 | 0.596 | 0.604 | 0.607 | 0.599 | 0.581 | 0.548 | 0.544 |
| El. 910 ft | $t_o$ | 41.2 | 45.6 | 53.8 | 64.2 | 71.6 | 81.1 | 85.9 | 85.9 | 77.5 | 67.6 | 52.6 | 43.9 |
| Tampa, Fla. | $\bar{H}$ | 1223.6 | 1461.2 | 1771.9 | 2016.2 | 2228 | 2146.5 | 1991.9 | 1845.4 | 1687.8 | 1493.3 | 1328.4 | 1119.5 |
| Lat. 27°55'N | $\bar{K}_t$ | 0.605 | 0.600 | 0.606 | 0.602 | 0.620 | 0.583 | 0.548 | 0.537 | 0.546 | 0.572 | 0.590 | 0.589 |
| El. 11 ft | $t_o$ | 64.2 | 65.7 | 68.8 | 74.3 | 79.4 | 83.0 | 84.0 | 84.4 | 82.9 | 77.2 | 69.6 | 65.5 |
| New York, N.Y. | $\bar{H}$ | 539.5 | 790.8 | 1180.4 | 1426.2 | 1738.4 | 1994.1 | 1938.7 | 1605.9 | 1349.4 | 977.8 | 598.1 | 476 |
| Lat. 40°46'N | $\bar{K}_t$ | 0.406 | 0.435 | 0.480 | 0.455 | 0.488 | 0.53 | 0.528 | 0.486 | 0.500 | 0.475 | 0.397 | 0.403 |
| El. 52 ft | $t_o$ | 35.0 | 34.9 | 43.1 | 52.3 | 63.3 | 72.2 | 76.9 | 75.3 | 69.5 | 59.3 | 48.3 | 37.7 |
| Oak Ridge, Tenn | $\bar{H}$ | 604 | 895.9 | 1241.7 | 1689.6 | 1942.8 | 2066.4 | 1972.3 | 1795.6 | 1559.8 | 1194.8 | 796.3 | 610 |
| Lat. 36°01'N | $\bar{K}_t$ | 0.382 | 0.435 | 0.471 | 0.524 | 0.541 | 0.551 | 0.536 | 0.534 | 0.542 | 0.527 | 0.438 | 0.422 |
| El. 905 ft | $t_o$ | 41.9 | 44.2 | 51.7 | 61.4 | 69.8 | 77.8 | 80.2 | 78.8 | 74.5 | 62.7 | 50.4 | 42.5 |
| Oklahoma City, Oklahoma | $\bar{H}$ | 938 | 1192.6 | 1534.3 | 1849.4 | 2005.1 | 2355 | 2273.8 | 2211 | 1819.2 | 1409.6 | 1085.6 | 897.4 |
| Lat. 35°24'N | $\bar{K}_t$ | 0.580 | 0.571 | 0.576 | 0.570 | 0.558 | 0.629 | 0.618 | 0.565 | 0.628 | 0.614 | 0.588 | 0.608 |
| El. 1304 ft | $t_o$ | 40.1 | 45.0 | 53.2 | 63.6 | 71.2 | 80.6 | 85.5 | 85.4 | 77.4 | 66.5 | 52.2 | 43.1 |
| Ottawa, Ontario | $\bar{H}$ | 539.1 | 852.4 | 1250.5 | 1506.6 | 1857.2 | 2084.5 | 2045.4 | 1752.4 | 1326.6 | 826.9 | 458.7 | 408.5 |
| Lat. 45°20'N | $\bar{K}_t$ | 0.499 | 0.540 | 0.554 | 0.502 | 0.529 | 0.554 | 0.560 | 0.546 | 0.521 | 0.450 | 0.359 | 0.436 |
| El. 339 ft | $t_o$ | 14.6 | 15.6 | 27.7 | 43.3 | 57.5 | 67.5 | 71.9 | 69.8 | 61.5 | 48.9 | 35 | 19.6 |
| Phoenix, Ariz | $\bar{H}$ | 1126.6 | 1514.7 | 1967.1 | 2388.2 | 2709.6 | 2781.5 | 2450.5 | 2299.6 | 2131.3 | 1688.9 | 1290 | 1040.9 |
| Lat. 33°26'N | $\bar{K}_t$ | 0.65 | 0.691 | 0.716 | 0.728 | 0.753 | 0.745 | 0.667 | 0.677 | 0.722 | 0.708 | 0.657 | 0,652 |
| El. 1112 ft | $t_o$ | 54.2 | 58.8 | 64.7 | 72.2 | 80.8 | 89.2 | 94.6 | 92.5 | 87.4 | 75.8 | 63.6 | 56.7 |
| Portland, Maine | $\bar{H}$ | 565.7 | 874.5 | 1329.5 | 1528.4 | 1923.2 | 2017.3 | 2095.6 | 1799.2 | 1428.8 | 1035 | 591.5 | 507.7 |
| Lat. 43°39'N | $\bar{K}_t$ | 0.482 | 0.524 | 0.569 | 0.500 | 0.544 | 0.536 | 0.572 | 0.554 | 0.546 | 0.539 | 0.431 | 0.491 |
| El. 63 ft | $t_o$ | 23.7 | 24.5 | 34.4 | 44.8 | 55.4 | 65.1 | 71.1 | 69.7 | 61.9 | 51.8 | 40.3 | 28.0 |
| Rapid City, S.D. | $\bar{H}$ | 687.8 | 1032.5 | 1503.7 | 1807 | 2028 | 2193.7 | 2235.8 | 2019.9 | 1628 | 1179.3 | 763.1 | 590.4 |
| Lat. 44°09'N | $\bar{K}_t$ | 0.601 | 0.627 | 0.649 | 0.594 | 0.574 | 0.583 | 0.612 | 0.622 | 0.628 | 0.624 | 0.566 | 0.588 |
| El. 3218 ft | $t_o$ | 24.7 | 27.4 | 34.7 | 48.2 | 58.3 | 67.3 | 76.3 | 75.0 | 64.7 | 52.9 | 38.7 | 29.2 |
| Riverside, Calif | $\bar{H}$ | 999.6 | 1335 | 1750.5 | 1943.2 | 2282.3 | 2492.6 | 2443.5 | 2263.8 | 1955.3 | 1509.6 | 1169 | 979.7 |
| Lat. 33°57'N | $\bar{K}_t$ | 0.589 | 0.617 | 0.643 | 0.594 | 0.635 | 0.667 | 0.665 | 0.668 | 0.665 | 0.639 | 0.606 | 0.626 |
| El. 1020 ft | $t_o$ | 55.3 | 57.0 | 60.6 | 65.0 | 69.4 | 74.0 | 81.0 | 81.0 | 78.5 | 71.0 | 63.1 | 57.2 |
| St. Cloud, Minn | $\bar{H}$ | 632.8 | 976.7 | 1383 | 1598.1 | 1859.4 | 2003.3 | 2087.8 | 1828.4 | 1369.4 | 890.4 | 545.4 | 463.1 |
| Lat. 45°35'N | $\bar{K}_t$ | 0.595 | 0.629 | 0.614 | 0.534 | 0.530 | 0.533 | 0.573 | 0.570 | 0.539 | 0.490 | 0.435 | 0.504 |
| El. 1034 ft | $t_o$ | 13.6 | 16.9 | 29.8 | 46.2 | 58.8 | 68.5 | 74.4 | 71.9 | 62.5 | 50.2 | 32.1 | 18.3 |
| Salt Lake City, Utah | $\bar{H}$ | 622.1 | 986 | 1301.1 | 1813.3 | - | - | - | - | 1689.3 | 1250.2 | - | 552.8 |
| Lat. 40°46'N | $\bar{K}_t$ | 0.468 | 0.909 | 0.529 | 0.579 | - | - | - | - | 0.621 | 0.610 | - | 0.467 |
| El. 4227 ft | $t_o$ | 29.4 | 36.2 | 44.4 | 53.9 | 63.1 | 71.7 | 81.3 | 79.0 | 68.7 | 57.0 | 42.5 | 34.0 |
| San Antonio, Tex | $\bar{H}$ | 1045 | 1299.2 | 1560.1 | 1664.6 | 2024.7 | 814.8 | 2364.2 | 2185.2 | 1844.6 | 1487.4 | 1104.4 | 954.6 |
| Lat. 29°32'N | $\bar{K}_t$ | 0.541 | 0.550 | 0.542 | 0.500 | 0.563 | 0.220 | 0.647 | 0.637 | 0.603 | 0.584 | 0.507 | 0.528 |
| El. 794 ft | $t_o$ | 53.7 | 58.4 | 65.0 | 72.2 | 79.2 | 85.0 | 87.4 | 87.8 | 82.6 | 74.7 | 63.3 | 56.5 |
| Toronto, Ontario | $\bar{H}$ | 451.3 | 674.5 | 1088.9 | 1388.2 | 1785.2 | 1941.7 | 1968.6 | 1622.5 | 1284.1 | 835 | 458.3 | 352.8 |
| Lat. 43°41'N | $\bar{K}_t$ | 0.388 | 0.406 | 0.467 | 0.455 | 0.506 | 0.516 | 0.539 | 0.500 | 0.493 | 0.438 | 0.336 | 0.346 |
| El. 379 ft | $t_o$ | 26.5 | 26.0 | 34.2 | 46.3 | 58 | 68.4 | 73.8 | 71.8 | 64.3 | 52.6 | 40.9 | 30.2 |
| Tucson, Arizona | $\bar{H}$ | 1171.9 | 1453.8 | - | 2434.7 | - | 2601.4 | 2292.2 | 2179.7 | 2122.5 | 1640.9 | 1322.1 | 1132.1 |
| Lat. 32°07'N | $\bar{K}_t$ | 0.648 | 0.646 | - | 0.738 | - | 0.698 | 0.625 | 0.640 | 0.710 | 0.672 | 0.650 | 0.679 |
| El. 2556 ft | $t_o$ | 53.7 | 57.3 | 62.3 | 69.7 | 78.0 | 87.0 | 90.1 | 87.4 | 84.0 | 73.9 | 62.5 | 56.1 |
| Upton, N.Y. | $\bar{H}$ | 583 | 872.7 | 1280.4 | 1609.9 | 1891.5 | 2159 | 2044.6 | 1789.6 | 1472.7 | 1102.6 | 686.7 | 551.3 |
| Lat. 40°52'N | $\bar{K}_t$ | 0.444 | 0.483 | 0.522 | 0.514 | 0.532 | 0.574 | 0.557 | 0.542 | 0.542 | 0.538 | 0.448 | 0.467 |
| El. 75 ft | $t_o$ | 35.0 | 34.9 | 43.1 | 52.3 | 63.3 | 72.2 | 76.9 | 75.3 | 69.5 | 59.3 | 48.3 | 37.7 |
| Washington, D.C. (WBCO) | $\bar{H}$ | 632.4 | 901.5 | 1255 | 1600.4 | 1846.8 | 2080.8 | 1929.9 | 1712.2 | 1446.1 | 1083.4 | 763.5 | 594.1 |
| Lat. 38°51'N | $\bar{K}_t$ | 0.445 | 0.470 | 0.496 | 0.504 | 0.516 | 0.553 | 0.524 | 0.516 | 0.520 | 0.506 | 0.464 | 0.460 |
| El. 64 ft | $t_o$ | 38.4 | 39.6 | 48.1 | 57.5 | 67.7 | 76.2 | 79.9 | 77.9 | 72.2 | 60.9 | 50.2 | 40.2 |
| Winnipeg, Man. | $\bar{H}$ | 488.2 | 835.4 | 1354.2 | 1641.3 | 1904.4 | 1962 | 2123.6 | 1761.2 | 1190.4 | 767.5 | 444.6 | 345 |
| Lat. 49°54'N | $\bar{K}_t$ | 0.601 | 0.636 | 0.661 | 0.574 | 0.550 | 0.524 | 0.587 | 0.567 | 0.504 | 0.482 | 0.436 | 0.503 |
| El. 786 ft | $t_o$ | 3.2 | 7.1 | 21.3 | 40.9 | 55.9 | 65.3 | 71.9 | 69.4 | 58.6 | 45.6 | 25.2 | 10.1 |

The data in Appendix A-3 is compiled from statistical data compiled by the U.S. Weather Bureau. The figures show the daily total (direct + diffuse) radiation, $\bar{H}$ on a horizontal surface for each of the twelve calendar months. $K_t$ = the fraction of the extraterrestial radiation transmitted through the atmosphere; $t_0$ = ambient temp., deg F.

Appendix A-4 *Sunpath Diagrams for Seven Latitudes (0-60°) Indicating the Sun's Altitude and Azimuth. Intermediate Latitudes can be Linearly Interpolated.*[1]

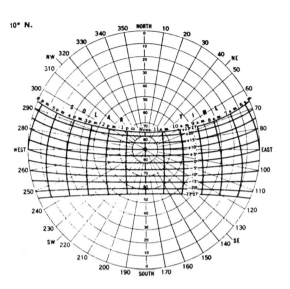

Figure 52.—Solar altitude and azimuth for selected days of the year at 10 degrees north latitude.

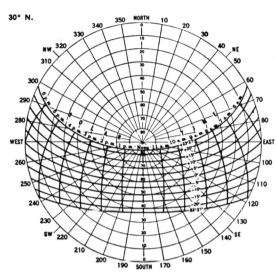

Figure 54.—Solar altitude and azimuth for selected days of the year at 30 degrees north latitude.

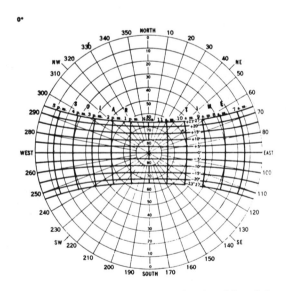

Figure 51.—Solar altitude and azimuth for selected days of the year at 0 degrees north latitude.

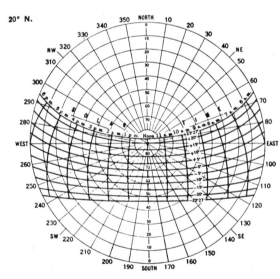

Figure 53.—Solar altitude and azimuth for selected days of the year at 20 degrees north latitude.

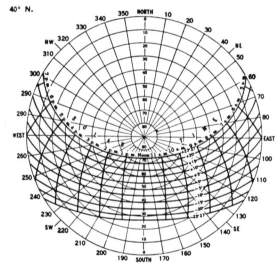

Figure 55.—Solar altitude and azimuth for selected days of the year at 40 degrees north latitude.

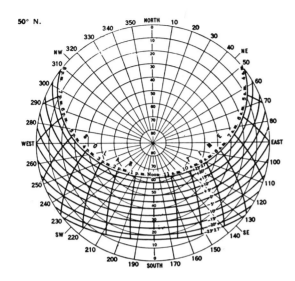

Figure 56.—Solar altitude and azimuth for selected days of the year at 50 degrees north latitude.

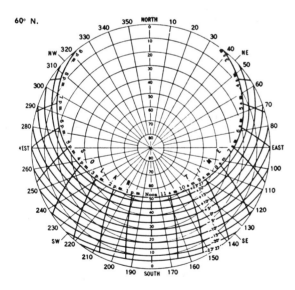

Figure 57.—Solar altitude and azimuth for selected days of the year at 60 degrees north latitude.

FOOTNOTES:

1. Buffo, John, *et.al.* "Direct Solar Radiation on Various Slopes from 0 to 60° North Latitude," *USDA Forest Service Research Paper*, 1972, (PNW-142).

2. "Solar Energy Utilization for Heating and Cooling," *ASHRAE 1974 Applications Handbook*, p. 59.6.

3. Jordan, Richard C., ed. "Low Temperature Engineering Application of Solar Energy," *ASHRAE*, 1967, Appendix 1-1.

REFERENCES:

1. Bennett, I. "Monthly Maps of Daily Insolation in the U.S.," *Solar Energy*, Vol. 9, No. 3, 1965, p. 145.

2. Jordan, R.C., *et.al.* "Low Temperature Engineering Applications of Solar Energy," *ASHRAE*, New York, 1967.

3. Lof, G.O.G.; J.A. Duffie; and C.O. Smith. *World Distribution of Solar Radiation*, Report No. 21, Solar Energy Lab, University of Wisconsin, July 1966.

4. Morrison, C.A. and E.A. Farber. "Development and Use of Solar Insolation Data for South-Facing Surfaces in Northern Latitudes," Paper No. 825 presented at ASHRAE Meeting, Montreal, June 1974.

5. Threlkeld, J.L. and R.C. Jordan. "Direct Radiation Available on Clear Days," *ASHRAE Transactions*, Vol. 64, 1958, p. 45.

APPENDIX B  *The Sundial and Its Aid in Building Design*

A sundial helps in understanding the geometry of the sunpath and how it varies with hour, date and latitude. This information can:

a. help to determine general precepts for building orientation,
b. allow to visualize the influence of structures, trees and vegetation on solar radiation gain or loss,
c. help to understand moving shadows, and
d. establish a shadow relationship between the building and its surroundings.

Method:

To depict the sun's influence on a building graphically the sundial becomes a useful aide that will simulate the sun's direction for various times and seasons at that latitude.

The sundial shows the sun shadow path by attaching it to a three dimensional model of the building and site. The site is oriented so that the sundial's meridian is oriented North/South.

When in sunlight the base of the model is tilted and pitched so that the shadow cast by the pin on the sundial corresponds to the right hour and season.

In order to fabricate the sundial the following needs to be done:

Calculate the direction and altitude of the sun from the following components:
a. latitude
b. season of year

By using the following formulae:
Sin Al = cosD cosL cosH + sinD sinL
Sin Az = cosD sinH + cosAl
Where:
Al = altitude of sun above the horizon
Az = azimuth of the sun
 L = latitude of place
 D = declination of the sun for the given season; northerly declination + southerly declination -
H = local hour angle of the sun (Each hour = 15°, H = 0 at noon, H = 15° at 11 a.m. or 1 p.m.; H = 30° at 10 a.m. or 2 p.m.)

Note: Since the sun is symmetrical the calculations need only be made once. Range and midpoint of sun positions need be calculated for only:
a. midwinter
b. midsummer
c. the two equinoxes
d. spring and fall
If exact declination is needed for a specific day of the year, it can be read from a solar ephemeris.

Construct a table for a particular place showing altitude and azimuth of the sun to the nearest degree for each hour of the day at the solstices and the equinoxes.

The construction of a sundial with the above information is as follows:

1. Through point 0 draw a straight line; this will become the north-south line.
2. A pin is placed at point 0; the height of the pin is recorded. (height=P)
3. Draw a line X from point 0.  The position and distance

**230**

of X is as follows:

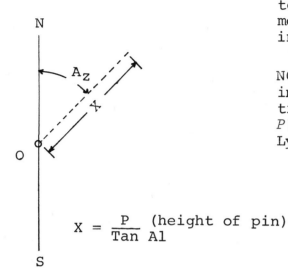

$$X = \frac{P}{Tan\ Al}\ (\text{height of pin})$$

the hour and season is to tilt the base of the model until the shadow intersects the line.

NOTE: The preceeding information was extracted from; *Site Planning* by Kevin Lynch.

The point determined at the end of the line represents the shadow tip at that hour and season. The above can be repeated for each hour of the day.

After the diagram is complete:
1. place dial flat on model with the NO line parallel to the north-south line of the model,
2. place a pin at point O the same height that you used in $X = \frac{P}{Tan}\ Al$, and
3. the shadow generated by the pin will represent the correct hour and season. All that is needed to change

# APPENDIX C
## *Conductivities, Conductances, and Resistances of Building and Insulating Materials.*
### *source: ASHRAE*

... Conductivities, Conductances, and Resistances of Building and Insulating Materials—(Design Values)[a]

**(For Industrial Insulation Design Values, see Table 38)**

These constants are expressed in Btu per (hour) (square foot) (Fahrenheit degree temperature difference). Conductivities (k) are per inch thickness, and conductances (C) are for thickness or construction stated, not per inch thickness

| Material | Description | Density (Lb per Cu Ft) | Mean Temp F | Conductivity (k) | Conductance (C) | Resistance[b] (R) Per inch thickness (1/k) | Resistance[b] (R) For thickness listed (1/C) | Specific Heat, Btu per (lb) (F deg) |
|---|---|---|---|---|---|---|---|---|
| BUILDING BOARD[c] Boards, Panels, Subflooring, Sheathing, Woodbased Panel Products[12] | Asbestos-cement board | 120 | 75 | 4.0 | — | 0.25 | — | |
| | Asbestos-cement board....⅛ in. | 120 | 75 | — | 33.00 | — | 0.033 | |
| | Asbestos-cement board....¼ in. | 120 | 75 | — | 16.50 | — | 0.07 | |
| | Gypsum or plaster board...⅜ in. | 50 | 75 | — | 3.10 | — | 0.32 | |
| | Gypsum or plaster board...½ in. | 50 | 75 | — | 2.25 | — | 0.45 | |
| | Plywood | 34 | 75 | 0.80 | — | 1.25 | — | 0.29 |
| | Plywood....................¼ in. | 34 | 75 | — | 3.20 | — | 0.31 | 0.29 |
| | Plywood....................⅜ in. | 34 | 75 | — | 2.13 | — | 0.47 | 0.29 |
| | Plywood....................½ in. | 34 | 75 | — | 1.60 | — | 0.62 | 0.29 |
| | Plywood or wood panels....¾ in. | 34 | 75 | — | 1.07 | — | 0.93 | 0.29 |
| | Insulating board Sheathing, regular density....½ in. | 18 | 75 | — | 0.76 | — | 1.32 | 0.31 |
| | ................................²⁵/₃₂ in. | 18 | 75 | — | 0.49 | — | 2.06 | 0.31 |
| | Sheathing intermediate density.½ in. | 22 | 75 | — | 0.82 | — | 1.22 | 0.31 |
| | Nail-base sheathing........½ in. | 25 | 75 | — | 0.88 | — | 1.14 | 0.31 |
| | Shingle backer...............⅜ in. | 18 | 75 | — | 1.06 | — | 0.94 | 0.31 |
| | Shingle backer............⁵/₁₆ in. | 18 | 75 | — | 1.28 | — | 0.78 | 0.31 |
| | Sound deadening board......½ in. | 15 | 75 | — | 0.74 | — | 1.35 | 0.30 |
| | Tile and lay-in panels, plain or acoustic | 18 | 75 | 0.40 | — | 2.50 | — | 0.32 |
| | ................................½ in. | 18 | 75 | — | 0.80 | — | 1.25 | 0.32 |
| | ................................¾ in. | 18 | 75 | — | 0.53 | — | 1.89 | 0.32 |
| | Laminated paperboard | 30 | 75 | 0.50 | — | 2.00 | — | |
| | Homogeneous board from repulped paper | 30 | 75 | 0.50 | — | 2.00 | — | 0.28 |
| | Hardboard Medium density siding....⁷/₁₆ in. | 40 | 75 | — | 1.49 | — | 0.67 | 0.28 |
| | Other medium density | 50 | 75 | 0.73 | — | 1.37 | — | 0.31 |
| | High density, service temp. service, underlay | 55 | 75 | 0.82 | — | 1.22 | — | 0.33 |
| | High density, std. tempered | 63 | 75 | 1.00 | — | 1.00 | — | 0.33 |
| | Particleboard Low density | 37 | 75 | 0.54 | — | 1.85 | — | 0.31 |
| | Medium density | 50 | 75 | 0.94 | — | 1.06 | — | 0.31 |
| | High density | 62.5 | 75 | 1.18 | — | 0.85 | — | 0.31 |
| | Underlayment.............⅝ in. | 40 | 75 | — | 1.22 | — | 0.82 | 0.29 |
| | Wood subfloor............¾ in. | | 75 | — | 1.06 | — | 0.94 | 0.34 |
| BUILDING PAPER | Vapor—permeable felt | | 75 | — | 16.70 | — | 0.06 | |
| | Vapor—seal, 2 layers of mopped 15 lb felt | | 75 | — | 8.35 | — | 0.12 | |
| | Vapor—seal, plastic film | | 75 | — | — | — | Negl. | |

### Design Heat Transmission Coefficients

.... Conductivities, Conductances, and Resistances of Building and Insulating Materials—(Design Values)[a] (Continued)

| Material | Description | Density (Lb per Cu Ft) | Mean Temp F | Conductivity (k) | Conductance (C) | Resistance[b] (R) Per inch thickness (1/k) | Resistance[b] (R) For thickness listed (1/C) | Specific Heat, Btu per (lb) (F deg) |
|---|---|---|---|---|---|---|---|---|
| FINISH FLOORING MATERIALS | Carpet and fibrous pad | — | 75 | — | 0.48 | — | 2.08 | 0.34 |
| | Carpet and rubber pad | — | 75 | — | 0.81 | — | 1.23 | |
| | Cork tile.................⅛ in. | — | 75 | — | 3.60 | — | 0.28 | |
| | Terrazzo.................1 in. | — | 75 | — | 12.50 | — | 0.08 | |
| | Tile—asphalt, linoleum, vinyl, rubber. | — | 75 | — | 20.00 | — | 0.05 | 0.30 |
| INSULATING MATERIALS BLANKET AND BATT | Mineral Fiber, fibrous form processed from rock, slag, or glass approx.* 2-2¾ in. | — | 75 | — | — | — | 7[d] | 0.18 |
| | approx.* 3-3½ in. | — | 75 | — | — | — | 11[d] | 0.18 |
| | approx.* 5½-6½ in. | — | 75 | — | — | — | 19[d] | 0.18 |
| BOARD AND SLABS | Cellular glass | 9 | 75 | 0.40 | — | 2.50 | — | 0.24 |
| | Glass fiber, organic bonded | 4-9 | 75 | 0.25 | — | 4.00 | — | 0.19 |
| | Expanded rubber (rigid) | 4.5 | 75 | 0.22 | — | 4.55 | — | |
| | Expanded polystyrene extruded, plain | 1.8 | 75 | 0.25 | — | 4.00 | — | 0.29 |
| | Expanded polystyrene extruded, (R-12 exp.) | 2.2 | 75 | 0.20 | — | 5.00 | — | 0.29 |
| | Expanded polystyrene extruded, (R-12 exp.) (Thickness 1 in. and greater) | 3.5 | 75 | 0.19 | — | 5.26 | — | 0.29 |
| | Expanded polystyrene, molded beads | 1.0 | 75 | 0.28 | — | 3.57 | — | 0.29 |
| | Expanded polyurethane[f] (R-11 exp.) | 1.5 | 75 | 0.16 | — | 6.25 | — | 0.38 |
| | (Thickness 1 in. or greater) | 2.5 | | | | | | | 0.38 |
| | Mineral fiber with resin binder | 15 | 75 | 0.29 | — | 3.45 | — | 0.17 |
| | Mineral fiberboard, wet felted Core or roof insulation | 16-17 | 75 | 0.34 | — | 2.94 | — | |
| | Acoustical tile | 18 | 75 | 0.35 | — | 2.86 | — | |
| | Acoustical tile | 21 | 75 | 0.37 | — | 2.73 | — | |
| | Mineral fiberboard, wet molded Acoustical tile[e] | 23 | 75 | 0.42 | — | 2.38 | — | |
| | Wood or cane fiberboard Acoustical tile[e]........½ in. | — | 75 | — | 0.80 | — | 1.25 | 0.30 |
| | Acoustical tile[e]........¾ in. | — | 75 | — | 0.53 | — | 1.89 | 0.30 |
| | Interior finish (plank, tile) | 15 | 75 | 0.35 | — | 2.86 | — | 0.32 |
| | Insulating roof deck Approximately.............1½ in. | — | 75 | — | 0.24 | — | 4.17 | |
| | Approximately.............2 in. | — | 75 | — | 0.18 | — | 5.56 | |
| | Approximately.............3 in. | — | 75 | — | 0.12 | — | 8.33 | |
| | Wood shredded (cemented in preformed slabs) | 22 | 75 | 0.60 | — | 1.67 | — | 0.38 |
| LOOSE FILL | Cellulose insulation (milled paper or wood pulp) | 2.5-3 | 75 | 0.27 | — | 3.70 | — | 0.33 |
| | Sawdust or shavings | 0.8-1.5 | 75 | 0.45 | — | 2.22 | — | 0.33 |
| | Wood fiber, softwoods | 2.0-3.5 | 75 | 0.30 | — | 3.33 | — | 0.33 |
| | Perlite, expanded | 5.0-8.0 | 75 | 0.37 | — | 2.70 | — | |
| | Mineral fiber (rock, slag or glass) approx.* 3 in. | — | 75 | — | — | — | 9[d] | 0.18 |
| | approx.* 4¼ in. | — | 75 | — | — | — | 13[d] | 0.18 |
| | approx.* 6½ in. | — | 75 | — | — | — | 19[d] | 0.18 |
| | approx.* 7½ in. | — | 75 | — | — | — | 22[d] | 0.18 |
| | Silica aerogel | 7.6 | 75 | 0.17 | — | 5.88 | — | |
| | Vermiculite (expanded) | 7.0-8.2 | 75 | 0.47 | — | 2.13 | — | |
| | | 4.0-6.0 | 75 | 0.44 | — | 2.27 | — | |
| ROOF INSULATION[h] | Preformed, for use above deck Approximately.............½ in. | — | 75 | — | 0.72 | — | 1.39 | |
| | Approximately.............1 in. | — | 75 | — | 0.36 | — | 2.78 | |
| | Approximately.............1½ in. | — | 75 | — | 0.24 | — | 4.17 | |
| | Approximately.............2 in. | — | 75 | — | 0.19 | — | 5.56 | |
| | Approximately.............2½ in. | — | 75 | — | 0.15 | — | 6.67 | |
| | Approximately.............3 in. | — | 75 | — | 0.12 | — | 8.33 | |
| | Cellular glass | 9 | 75 | 0.40 | — | 2.50 | — | 0.24 |
| MASONRY MATERIALS CONCRETES | Cement mortar | 116 | | 5.0 | — | 0.20 | | |
| | Gypsum-fiber concrete 87½% gypsum, 12½% wood chips | 51 | | 1.66 | — | 0.60 | | |
| | Lightweight aggregates including expanded shale, clay or slate; expanded slags; cinders; pumice; vermiculite; also cellular concretes | 120 | | 5.2 | — | 0.19 | | |
| | | 100 | | 3.6 | — | 0.28 | | |
| | | 80 | | 2.5 | — | 0.40 | | |
| | | 60 | | 1.7 | — | 0.59 | | |
| | | 40 | | 1.15 | — | 0.86 | | |
| | | 30 | | 0.90 | — | 1.11 | | |
| | | 20 | | 0.70 | — | 1.43 | | |

.... Conductivities, Conductances, and Resistances of Building and Insulating Materials—
(Design Values)ᵃ (Continued)

| Material | Description | Density (Lb per Cu Ft) | Mean Temp F | Conductivity (k) | Conductance (C) | Resistanceᵇ (R) Per inch thickness (1/k) | Resistanceᵇ (R) For thickness listed (1/C) | Specific Heat, Btu per (lb)(F deg) |
|---|---|---|---|---|---|---|---|---|
| MASONRY MATERIALS CONCRETES (Continued) | Sand and gravel or stone aggregate (oven dried) | 140 | | 9.0 | — | 0.11 | — | |
| | Sand and gravel or stone aggregate (not dried) | 140 | | 12.0 | — | 0.08 | — | |
| | Stucco | 116 | | 5.0 | — | 0.20 | — | |
| MASONRY UNITS | Brick, commonⁱ | 120 | 75 | 5.0 | — | 0.20 | — | |
| | Brick, faceⁱ | 130 | 75 | 9.0 | — | 0.11 | — | |
| | Clay tile, hollow: | | | | | | | |
| | 1 cell deep........3 in. | — | 75 | — | 1.25 | — | 0.80 | |
| | 1 cell deep........4 in. | — | 75 | — | 0.90 | — | 1.11 | |
| | 2 cells deep.......6 in. | — | 75 | — | 0.66 | — | 1.52 | |
| | 2 cells deep.......8 in. | — | 75 | — | 0.54 | — | 1.85 | |
| | 2 cells deep......10 in. | — | 75 | — | 0.45 | — | 2.22 | |
| | 3 cells deep......12 in. | — | 75 | — | 0.40 | — | 2.50 | |
| | Concrete blocks, three oval core: | | | | | | | |
| | Sand and gravel aggregate....4 in. | — | 75 | — | 1.40 | — | 0.71 | |
| | ....8 in. | — | 75 | — | 0.90 | — | 1.11 | |
| | ....12 in. | — | 75 | — | 0.78 | — | 1.28 | |
| | Cinder aggregate....3 in. | — | 75 | — | 1.16 | — | 0.86 | |
| | ....4 in. | — | 75 | — | 0.90 | — | 1.11 | |
| | ....8 in. | — | 75 | — | 0.58 | — | 1.72 | |
| | ....12 in. | — | 75 | — | 0.53 | — | 1.89 | |
| | Lightweight aggregate          3 in. | — | 75 | — | 0.79 | — | 1.27 | |
| | (expanded shale, clay, slate   4 in. | — | 75 | — | 0.67 | — | 1.50 | |
| | or slag; pumice)              8 in. | — | 75 | — | 0.50 | — | 2.00 | |
| | 12 in. | — | 75 | — | 0.44 | — | 2.27 | |
| | Concrete blocks, rectangular core:ʲ | | | | | | | |
| | Sand and gravel aggregate | | | | | | | |
| | 2 core, 8 in. 36 lb.ᵏ | — | 45 | — | 0.96 | — | 1.04 | |
| | Same with filled coresˡ | — | 45 | — | 0.52 | — | 1.93 | |
| | Lightweight aggregate (expanded shale, clay, slate or slag, pumice): | | | | | | | |
| | 3 core, 6 in. 19 lb.ᵏ | — | 45 | — | 0.61 | — | 1.65 | |
| | Same with filled coresˡ | — | 45 | — | 0.33 | — | 2.99 | |
| | 2 core, 8 in. 24 lb.ᵏ | — | 45 | — | 0.46 | — | 2.18 | |
| | Same with filled coresˡ | — | 45 | — | 0.20 | — | 5.03 | |
| | 3 core, 12 in. 38 lb.ᵏ | — | 45 | — | 0.40 | — | 2.48 | |
| | Same with filled coresˡ | — | 45 | — | 0.17 | — | 5.82 | |
| | Stone, lime or sand | — | 75 | 12.50 | — | 0.08 | — | |
| | Gypsum partition tile: | | | | | | | |
| | 3 × 12 × 30 in. solid | — | 75 | — | 0.79 | — | 1.26 | |
| | 3 × 12 × 30 in. 4-cell | — | 75 | — | 0.74 | — | 1.35 | |
| | 4 × 12 × 30 in. 3-cell | — | 75 | — | 0.60 | — | 1.67 | |
| METALS | (See Chapter 30, Table 3) | | | | | | | |
| PLASTERING MATERIALS | Cement plaster, sand aggregate | 116 | 75 | 5.0 | — | 0.20 | — | |
| | Sand aggregate......⅜ in. | — | 75 | — | 13.3 | — | 0.08 | |
| | Sand aggregate......¾ in. | — | 75 | — | 6.66 | — | 0.15 | |
| | Gypsum plaster: | | | | | | | |
| | Lightweight aggregate........½ in. | 45 | 75 | — | 3.12 | — | 0.32 | |
| | Lightweight aggregate........⅝ in. | 45 | 75 | — | 2.67 | — | 0.39 | |
| | Lightweight agg. on metal lath..¾ in. | — | 75 | — | 2.13 | — | 0.47 | |
| | Perlite aggregate | 45 | 75 | 1.5 | — | 0.67 | — | |
| | Sand aggregate | 105 | 75 | 5.6 | — | 0.18 | — | |
| | Sand aggregate......½ in. | 105 | 75 | — | 11.10 | — | 0.09 | |
| | Sand aggregate......⅝ in. | 105 | 75 | — | 9.10 | — | 0.11 | |
| | Sand aggregate on metal lath..¾ in. | — | 75 | — | 7.70 | — | 0.1 | |
| | Vermiculite aggregate | 45 | 75 | 1.7 | — | 0.59 | — | |
| ROOFING | Asbestos-cement shingles | 120 | 75 | — | 4.76 | — | 0.21 | |
| | Asphalt roll roofing | 70 | 75 | — | 6.50 | — | 0.15 | |
| | Asphalt shingles | 70 | 75 | — | 2.27 | — | 0.44 | |
| | Built-up roofing.......⅜ in. | 70 | 75 | — | 3.00 | — | 0.33 | 0.35 |
| | Slate.......½ in. | — | 75 | — | 20.00 | — | 0.05 | |
| | Wood shingles, plain a plastic film faced | — | 75 | — | 1.06 | — | 0.94 | 0.31 |
| SIDING MATERIALS (ON FLAT SURFACE) | Shingles | | | | | | | |
| | Asbestos-cement | 120 | 75 | — | 4.76 | — | 0.21 | |
| | Wood, 16 in., 7½ exposure | — | 75 | — | 1.15 | — | 0.87 | 0.31 |

(Design Values)ᵃ (Concluded)

| Material | Description | Density (Lb per Cu Ft) | Mean Temp F | Conductivity (k) | Conductance (C) | Resistanceᵇ (R) Per inch thickness (1/k) | Resistanceᵇ (R) For thickness listed (1/C) | Specific Heat, Btu per (lb)(F deg) |
|---|---|---|---|---|---|---|---|---|
| SIDING MATERIALS (ON FLAT SURFACE) (Continued) | Wood, double, 16-in., 12-in. exposure | — | 75 | — | 0.84 | — | 1.19 | 0.31 |
| | Wood, plus insul. backer board, 5/16 in. | — | 75 | — | 0.71 | — | 1.40 | 0.31 |
| | Siding | | | | | | | |
| | Asbestos-cement, ¼ in., lapped | — | 75 | — | 4.76 | — | 0.21 | |
| | Asphalt roll siding | — | 75 | — | 6.50 | — | 0.15 | |
| | Asphalt insulating siding (½ in. bd.) | — | 75 | — | 0.69 | — | 1.46 | |
| | Wood, drop, 1 × 8 in. | — | 75 | — | 1.27 | — | 0.79 | 0.31 |
| | Wood, bevel, ½ × 8 in., lapped | — | 75 | — | 1.23 | — | 0.81 | 0.31 |
| | Wood, bevel, ¾ × 10 in., lapped | — | 75 | — | 0.95 | — | 1.05 | 0.31 |
| | Wood, plywood, ⅜ in., lapped | — | 75 | — | 1.59 | — | 0.59 | 0.29 |
| | Aluminum or Steelᵐ, over sheathing | | | | | | | |
| | Hollow-backed | — | | — | 1.61 | — | 0.61 | |
| | Insulating-board backed nominal ⅜ in. | — | | — | 0.55 | — | 1.82 | |
| | Insulating-board backed nominal ⅜ in. foil backed | — | | — | 0.34 | — | 2.96 | |
| | Architectural glass | — | 75 | — | 10.00 | — | 0.10 | |
| WOODS | Maple, oak, and similar hardwoods | 45 | 75 | 1.10 | — | 0.91 | — | 0.30 |
| | Fir, pine, and similar softwoods | 32 | 75 | 0.80 | — | 1.25 | — | 0.33 |
| | Fir, pine, and similar softwoods....¾ in. | 32 | 75 | — | 1.06 | — | 0.94 | 0.33 |
| | ....1½ in. | 32 | 75 | — | 0.53 | — | 1.89 | 0.33 |
| | ....2½ in. | 32 | 75 | — | 0.32 | — | 3.12 | 0.33 |
| | ....3½ in. | 32 | 75 | — | 0.23 | — | 4.35 | 0.33 |

**Notes for Table 3A**

ᵃ Representative values for dry materials is selected by the ASHRAE Committee 2.4 on Insulation. They are intended as design (not specification) values for materials of building construction in normal use. For conductivity of a particular product, the user may obtain the value supplied by the manufacturer or secure the results of unbiased tests.

ᵇ Resistance values are the reciprocals of C before rounding off C to two decimal places.

ᶜ See also Insulating Materials, Board.

ᵈ Includes paper backing and facing if any. In cases where the insulation forms a boundary (highly reflective or otherwise) of an air space, refer to Tables 1 and 2, to obtain the insulating value of air space for the appropriate effective emissivity and temperature conditions of the space.

ᵉ Conductivity varies also with fiber diameter. See also Factors Affecting Thermal Conductivity and Fig. 1, Chapter 17. Insulation is produced by different densities, therefore, there is a wide variation in thickness for the same R-value between various manufacturers. No effort should be made to relate any specific R-value to any specific thickness. The commercial thicknesses generally available range from 1½ to 7 in.

ᶠ These are values for aged board stock. For discussion on the change in conductivity with age of Refrigerant 11 expanded urethane see Chapter 17, Factors Affecting Thermal Conductivity.

ᵍ Insulating values of acoustical tile vary depending on density of the board and on the type, size, and depth of the perforations. An average conductivity k value is 0.40.

ʰ The U. S. Department of Commerce, *Simplified Practice Recommendation for Thermal Conductances Factors for Performed Above-Deck Roof Insulation*, No. R 257-55, recognizes the specification of roof insulation on the basis of the C values shown. Roof insulation is made in thicknesses to meet these values. Therefore, thickness supplied by different manufacturers may vary depending on the conductivity k value of the particular material.

ⁱ Face brick and common brick do not always have these specific densities. When the density is different from that shown, there will be a change in the thermal conductivity.

ʲ Data on rectangular core concrete blocks differs from the above data on oval core blocks due to core configuration, different mean temperatures and possibly differences in unit weights. Weight data on the oval core blocks tested is not available.

ᵏ Weights of units approximately 7⅝ in. high and 15⅝ in. long. These weights are given as a means of describing the blocks tested, but conductance values are all for one square foot of area.

ˡ Vermiculite, perlite or mineral wool insulation. Where insulation is used vapor barriers or other precautions must be considered to keep insulation dry.

ᵐ Value for metal siding applied over flat surfaces vary widely depending upon the amount of ventilation of air space beneath the siding, whether the air space is reflective or nonreflective, and on the thickness, type, and application of insulating backing-board used. Values given are averages intended for use as design guide values and were obtained from several guarded hot-box tests (ASTM C236) on hollow-backed types and on types made using backer-board of wood-fiber, foamed plastic, and glass fiber. Departures of ± 50 percent, or more, from the values given may occur.

APPENDIX D  *Sizing a Wind Installation for a determined Energy Demand*

SAMPLE CALCULATION #1 (Generalized Design Calculation)
Supply the energy demands for 1500 people in a commercial office space with an average wind velocity of 14 mph using an airfoil collector. Determine the size of the airfoil needed.

SAMPLE CALCULATION #2 (Specific Wind Plant Installation)
Supply the energy demands for a house having the following appliances. The average wind velocity is 8 mph. Determine the size of the airfoil needed.

A. Establish the Energy Needs

Calc. #1
(# people) (Consumption in kwhr/person/year)
Table #1 Appendix D

(1500 people)(10,000 kwhr/person/year)
$= 1.5 \times 10^7$ kwhr/year

8-75W Light Bulbs 192.0 kwhr
1 - Water Pump    20.0 kw
1 - Refrigerator   9.5 kw
    Freezer
1 - Washing Machine 9.0 kw
1 - Stereo       3.0 kw
                 _____
                 233.5 kwhr/month

---

Calc. #2
Determine yearly kw-hr consumption from Table #2 Appendix D

$(233.5)(12) = 2.8 \times 10^3$ kwhr/yr

---

B. Establish Useful Collection Period

Total Energy Needs
Total # hrs/yr a windplant can produce energy. There are 8760 hours in one year. There is only a certain percentage in those hours that can produce a useful output, i.e., those over 7 mph for airfoil collectors or 5 mph for savonious rotors. Determine this value from weather bureau records.

Use 7500 hrs as useful collection period:

$$\frac{1.5 \times 10^7 \text{ kwhr/year}}{7.5 \times 10^3 \text{ hr}}$$
$= 2.0 \times 10^3$ kwhr

Use 7500 hrs as useful collection period:

$$\frac{2.8 \times 10^3 \text{ kwhr/year}}{7.5 \times 10^3 \text{ hr}}$$
$= 3.73 \times 10^{-1}$ kwhr

C. Determine monthly wind velocity in feet per second obtained from National Weather Bureau or onsite measurements.

To convert mph to feet per second (fps) multiply by 1.43:

14 mph = 20 fps (average)

8 mph = 11.4 fps (average)

D. Power Capacity for a Specific Collector.

Airfoil type $P(kw) = 2.0 \times 10^{-6}R^2V^3$
Savonious $P(kw) = 3.2 \times 10^{-7}AV^3$

*Note: If average wind velocity is used, double power capacity

airfoil $= 4.0 \times 10^{-6}R^2V^3$
savonious $= 6.4 \times 10^{-7}AV^3$

$KW = 4.0 \times 10^{-6}R^2V^3$
$2.0 \times 10^3 = 4.0 \times 10^{-6}R^2 20^3$
$R^2 = \dfrac{(2.0 \times 10^3)(1.0 \times 10^6)}{3.2 \times 10^4}$
$R^2 = 6.25 \times 10^4$
$R = 250'$ radius
or
$500'$ Diameter Airfoil

The same energy demands can be met with 4 collectors 250' in diameter, 8 collectors 125' in diameter, etc.

$KW = 4.0 \times 10^{-6}R^2V^3$
$(3.73 \times 10^{-1}) = 4.0 \times 10^{-6}R^2(11.4)^3$
$R^2 = \dfrac{(3.73 \times 10^{-1})(1.0 \times 10^6)}{1.48 \times 10^3}$
$R = 16'$ or $32'$ diameter airfoil

The above mentioned sizing diameters for the airfoil are deceiving for several reasons. The average wind velocity disregards a possible increase in velocity due to topographic form or built form. The effective diameter size could also be reduced by utilizing energy conservation methods to reduce overall energy consumption. The total energy needs should not be strictly supplied by wind power but should be in combination with other alternative sources.

# TABLE 1

| APPLIANCES | POWER IN WATTS | CURRENT REQUIRED IN AMPS AT 12V | AT 115V | TIME USED PER MO. (HR.) | TOTAL KW-HRS. PER MO. |
|---|---|---|---|---|---|
| Air Cond. | 1566 | 130. | 13.7 | 74. | 116. |
| Blanket, electric | 177 | 14.5 | 1.5 | 73. | 13. |
| Blender | 350 | 29.2 | 3.0 | 1.5 | 0.5 |
| Blower (forced air furn.) | 450 | 37. | 3.9 | 300. | 135. |
| Broiler | 1436 | 120. | 12.5 | 6. | 8.5 |
| Clother Dryer | 4856 | 405. | 42.0 | 18. | 86. |
| Coffee Pot | 894 | 75. | 7.8 | 10. | 9. |
| Dishwasher | 1200 | 100. | 10.4 | 25. | 30. |
| Drill (1/4" elec.) | 250 | 20.8 | 2.2 | 2. | .5 |
| Fan (attic) | 370 | 30.8 | 3.2 | 65. | 24. |
| Freezer (15 cu.') | 341 | 28.4 | 3.0 | 29. | 10. |
| Freezer (15 cu.') (frostless) | 440 | 36.6 | 3.8 | 33. | 14.7 |
| Frying Pan | 1196 | 99.6 | 10.4 | 12. | 15. |
| Garbage Disposal | 445 | 36. | 3.9 | 6. | 3. |
| Heat, elec. baseborad, avg. size home(1500'2) | 10000 | 832. | 87. | 160. | 1600. |
| Iron | 1088 | 90.5 | 9.5 | 11. | 12. |
| Lightbulb, 75W | 75 | 6.25 | .65 | 320. | 2.4 |
| Lightbulb, 40W | 40 | 3.3 | .35 | 320. | 1.3 |
| Lightbulb, 25W | 25 | 2.1 | .22 | 320. | .8 |
| Oil Burner, 1/8 HP | 250 | 20.8 | 2.2 | 64. | 16. |
| Radio | 70 | 5.7 | .61 | 100. | 7. |
| Range | 12207 | 1020. | 106. | 8. | 98. |

| APPLIANCES | POWER IN WATTS | CURRENT REQUIRED IN AMPS AT 12V | AT 115V | TIME USED PER MO. (HR.) | TOTAL KW-HRS. PER MO. |
|---|---|---|---|---|---|
| Record Player (tube) | 150 | 12.5 | 1.3 | 50. | 7.5 |
| Record Player (solid st.) | 60 | 5. | .52 | 50. | 3. |
| Refrigerator-Freezer (14 cu.') | 326 | 27.2 | 2.8 | 29. | 9.5 |
| Refrigerator-Freezer (14 cu.'), frostless | 615 | 51.3 | 5.35 | 25. | 15.2 |
| Skill Saw | 1000 | 83.5 | 8.7 | 6. | 6. |
| Sun Lamp | 279 | 23.2 | 2.4 | 5.4 | 1.5 |
| Television, B/W | 237 | 19.8 | 2.1 | 110. | 25. |
| Television, Color | 332 | 27.6 | 2.9 | 125. | 42. |
| Toaster | 1146 | 95.5 | 10. | 2.6 | 3. |
| Typewriter | 30 | 2.5 | .26 | 15. | .45 |
| Vacuum Cleaner | 630 | 52.5 | 5.5 | 6.4 | 4. |
| Washing Machine (automatic) | 512 | 42.5 | 4.5 | 17.6 | 9. |
| Washing Machine (wringer) | 275 | 23. | 2.4 | 15. | 4. |
| Water Heater | 474 | 38.3 | 4.0 | 89. | 40. |
| Water Pump | 460 | 37.2 | 3.9 | 44. | 20. |

POWER, CURRENT AND MONTHLY KW-HR CONSUMPTION OF VARIOUS HOME APPLIANCES

# TABLE 2

| AREA | PERCENT | KWHR/PERSON/YEAR |
|---|---|---|
| Industry | 30% | $3.0 \times 10^4$ |
| Transportation | 25% | $2.5 \times 10^4$ |
| Utilities/Electricity | 25% | $2.5 \times 10^4$ |
| Commercial | 10% | $1.0 \times 10^4$ |
| Domestic | 10% | $1.0 \times 10^4$ |

1972 Energy Consumption for Five Major Areas (from Hottel, New Energy Tech)

## WIND GENERATOR DEALERS

| Agent | Product |
|---|---|
| Solar Wind Co. R.F.D. 2 East Holden, ME 04429 | Agents for Dunlite of Australia; Elektro of Switzerland; Dyna Technology of USA; Sencenbaugh, USA (plans only). |
| Sencenbaugh Electric P.O. Box 11174 Palo Alto, CA 94306 | Sencenbaugh carries their own plans, Dunlite, and Elektro. |
| Pennwalt Corp. Automatic Power Division P.O. Box 18738 Houston, TX 77023 | Distributes Aerowatt from France. |
| Real Gas & Electric Co., Inc. P.O. Box A Guerneville, CA 95446 and Environmental Energies, Inc. 11350 Schaefer Detroit, MI 48227 | Quirk's, Dyna Technology and Elektro as well as batteries and other related equipment. They also stock Solerator collectors and Solarex solar cells. |
| Independent Power Developers P.O. Box 618 Noxon, MT 59853 | Agency for Dunlite, Elektro, Dyna Technology, and a variety of water turbines & rams. |
| Lubing Maschinenfabrik Ludwig Bening 2847 Barnstorf P.O.B. 110 Germany (West) | Manufacture the Lubing water pumping & electricity producing windmills which are highly regarded in Europe. |

APPENDIX D-1 *Determining Battery Storage Capacity for a Given Wind Plant Installation.*

The storage capacity is determined by the maximum period of time that adequate power can be supplied when there is no usable wind available. How much of this storage capacity that is provided is also determined by the percentage of auxiliary power versus battery storage.

*Battery Storage Capacity Sample Calculation:*

Calculate the battery storage capacity required for 233.5 kwhr/mo power consumption at 115 volts for four windless days.

| | |
|---|---|
| A. Total kwhr/month = consumption (Table 2) | From Step A preceeding problem. 233.5 kwhr/month |
| B. Average daily consumption | 233.5/30 = 7.78 kwhr/day |
| C. Convert Step B into Watt-hrs per day (1 kw = 1000W) | 7780 watt-hrs/day |
| D. Convert Watt-hrs/day to amp-hrs<br><br>amps = watts/volts | $A = \dfrac{7780 \text{ watt-hrs/day}}{115V}$<br>A = 67.65 amp-hrs at 115V<br>(67.65)(4) = 270 amp-hrs |
| E. Average number of windless days (determined from weather records) | The amount equals battery storage capacity for four (4) windless days. |

Another important factor is the maximum amount of current to be drawn at one time in order to keep within the maximum current rating of the battery. This can be totaled from the maximum amount of applicances on at one time (Table 2).

Total maximum number of amps drawn at any one time:

Water Pump    3.9 amps at 115V
Refrig.       2.8 amps at 115V
Washing       2.4 amps at 115V
  Machine
3-75W Bulbs   2.0 amps at 115V
TOTAL        11.4 amps at 115V

This figure should be within the current rating of the battery.

**237**

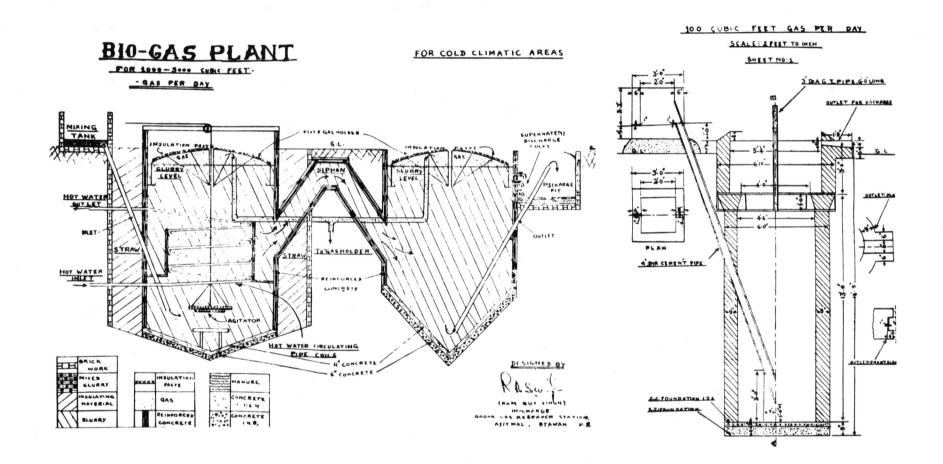

BIO-GAS PLANT

FOR 1000-3000 CUBIC FEET GAS PER DAY

FOR COLD CLIMATIC AREAS

100 CUBIC FEET GAS PER DAY

SCALE: 2 FEET TO INCH

SHEET NO. 1

**238**

# BIO GAS PLANT

## 150 CU.FT PER DAY

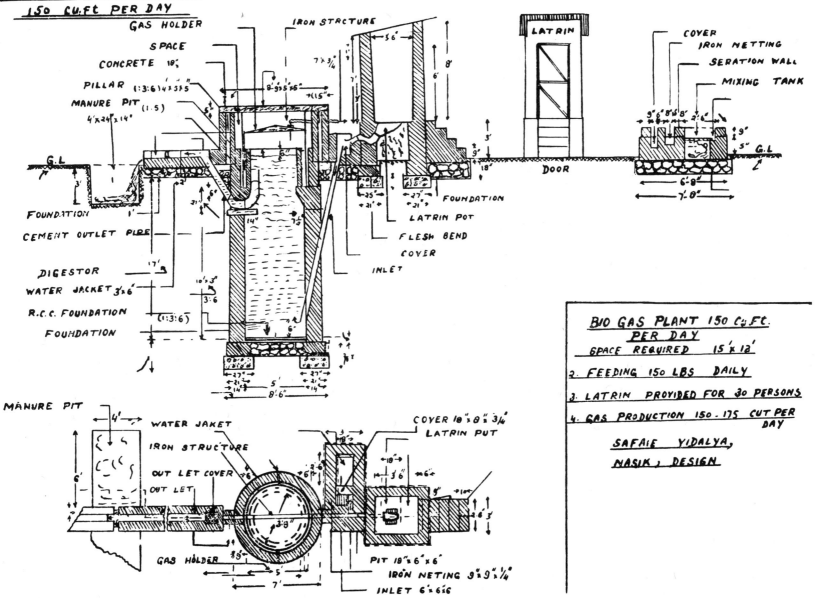

GAS HOLDER
SPACE
CONCRETE 10"
PILLAR (1:3:6) 4'x3'x5'
MANURE PIT (1.5) 4'x24'x14'
IRON STRUCTURE
LATRIN
COVER
IRON NETTING
SERATION WALL
MIXING TANK
G.L
FOUNDATION
CEMENT OUTLET PIPE
DIGESTOR
WATER JACKET 3'x6'
R.C.C. FOUNDATION
FOUNDATION
LATRIN POT
FLESH BEND
COVER
INLET
DOOR
FOUNDATION

MANURE PIT
WATER JAKET
IRON STRUCTURE
OUT LET COVER
OUT LET
GAS HOLDER
COVER 10"x8"x3/4"
LATRIN PUT
PIT 18"x6"x6'
IRON NETING 9"x9"x1/4"
INLET 6"x6'6"

BIO GAS PLANT 150 Cu.Ft.
PER DAY
SPACE REQUIRED   15'x12'
2. FEEDING  150 LBS  DAILY
3. LATRIN  PROVIDED FOR 30 PERSONS
4. GAS PRODUCTION 150-175 CUT PER DAY

SAFAIE  YIDALYA,
NASIK ; DESIGN

239

APPENDIX F    *Ecologic*
              *Standards*
              *for*
              *Construction*

The following is reproduced
with the kind permission of
the author, Malcolm B.
Wells, Architect/Conserva-
tionist.  Any suggestions
regarding this appendix
should be directed to
Malcolm B. Wells, Box 183,
Cherry Hill, New Jersey
08034.

*Introduction*

The American land is dying.
Centuries of careless
lumbering, mining, and
farming have depleted its
rich soils, along with its
vast communities of living
plants and animals.  From
Hawaii to Maine (and, in
fact, across most of the
Northern Hemisphere) the air
and the water are dangerously polluted.  More radio-
active and conventional
wastes spew into them each
year.  And overpopulation,
combined with all the rest,
is further deteriorating the
quality of all human life.
But one of the greatest
ecologic dilemmas of all has
gone relatively unnoticed.

It is what we now call
overpaving, and it includes
not only highways, air-
ports, and parking lots
but buildings, too; homes,
churches, schools, factories and shopping centers--
even many lawns; every-
thing, in fact, that
smothers the once-living
face of the land.

As the seriousness of
nationwide overpaving has
come to light, growing
numbers of the nearly four
million Americans involved
in construction-- building
tradesmen, suppliers,
contractors, owners, de-
velopers, regulatory
agents, planners, archi-
tects, and engineers--
have begun to look for new
ways to build, to design,
and to manage natural re-
sources; ways that will do
less damage to the life-
giving earth.  Their search
has generated these
suggested ecologic stan-
dards for the modification
of conventional construc-
tion practices.  Much of
the outline is based on
survival practices that
were developed by what we
call wilderness, eons
before man existed.

Building codes provide for
the life-safety of the
human species.  But no code
concerns itself with the
living land, or with the
millions of other species
with which we share this
planet.  All construction
sites, even those almost
covered with buildings and
paving, deserve new ecological standards, not only to
protect and restore land
health but also to help
insure our own survival.  If
we survive, it will happen
because we learned to care
about the land.  Land
developers will have become
highly-trained professionals
held responsible by law for
the health of the land in
their care.

Construction projects always
have double impacts upon the
land:  the ravages of
construction itself, when
great earth-wounds sometimes
lie open for years, and the
never-ending effect of the
actual "improvements."  It
is into these two corres-
ponding sections, *"Building
the Project"* and *"The Project
Itself,"* that this outline is
divided.

**240**

*Section I. Building the
Project*

A. *Protection of Existing
Site-Resources*

1. Living plants. Con-
struction activities
tend to spread out over
all the land made
available to them.
That's why we must limit
construction-use areas
to the absolute minimums
compatible with effi-
cient work. Fence all
green land on site
outside construction
areas. Use ditches and
low earth-dikes to pre-
vent construction-site
runoff from flooding,
silting, contaminating,
or eroding green areas.
Prevent brush fires.
Maintain adequate fire-
fighting equipment. Do
not store materials or
change grades above roots
of trees that remain.

2. Wildlife. Follow 1.
above, plus: prevent
accidental poisonings.
If pest control must be
used at construction
site, use methods harm-
less to wildlife.
Temporary fencing at
green areas is to pre-
vent human trespass;
fence-openings must be
large enough to allow
escape of wildlife in
event of fire or flood.

3. Soils. Protect adja-
cent properties from
damage by fire,
flooding, silting,
erosion, and pollution.
Natural areas, parti-
cularly streams and
swamps, have great
biological importance.

4. Manmade improvements.
Stress salvage and re-
use. Fence and protect
improvements which
remain.

B. *Temporary Structures*

1. Offices. See general
waste-management and
temporary-heating
requirements below.
Construction offices
should be models of
land-concern for their
projects.

2. Storage buildings. See
runoff controls on the
following pages.

3. Parking and other
vehicle-access areas.
Use porous paving, and
follow runoff controls
shown on the following
pages.

4. Canteens and housing
for workmen. See runoff
controls and waste-
management requirements
below.

5. Mix plants. Prevent
runoff from causing
pollution of streams
or other drainage areas
by draining the plant-
site to a separate pit
area. Require ecolo-
gically-safe neutraliz-
ing agents, to be
supplied by the manu-
facturers. Inspect for
compliance before
approving backfill at
plant areas.

6. Chemical, oil, and
solvent storage areas.
Prevent runoff from
causing pollution of
streams or other drain-
age areas. Prevent
leaching into soil (use
plastic sheeting under
sand layer, or a layer
of clay, or drip-pans).
Require ecologically-
safe neutralizers of

each material from its manufacturer. Inspect for compliance before approving this work.

C. *Topsoil Storage*

1. <u>Topsoil is alive.</u> Bacteria, enzymes, and decaying plant materials, built up over long centuries, give it its great life-growing powers. Do not mix topsoil with subsoils; store it carefully, clear of pollutants and erosion hazards. Dike foot of pile to prevent erosion and creepage. Seed slopes with annual grasses if growth seasons occur during construction.

D. *Runoff, and Erosion Control*

1. <u>Create temporary grades</u> (not necessarily the same as final grades) in nearly flat terraces for slowest runoff. Drain all construction areas. plus new structure itself, into water-conservation areas as described below.

2. <u>Water-conservation pits.</u> Excavate to accommodate maximum probable runoff, considering percolation and evaporation. Where percolation is possible, line floor of pit with pebbles. Locate and size overflow pipe for slowest safe drainage from site.

3. <u>Cover all exposed subsoil,</u> during entire construction period, with approved mulch, composted waste materials (see E. on the following page) and/or temporary living ground-covers, as needed to prevent mud, erosion, siltation, and blown dust.

E. *Waste Management*

1. <u>Allow no burning of wastes</u> or demolished materials on or off site.

2. <u>Cleared brush and humus.</u> Use as mulch on exposed soils.

3. <u>Tree removal.</u> Trees may be sold for lumber or pulp. Branches must be mechanically chipped for use as mulch. Unsalable trunks and large branches: cut into uniform convenient (8 foot?) lengths and stack where directed (excellent small-game cover, picturesque landscape feature, children's play area). Stumps, if pulled for project requirements, must be placed in orderly piles where directed, and later made a part of the landscape design.

4. <u>Demolished materials.</u>
   a. Organic materials. Sell lumber for reuse, or stack on site where directed by the architect after removal of nails. Small wood members and paper trash; use as mulch on exposed soils.
   b. Inorganic materials. Relatively inert materials (brick, stone, steel) may be removed and/or sold, or buried on site if permitted. Poisons and other dangerous materials must be

chemically neutralized, then inspected and approved before burial.

5. Trash. Allow no disposable food or drink containers to be dispensed free or sold on site. Disposable containers, wrappings and cigarets brought by workmen must be placed in proper receptacles. NO LITTERING WILL BE TOLERATED. Repeated offenses will be subject to (union-approved) fines. All paper, plastic, and cardboard trash on the project, along with all garbage, must be mechanically pulped for use on exposed land surfaces. At final grading of site, wastes used as temporary mulch shall be left as part of the subsoil material.

6. Sewage. When the recycling toilets mentioned on page 9 are available, and approved by local authorities, their use should be made mandatory.

7. Toxic materials. (See sections A.2, B.5 and B.6).

8. Smoke. No open fires permitted for any purpose. No internal-combustion-powered equipment (from bulldozers and cranes to generators and compressors) allowed on site unless equipped with approved air pollution abatement devices. Temporary heating units, roofing-material heaters, and the like must be electrically-powered or, if fossil-fueled, fitted with approved air pollution abatement devices.

*Section II. The Project Itself--Design Considerations*

*A. The Site*

1. The building and the land. If the total site including paving and structures cannot be improved by the work, the project will be a failure. There are many ways to pave and

build that improve sites. A fifteen-point checklist for use in evaluating a project's ecologic impact can be found at the end of these standards.

2. Prohibited areas. It is evident now that construction in swamps, flood plains, and wilderness areas cannot be justified. Such areas are national treasures; they are the life-generating parts of our planet. (Lakes and seas must be considered as wilderness areas in this sense.)

3. Restricted areas. Because of the ecologic crisis it is best not to build in any green areas; fields, forests, or farms. If man is to survive, world restrictions on all further green-area destruction must come within a decade. Vast, non-green, urban and suburban areas are available for rehabilitation or reconstruction. If green-area disruption is unavoidable it is extremely important that all possible precautions against land-damage

be taken. Such pre-
cautions grow from a
healthy respect for
existing contours and
existing plant materi-
als.

4. Paved areas. Roofs,
   plazas, highways, parking lots, airports and
   walks create massive
   land waste. A paved
   acre repels 27,000
   gallons of water during
   a one-inch rain. Many
   factories and shopping
   centers repel millions
   of gallons each year.
   Highways repel and
   waste billion; so do
   suburbs and cities.
   Sound planning includes
   incentives not to drive
   (bike, walk). Whenever
   possible, retain runoff
   on site. Use sunken
   pebble gardens for percolation and erosion
   control. Investigate
   reverse wells and ponding in non-absorbent
   soils. Surprising
   benefits usually appear.
   Buildings and other
   paved areas not only
   waste rainwater; they
   wipe out oxygen-produc-
   ing, pollution-absorbing
   green areas, they deny
   living space to all

other animals, they
intensify noise and
weather, they destroy
rich soils, and they
are ugly. But their
sting can be reduced
if ecologic standards
are adopted.

5. Wildlife habitat. As
   farmers long ago dis-
   covered to their
   advantage, even a
   small proportion of a
   site, left wild, will
   attract and provide
   cover for the birds,
   small game, insects,
   and other creatures
   needed to restore land
   health. Wild areas
   provide beautiful
   foliage and offer
   zero-maintenance land-
   scaping. As important
   in the city as in the
   country.

6. Erosion control. Ab-
   sorbent surfaces, such
   as natural humus and
   mulch, are ideal rain-
   holders. Underground
   structures present
   these absorbent sur-
   faces to the rains.
   If above-surface
   structures must be
   used, control erosion
   by reducing the speed

and volume of runoff
(by using nearly-flat
grades, baffles,
multiple drains) and
protect land surfaces
with deep mulch and
living plants. Retain-
ing rainwater on site
will save many small
streams otherwise due
for destruction if con-
ventional drainage is
used.

7. Soil enrichment. Chemical fertilizers and
   pesticides destroy fertility. Slow, natural
   enrichment seems preferable, and costs far less.
   Starting with mulch and
   living plants, use pulped
   and composted trash and
   garbage (plus dried
   sewage where allowed)
   for added absorption and
   soil enrichment. Plant
   zero-maintenance ground-
   covers like Crown Vetch,
   which puts nitrogen into
   the soil, grows under the
   worst conditions, blooms
   for months each year, and
   never needs mowing.

8. Lighting control. Night
   no longer exists in and
   around American cities.
   The deadly, all-night
   glare of high-efficiency

lighting reaches farther into the country each year, preventing deep rest, confusing nocturnal animals, denying the wonders of a starry night to whole generations of Americans, and allowing lighting designers to get away with soul-crushing thoughtlessness. All lighting, both existing and future, whether it exists for decoration, advertising, or safety, must be so shaded that light *sources* cannot be seen from any adjoining site, or from the sky. This will not only increase lighting efficiency but will make good neighbors of lighted areas now totally out of control.

*The Structure*

Is this project REALLY necessary? (This must henceforward and forever be the first question asked by all who build. It is a very tough question, demanding the kinds of honesty and guts that too few of us seem to have.) Have all the less damaging alternatives such as rehabilitation of existing structures been explored? Have all ecologic costs (environment, resources, the future, etc.) been included in the project estimates?

2. What will be its impact on the land? Will the neighborhood benefit? How about the community? The nation?

3. What kinds of structures will do the least harm to the land? Has underground construction been given first consideration? How long should a structure last? Will it be useful in 1990? 2000? 2050? The planetary cycles around us have fixed rhythms; days, seasons, years; cycles of growth and rest that range from minutes to centuries. Are we in step? Can we uproot a forest today, build tomorrow, and demolish, for another use, the day after that without crippling natural cycles? Will the project be flexible enough to accommodate future uses?

4. Materials. Use no products from threatened species (redwood). Use no hazardous materials (asbestos). Use the least amount of material consistent with the life of the structure. The days of the throw-away society and of planned obsolescence are numbered.

5. Shape and color. Are man's rights unlimited in intruding upon a formerly wild landscape? How will shape, color, and texture affect the microclimate? The interior? Are fuel and energy savings possible through intelligent use of exterior colors and shapes? Many architects are now convinced that ecologically-sound buildings will be beautiful automatically. They will express the land ethic as gracefully as do living creatures.

6. Radiation protection. Radiation is the

ultimate pollution.
Shielding techniques
are imperfect and acci-
dents are commonplace,
yet atomic power plants
proliferate and the
uses of X-rays and
radioactive materials
multiply. Unthinkable
suffering for all liv-
ing creatures is only
an accident away.
There is *no* radiation
threshold below which
no damage occurs.
Shield not only man but
all living plants and
animals in every way
possible.

7. Noise control, privacy.
This is one of the
pollutions which shows
no sign of abatement,
and yet it is the one
most closely linked to
man's mental health.
Escape from noise and
crowding, for each of
us, is imperative. No
new housing must be
built without really
soundproof partitions,
walls and doors. Surely
this is a basic right
for all occupants of
what is accurately
called the human zoo.

C. *Energy and Resource
Conservation*

1. Power and fuel wastes.
Conservation practices
include underground
construction (natural
insulation), high-
efficiency artificial
insulations, solar
designs, heat-captur-
ing devices on ventila-
tor exhausts and at
process water drains,
efficient heating,
cooling, and lighting
systems, compactness
of building, and tak-
ing advantage of the
new engineering prac-
tices being perfected
each year.

2. Waste management. (See
comparable paragraphs
under Section I.)
Pollution "controls"
have proven themselves
utterly ineffective.
Business-like waste-
management practices
that recognize pollu-
tants as illegally-
dumped property are
finally becoming estab-
lished. There is no
right to dump private-
ly-owned materials
(wastes) into the

public domain, regard-
less of whether those
materials are dumped
into the water as pollu-
tion, into the air as
smoke, or onto land as
litter. Both old and
new construction pro-
jects must be made to
manage their wastes
rather than dump them.
Waste management devices
are improving almost
daily. At this time,
the following practices
seem to be best.
a. Trash and garbage.
Always segregate
wastes. Remove
metals for sale as
scrap; heavy plas-
tics for convention-
al disposal. Use
water-recycling
waste-pulping de-
vices for reduction
of all paper, card-
board, light pastics,
glass, small metal
wastes, and garbage.
The resulting pulp
is a light-colored,
damp, odorless
material. If harm-
less dyes are added
to the pulping water
system, resultant
pulp can be made the
color of peatmoss.
Use pulped wastes as

mulch on the land, or-- ideally-- mechanically compost the pulp (along with treated and dried sewage as soon as we revise our archaic prejudices) and use the mixture as a soil-building mulch/ nutrient. If site is limited, such material can be sold.

b. Sewage. If sewage may not be used on site as described above, investigate recycling toilets of the kind now used experimentally in Canada (Societe Centrale d'Hypotheques et de Logement, Ottawa 7). If neither is possible, use all water-conservation practices possible and push local municipality to employ full tertiary treatment.

c. Process wastes. Some of these materials can be used on the land as described in (a.) above. Harmful or toxic materials must be cooled and/or neutralized to an ecologically-safe level before their release into the public domain.

d. Smoke. Fit all chimneys and exhausts with efficient and appropriate precipitators, filters, after-burners, bag-houses, and the like. Arrange for highest combustion efficiencies. Ban all incineration.

3. Water conservation. See discussions of runoff and percolation in the paragraphs above. Conserve city water by banning all lawn and garden sprinkling, prohibiting single-use dumping of cooling waters, installing automatic shut-off timers on washroom lavatories, and using best engineering practices to increase water use efficiency and prevent leaks.

D. *Land Reclamation Bonds*

1. Abandoned, incomplete projects. Bankruptcy, whimsy, changed conditions, disaster...any of these can halt a project for months or for years. When this happens the land lies exposed, open to tremendous damage from many sources. Whole neighborhoods, communities, and natural drainage systems can be downgraded by blown dust, erosion, mudslides, siltation, flooding, fire, weather intensification, vandalism, and ugliness. To allow these common disasters to recur is madness, especially when a simple land reclamation policy, written by insurance companies and providing for the restoration of an abandoned or inactive site to healthy green condition, can prevent all damage.

2. Unused, completed projects. Conventional structures-- factories, shopping centers, roads, parking lots-- offer some justification for their land destruction when they are in use, but abandoned structures have no justification

whatsoever.  They wreck
the land but offer no
compensating benefits.
It is inevitable that as
ownerships and condi-
tions change many
facilities will stand
idle for short periods.
But prolonged disuse,
along with constant
landwaste, is ecologi-
cally intolerable.  Land
reclamation bonds, post-
ed by those who most
recently owned or oper-
ated such facilities,
can assure the return of
long-vacant idle struc-
tures to living green
land.  Wasteful?  Per-
haps, but nowhere
near as costly to future
generations as are un-
used buildings, endless-
ly smothering the land.

# Index